GOLDSTRIKE!

BILL JAMIESON

GOLDSTRIKE!

THE
OPPENHEIMER
EMPIRE
IN CRISIS

Hutchinson
Business
Books

Copyright © Bill Jamieson 1990

The right of Bill Jamieson to be identified as the author of this work has been
asserted by him in accordance with the Copyright, Designs and Patents Act, 1988

First published in Great Britain by
Hutchinson Business Books Limited
An imprint of Random Century Limited
20 Vauxhall Bridge Road, London SW1V 2SA

Century Hutchinson Australia (Pty) Limited
20 Alfred Street, Milsons Point
Sydney, NSW 2061, Australia

Century Hutchinson New Zealand Limited
PO Box 40–086, 32–34 View Road, Glenfield
Auckland 10, New Zealand

Century Hutchinson South Africa (Pty) Limited
PO Box 337, Bergvlei 2012, South Africa

British Library Cataloguing in Publication Data
Jamieson, Bill
  Goldstrike : the Oppenheimer empire in crisis.
  1. South Africa. Mining industries. Anglo American
  Corporation of South Africa, history
  I. Title
  338.7′622′0968

ISBN 0–09–174260–9

Phototypeset by Input Typesetting Ltd, London
Printed and bound in Great Britain by
Mackays of Chatham PLC, Chatham, Kent

This book is dedicated to

Fallang Mobe
Nkosiyakhe Mqungwana
Polao Kheola
61/W1 stope machine operators, Western Deep Mine

and all their children.

In eigner Fessel;
fing ich mich.
Ich Unfreiester aller.

– Wotan, Act II,
   Die Walküre

(*I forged the fetters;*
now I am bound.
I, least free of all living.)

Acknowledgments

■

To my wife Elaine and my son Alastair, for their understanding and forbearance.

To the directors and staffs of Anglo American Corporation, De Beers, Minorco and Consolidated Gold Fields for their assistance and their courtesy. While Anglo American has been fully co-operative, the views expressed by the author should not be taken as representing those of Anglo American or executives within it.

In particular, to Gavin Relly, Julian Ogilvie Thompson and Michael Spicer; Rudolph Agnew, Antony Hichens, Hugh Impey and Graham Williams; Sir Michael Edwardes, Hank Slack, Roger Phillimore and Tony Lea, all of whom gave extensive interviews and assistance.

To the mining analysts at Phillips & Drew, BZW, Shearson Lehman, Martin & Co and, in particular, Mark Wood at Kleinwort Benson Securities and Mick Oliver at James Capel.

To Peter Cadbury of Morgan Grenfell and Gerry Grimstone of Schroders.

To my colleagues at the *Sunday Telegraph* for their understanding and patience.

To Harry Oppenheimer. His courtesy is everything I was told it would be. I am sorry about the diamond encrusted cigar cutters which came apart in my hands during lunch. It worried me for days until I found out the truth.

Hank Slack broke them first, but he never said.

Dramatis Personae

∎

Agnew, Rudolph: chairman and chief executive, Consolidated Gold Fields (until July 1989).

Agostinelli, Robert: London manager, Lazard Freres, advisers to Minorco.

Anderson, Campbell: managing director, Renison Goldfields of Australia; director, Consolidated Gold Fields.

Anderson, Eugene: chief executive, Johnson Matthey (until December 1989).

Beckett, Michael: joint managing director, Consolidated Gold Fields; director, Renison Goldfields (until July 1989).

Boustred, Graham: executive director and deputy chairman, Anglo American Corporation.

Boyd, Leslie: executive director, Anglo American Corporation; chairman, Highveld Steel and Vanadium.

Cadbury, Peter: director, Morgan Grenfell, advisers to Minorco.

Clarke, Neil: director, Anglo American Corporation; former deputy chairman and chief executive, Charter Consolidated; former director, Minorco and Consolidated Gold Fields.

De Beer, Zach: former executive director, Anglo American Corporation; co-leader, Democratic Party.

Diemont, Nick: group managing director, Anglo American Farms.

Edwardes, Sir Michael: chief executive and deputy chairman, Minorco (until December 1989); chairman, Charter Consolidated (since November 1988).

Epstein, Jeremy: corporate attorney, Shearman & Sterling, New York, legal advisers to Minorco.

Godsell, Bobby: director, Anglo American Corporation; group consultant, industrial relations and public affairs.

Grimstone, Gerry: director, J Henry Schroder Wagg; adviser to Consolidated Gold Fields.

Gush, Peter: executive director, Anglo American Corporation; chairman, gold and uranium division (until December 1989).

Hanson, Lord: chief executive, Hanson Group.

Hichens, Antony: joint managing director and chief financial officer, Consolidated Gold Fields (until July 1989).

Hofmeyer, Murray: executive director, Anglo American Corporation; chairman, Johannesburg Consolidated Investments; former chairman and managing director, Charter Consolidated.

Kaplan, Lewis: corporate attorney, Paul Weiss, Rifkind, Wharton & Garrison, New York: legal advisers to Consolidated Gold Fields.

King, Mike: executive director, Anglo American Corporation; head of finance division.

Lea, Tony: 'Young Turk'; former director, Anglo American Corporation; finance director, Minorco; now joint managing director.

Loomis, Bill: director, Minorco; director, Lazard Freres.

Mukasey, Michael: US circuit judge, Southern District Court, New York.

Oppenheimer, Harry: son of Sir Ernest Oppenheimer; former chairman, Anglo American Corporation; director, Anglo American (retired December 1982) and Minorco (until May 1989); director, De Beers.

Oppenheimer, Nicholas: son of Harry; deputy chairman, De Beers; chairman, Central Selling Organisation (London); joint deputy chairman and managing director, Anglo American Corporation; director, Minorco (from June 1989).

Parker, Gordon: president and chief executive, Newmont Mining Corporation; director, Consolidated Gold Fields.

Phillimore, Roger: 'Young Turk'; strategy director, Minorco; now joint managing director; former marketing manager, Anglo American gold division.

Plumbridge, Robin: chairman and chief executive, Gold Fields of South Africa; director, Consolidated Gold Fields; director, Newmont Mining Corporation.

Relly, Gavin: chairman, Anglo American Corporation; director, Minorco and De Beers.

Slack, Hank: 'Young Turk'; son-in-law of Harry Oppenheimer (third husband of Mary Oppenheimer); former personal assistant to Harry

Oppenheimer; director, Anglo American Corporation; president of Minorco (in charge of North American operations); now joint managing director.

Spicer, Michael: personal assistant to Gavin Relly.

Spiro, Sidney: founder, Union Acceptances; former chairman and chief executive, Charter Consolidated; former director, Anglo American Corporation and Minorco (until June 1989); director, De Beers.

Sunter, Clem: director and chairman, administrative committee, Anglo American Corporation (until January 1990); now chairman, Gold and Uranium division.

Sykes, Allen: joint managing director, Consolidated Gold Fields, responsible for corporate development.

Thompson, Julian Ogilvie: chairman, De Beers; deputy chairman, Anglo American Corporation; chairman, Minorco; director, Consolidated Gold Fields (until July 1989).

Watson, Anthony Richmond: director, Morgan Grenfell, advisers to Minorco.

Williams, Graham: senior press officer, Consolidated Gold Fields.

Wood, Humphrey: joint managing director, responsible for public affairs, Consolidated Gold Fields (until July 1989).

Simple isn't it? The Byzantine web of the Anglo American, De Beers and Gold Fields empires, as at January 1990.

RTZ · PALABORA · PALAMIN · RICHARDS BAY MINERALS · AUSTRALIAN NATIONALS

SANLAM · IDC · GENCOR · GENBEL · IMPALA · KARBE · SA GOLD MINES · CUDGEN · CONS RUTILE

REMBRANDT · GENCOR BESHERBEND

BARLOW RAND · RAND MINES · VANSA VANADIUM · BARPLATS · BARDINE · RHODIUM REEFS · CROCODILE MINE · SA GOLD MINES

SA MUTUAL · OPPENHEIMER FAMILY INTERESTS

MINORCO · ADOBE RESOURCES · CHARTER CONSOLIDATED · JOHNSON MATTHEY · INSPIRATION RESOURCES · WESTGOLD · ENGELHARD · LIBERTY

DEBEERS · AMSA · AMGOLD · EASTERN · HANSON

ANGLO AMERICAN · LYDENBURG · JCI · RUSTENBURG PLATINUM HOLDINGS · RUSTENBURG MINE · LEBOWA

AMCOAL · SA INDUSTRIALS · SA GOLD MINES · WEST COAST MINERAL SANDS · SOUTHERN LIFE

CONSOLIDATED GOLDFIELDS · GFSA HOLDINGS · GFSA · ARC · GFMC · NEWMONT MINING · NEWMONT GOLD · RENISON · DRIEFONTEIN · NORTHAM · SA GOLDMINES · ASTEROID

DRAWING REF: MINORCO1
DATE: 1/12/89
DRAWN BY: LOUISE STEWART
COMPANY: JAMES CAPEL & CO.

Courtesy of James Capel & Co

Contents

■

Plates

∎

1. Harry Oppenheimer. All photographs by John Chapman, courtesy of the *Sunday Telegraph*.

2. Anglo American. Photograph courtesy of Anglo American Corporation.

3. Robin Plumbridge. Photograph courtesy of Consolidated Gold Fields.

4. Gordon Parker. Photograph courtesy of Consolidated Gold Fields.

5. Michael Edwardes. Photograph by Richard Olivier, courtesy of the *Daily Telegraph*.

6. Tony Lea, Roger Phillimore and Hank Slack. All photographs by Keith Bernstein, courtesy of the *Sunday Telegraph*.

7. Minorco press conference. Photograph courtesy of the *Sunday Telegraph*.

8. Gold Fields press conference. Photograph by Matthew Ford, courtesy of the *Sunday Telegraph*.

9. Michael Mukasey. Photograph courtesy of Ricke-Hultes.

10. Rudolph Agnew. Photograph by Matthew Ford, courtesy of the *Daily Telegraph*.

11. Nicholas Oppenheimer. Photograph by Judah Passon, courtesy of the *Sunday Telegraph*.

Prologue

In the Library of the World

■

There is a mural called 'The Bridge'.

It is the most disturbing painting in South Africa: a nightmare vision of apocalypse, a terrible Armageddon.

The mural, by the Australian artist Leonard French, measures some 12 feet by six, and is painted in medieval colours of golds and browns and greens. It shows a primitive arched bridge, made of wooden struts nailed crudely together. Two white armies have converged on the bridge and at its apex they are fighting and killing. Below the bridge, as if pouring out towards the viewer, is a tangle of black people.

The bridge is on fire. The faces of the people are robotic and distraught. Only when you step closer do you see that each face is the mouth of a cannon.

Ripping through the middle of this raging mural, running from top to bottom, is a violent black tear, a splintering fault like Africa's Great Rift. Any unity in the picture is impossible. For many, it exactly represents South Africa and its bridge of crisis.

Standing in front of the mural, it is difficult to look for long. But it is like a mirror: those who catch their reflection in it are compelled to look back. Its haunting power stems from a powerful psychological alchemy of premonition and *déjà vu*.

As remarkable as the mural itself is the place where it stands. It is in the central hallway of the Brenthurst Library, the private library of one of the world's richest, most powerful and most fascinating men: Harold Frederick Oppenheimer.

The library, built in 1984, is situated like a gateway to Oppenheimer's lush, 40-acre private estate in Houghton, in the northern

1

suburbs of Johannesburg. When it was opened, Oppenheimer's guests, among them the most powerful and influential in international mining and finance, were stunned and appalled by the painting. It created – and stopped – conversation. At the opening ceremony, the writer and anti-Apartheid activist, Alan Paton, said: 'The meaning is painful to me. Mr French's painting is a forecast of the cataclysm, and the irony of the painting is that if it is true, there will be no libraries left in which such a painting can be displayed.'

Of all the words written about Harry Oppenheimer, this library is the gateway to the inner man, and this mural the apocalypse on which his empire, Anglo American Corporation of South Africa, now rests.

Has the Armageddon come nearer? Oppenheimer himself says: 'I don't think so. I see the painting as a warning, not a prophesy. And I have a stupid optimism. I couldn't take it as a literal truth. It would so contradict everything that Anglo American is about. And it is all about the development of this entire country.'

It is at the Brenthurst Library that Oppenheimer has spent much time of late, reflecting on an empire he ruled that is the world's largest gold producer, the world's largest platinum producer, controller of the world's diamond supply, and South Africa's largest private sector employer, with a payroll of 200,000 and a vast cobweb of businesses accounting for more than 30 per cent of the Republic's gross domestic product.

In any inner cabinet of Earth Incorporated, Oppenheimer would have powerful claim to the chairman's seat.

In this library he has a private study, where visitors are rarely allowed. It is like a turret, filled with books, and is reached through a small ante-room with a display of some of the world's rarest stones. In the study are four dark red armchairs, grouped in a semicircle.

On the wall is a painting by Thomas Baines, of galleons at anchor in the arc of Table Bay. A tall narrow slit of window, running from floor to ceiling, looks out on to a pond that forms a moat round the library.

By the window is a writing desk with some rare American stamps tucked into the corner of a leather-bound blotting pad; there is a Desiderata, and an informal snapshot of Harry Oppenheimer with Alan Paton. Above the desk is a painting of a man who presents a questioning and hesitant face to the world: his father, Sir Ernest Oppenheimer.

On the shelves are some of the world's rarest books on African natural history and wildlife. Then there are the volumes of Oppenheimer's most loved writers – Keats, Shelley, and his greatest love of all, Byron. Nowhere in the room is there a single book about mining, finance or industry.

Oppenheimer, a man of extraordinary intellectual suppleness, is encased by a persona that belies hardness and guile. Yet he has sustained the largest and most patriarchal precious metals empire in the world by a hereditary obsession with power, position, hands-on control, and antennae for potential threat that are among the keenest anywhere.

The library, looked after by Marcelle Weiner, houses the world's most valuable collection of Afrikaner; 12,000 books; 14,000 items altogether. It is air-conditioned with an intricate filter process that excludes dust and pollutants. It has controls to maintain constant humidity; fire protection and automatic alarm systems; filters to eliminate ultra-violet rays; and shelf lights that automatically switch off after four minutes to prevent the light from damaging the books. Such technology is matched only by the Library of Congress in Washington.

It is intriguing that for all the top-trained accountants, lawyers and auditors hired to insure every division of the Oppenheimer empire – embracing Anglo American and the diamond giant De Beers (what is known in Main Street as 'the greater group'), and extending into every corner of South African economic life (a total, it is said, of 1,300 companies to which the greater group is connected) – here at the centre is one operation, the smallest but most loved of all, that is allowed to lose Oppenheimer £40,000 a year.

The library lies to the right of the entrance to Brenthurst, flanked by uniformed Anglo American guards. In the central gallery, where the Leonard French mural stands, Oppenheimer frequently entertains. Here he reveals himself with a persona that instantly and disturbingly demolishes all popular preconceptions of what a global tycoon should be. Oppenheimer has been the world's shyest and least noisesome millionaire. He is without doubt one of the best read and the cleverest. He is not just alien to the powerfully entrenched money set in Johannesburg – a caste more deeply driven and obsessed by money and its trappings than perhaps any in the world, and from which Oppenheimer was at telling points socially distant – he is a class traitor to the mega-rich.

At the library's opening, he presented each guest with a facsimile of a letter written in 1910 by Leo Tolstoy to Gandhi, then living in South Africa. 'The whole life of the Christian people,' it read, 'is a ceaseless contradiction between what they preach and on what they build their lives.' Quite a contrast to his father, Sir Ernest, who was known to quietly slip into the palms of each of the wives of business friends after dinner parties at Brenthurst a 'little token' of a gem diamond.

The library is where Harry Oppenheimer now reflects upon his private empire in a stricken country, one by whose ruling group he has also been treated as an *uitlander* – and at times a traitor.

Anglo American, founded by his father, reached its pre-eminence under Harry. He has much time to reflect on the profound dilemmas of corporate stance and action that it faces now. Darkest shadows steal across the moat. Here, as in the legend of Parsifal, is English South Africa's stricken Monsalvat, its troubled Grail. On the world stage, it battles against isolation and the pariah status accorded to South Africa.

Although now in his 80s, and long retired from the minutiae of Main Street, his standback position should never obscure the stranger's view of the breadth and depth of the Oppenheimer grip on the gold, diamond and natural resources markets.

Oppenheimer is enjoying a style of retirement enjoyed by few other men in the world, largely by virtue of other people's underestimation of him. Doing business with Anglo American was an experience likened by one survivor to being attacked, in the dark, from behind.

The world view of the Oppenheimer empire is essential to an understanding of it, and its crisis. More than any other industry, the world of natural resources and precious metals is a complex intermeshing of an extended family. The proper study of it is as much the prerogative of the social anthropologist as the stockbroker's analyst.

Frequently in the story of the building of the Oppenheimer empire, the same names, or the relations of names, crop up: Newmont, a current foe of Anglo American, was once a founding shareholder in it; Gold Fields of South Africa, in other areas a financial cousin and partner, is here, in this story, an implacable opponent; Engelhard and Johnson Matthey, two extensions of a platinum empire, are held in fraught and uneasy relation; Salomon Brothers,

Wall Street's biggest bond trading house, was at one time gripped and divided by the Oppenheimer hand; Warburgs, one of London's biggest merchant banks, was intimately connected with the Anglo American empire and at the same time divided by it. Allies and enemies, kindred friends and kindred foes: Anglo American is at the apex of a Byzantine web of conflicting crossholdings, not just within itself, but in its relations with the world.

Over all this – the central nodes of gold, diamond and platinum production and an industrial grip on South Africa – the empire has come to be a dominant player in its markets. Control by market dominance has been a recurring theme. And that dominance has been achieved, not by a wave of hostile takeovers, but by a relentless extrusion of value from its core businesses.

Over this machine, the family has presided with an outward open palm – the nearest the Republic has got to a Royal family – and an inner clenched fist.

In any analysis of Anglo American, one is driven to an analysis of its relationships. And it is suffering a crisis of relationships. Nothing more illuminated this crisis than defeat on the world stage in the £3.5 billion battle for Consolidated Gold Fields. Not only did this battle reveal a managerial disarray within Anglo American, but it also dramatically aggravated the group's increasing isolation on the world stage.

A defeat abroad, and at home the inexorable demographic march of black empowerment: these combine to make this a problematic empire. Nothing more encapsulates this crisis than the super tensions within Anglo American, and in particular its tight élite of Rhodes scholars at the top. It is an élite at elegant war.

The tangible financial bonds that link the Oppenheimer family with the Anglo American empire seem like frail threads against the power that they carry: E Oppenheimer & Sons owns a holding of just 8.3 per cent in Anglo American (worth some £300 million) and seven per cent of Minorco (£123 million). But the family influence, and the sense of patriarchy that imbues the empire, are immense.

Oppenheimer's son, son-in-law and godsons have risen through the hierarchy with astonishing speed and have found themselves in the highest positions of power. Huge though the empire has grown, it has remained at heart a family affair. Harry Oppenheimer's kith and kin and the greater group's inner cabinet are paid and rewarded, not by salaries from Anglo American and De Beers, but through disbursements through a private Oppenheimer Swiss account: Central Holdings Ltd, controlled by Oppenheimer. The disbursements are kept secret, as are the names of all the beneficiaries. That system of reward helps sustain a keen loyalty and protection at the centre of the Anglo American group.

But the patriarchy until recently was sustained by a wider loyalty. The Oppenheimers brought to the group a set of values which conferred on it a legitimizing purpose over and above successful capital accumulation. That is what gave the group its distinctive complexion and progressive flavour. It was commonly understood that 44-year-old Nicholas Oppenheimer will inherit the chairmanship. It would pass to him less by the power of that shareholding or sense of founding family right – powerful though the latter is in this case – than by a loyalty and consensus that the family culture has engendered. This, coupled with a continuing ability to deliver the goods, is where the legitimacy of family power resides.

It is a unique consent. No one votes the Oppenheimers to their stations. Nor does their continuing pre-eminence at Anglo American rest on any legal or formal fiduciary base. It derives from voluntary support and endorsement of the culture. The loyalty it engenders gives the group its cohesiveness.

This legitimizing force flows two ways: the values, and the obligations these values impose on Anglo American as a catalyst for political change in South Africa, have given the company a distinctiveness of which the Oppenheimers are guardians. In a sense, were they not there, it would have been necessary to invent them.

But the voluntary base of such control, in the absence of power deriving from a large shareholding or from any formal legal arrangement of trusteeship, is fluid and unstable at heart: the event of succession and transfer of that power presents a natural crisis to the group, particularly so when there is an interregnum. The voluntary base needs renewal if crisis is to be avoided, and such a period is now upon it. This is when the consensus is most vulnerable to the consequences of a setback at home or failure abroad. Both for the family and for those involved in the interregnum, danger and opportunity have never been more present. Without a necessary renewal, the dynastic impulse begins to fade. And when it fades, competing pressures build upon the centre: a patriarchal rockburst is in the making.

The bigger Anglo American has grown, the deeper it has mined into South African life: the more susceptible is the grip to pressure.

At the heart of Anglo American's greater crisis is one of inheritance and succession and the need for renewal of ideas. Both outer pressures on the group and inner ones present the Oppenheimers with a familiar but deadly dilemma: a clash between the compulsion to hold on and the necessity of letting go. Nothing is more potent, more creative or more destructive, depending on how it is handled, than the crisis of letting go.

How deceptive the peace of a library can be. Opera producer David Pountney recently staged a production of the *Wagner Ring*, the epic story of stolen gold and the crisis of relationships that this unleashes. In Act Two of *Die Walküre*, there is a confrontation between the compulsion of control and the necessity of release. According to Wagner's instructions, this epic act was to unfold 'in a wild, craggy place'. Designer Maria Bjørnson set it in a library: a vast turret of books.

It is hard not to see in this setting the Oppenheimers similarly confronted. For all its power, Anglo American has been unable to change the nature of the pariah state in which it operates. For all that it has sought to be a catalyst for change, it has been kept at the margin of political power for more than 40 years. When the empire has sought to break out it has been denied access to other markets and other theatres of corporate action by regulatory authorities and legal rulings. The United States in particular has allowed little corporate room for Anglo American; the threat of anti-trust kept Oppenheimer's apartment in New York empty for years.

The distrust initially stemmed from the greater group's world monopoly of the very product that has financed the expansion of Anglo American to its current size and power: diamonds. Four out of five diamonds on the fingers of women around the world have passed through Oppenheimer hands. To this has been added growing international pressure on South Africa to reform Apartheid by means of sanctions, disinvestment and a clampdown on international lending. Such pressure does not discriminate between the agents working for Apartheid's continuance and those working for its change. That is why the Oppenheimers feel they have been unfairly treated.

Nothing has more brought home the status of the untouchable for Anglo American than the battle for Consolidated Gold Fields, the world's second largest gold producer. Defeat in that bid shattered the unity and sense of omnipotence (some might say the God-like arrogance) of the inner élite of Oppenheimer Inc. It forced it to confront a numbing truth about its growing isolation in the world, its loss of influence and following, and the need for new ideas.

That isolation is reflected in the market's treatment of its equity. Its shares in 1989 traded at a discount of between 28 and 35 per cent to the asset worth of the company. Between 1980 and 1989, net asset value has risen by 22 per cent a year and equity accounted earnings by 20 per cent. But the world markets rate the shares at less than half the value they assign to the average equity.

More tellingly, since 1980 the proportion of Anglo American stock held outside South Africa has more than halved: from 25 per cent to 11 per cent. For all that profits, assets and dividends have moved ahead, at the base of Anglo American there has been a worrying attrition. There is a sense less of growth and spreading out, than of a closing in.

Meanwhile, at home, there is no confidence – in the inner conversations of the Anglo American set, of certainty in the future, as once there was, or that the centrifugal drive will hold for much longer. Ideas are running out. The pulse of a necessary re-enervation cannot be felt.

In the library the clues to this crisis can be found: the moat a symbol of isolation, the mural of 'The Bridge' – the bridge over a moat, but a bridge on fire and with its people at war – an awesome bridge between prophecy and warning. It is not an unbridgeable crisis. But it is a necessary one.

1

A World Lit by Diamonds

■

At the centre of the 'greater group' of Anglo American and De Beers is a hole – one of the biggest man-made holes in the world. It is the Big Hole, Kimberley, and in it were diamonds: more than 14 million carats of them.

There was great scepticism about the African diamond discoveries at first: it was thought by some that the diamonds had been dropped from the sky, by ostriches. But then another one was found. Then another.

The first discovery was in 1866, close to the junction of the Orange and Vaal rivers, when a struggling farmer, Schalk van Niekerk, noticed children playing the familiar game of 'klip-klip' (five stones) with an assortment of pebbles. One of them was a 21¼ carat diamond.

Before long the diamond hunters, in their tens, hundreds and hundreds of hundreds came to this grey and stony place. They would camp out along the banks of the Vaal, and at night their candle-lit tents would bob in the evening breeze like fairy balloons: the first lights in a world that would be lit by diamonds.

To get at the diamonds in the Kimberley Hole men removed 22½ million tons of earth. They began by scrambling at little plots which measured 30 feet by 30, and scrambled and dug until Kimberley became a grotesque honeycomb of hundreds of little mines, digging deeper to the core of the diamond Kimberlite pipe. When Cecil Rhodes first came upon the scene he likened it to a mountain of ants 'around a monumental stilton of cheese'. The Hole is one of the most awesome sights of the world. Today, a suspended platform enables the visitor to gaze down into a now silent abyss. It has an ominous and haunting stillness of a grave. The Hole has a perimeter of almost a mile, and plunges 165 metres to a reservoir with a depth of 230 metres.

The Kimberley Hole, and the neighbouring holes of the Bultfontein, Dutoitspan and Koffiefontein mines, were fonts of diamonds that lit the fingers of millions of women. They also lit up South Africa and the fastest phase of expansion of the British Empire. Some of the most exciting jewels were in the original mine of Vooruitzicht. Rhodes and the early settlers could never pronounce it, so they changed the name to Kimberley, after the then British Colonial Secretary. The two pipes were on a farm which had been owned by two brothers – the De Beer brothers. To give an idea of the quantity of diamonds produced, there stands, by the platform overlooking the Big Hole, three freight wagons filled to the brim with pebbles of glass. These are the volume equivalent of the Kimberley diamonds.

Any story of Anglo American must start here. Not only did the diamond discoveries mark the opening up of South Africa's huge mineral wealth, but they also released the most powerful centrifugal forces that have resulted today in the world diamond market being the biggest, richest, reticent and most enigmatic cartel outside of OPEC. Its astonishing sophistication, durability and reach was the product of the intellect and drive of one man: Ernest Oppenheimer.

The surviving company, De Beers, produces between 40 and 50 per cent of the world's gem diamonds and markets through the General Selling Organisation, set up in 1930, more than 80 per cent of world production. It has never been driven to reduce the price of a diamond once. Today the lights of De Beers have never shone brighter. For Anglo American – the largest single shareholder in De Beers with 34.3 per cent of the shares – diamonds have truly proved forever. In 1988, pre-tax profits of De Beers more than doubled to $1.2 billion on the back of diamond sales by the CSO, up 35 per cent to a record $4.2 billion.

That shareholding in De Beers brings to Anglo American more than £1 in every £4 of its equity accounted earnings. The De Beers shareholding, together with its dividend income, is set to overtake the contribution from gold and mining finance. Diamonds light up the Anglo American empire. How did it start?

*   *

On to the primal and chaotic scene of hundreds of diggers fighting and scrambling for diamonds at Colesberg Kopje, the paths between the digs constantly crumbling and carts tumbling into the abyss, came Cecil John Rhodes. Two points immediately struck him: first, the 'diggers' democracy' of small producers would have to go if serious mining was to progress; second, if the industry was to survive, the price of diamonds must be controlled.

The history of precious stone and metal discoveries had been a history of wild and self-destructive boom–bust cycles. The Kimberley boom was shaping to be no exception. In less than ten years, 20,000 men had scrambled to stake 3,600 claims at Kimberley. If the diamond price tumbled the edifice would collapse. This was a constant fear from the beginning.

There were scenes of chaos, road collapses, theft and fighting. The historian, Hedley Chilvers, noted: 'The need for combination, centralization, increased from day to day.' Rhodes set out to bring the diamond claims under one control. His partners in buying out the diggers' democracy at the De Beers mine included Alfred Beit and Charles Rudd. Others came in, leading to the formation of De Beers Mining Company with capital of £200,000. Such amalgamations had to come: not only was the old system creating huge physical hazards, such as reef falls and fires with appalling loss of life, but the full opening of the diamondiferous pipe required technology, mechanization and finance on a scale beyond the means of the small independent producers.

After merging the small producers, Rhodes went after the buyers to achieve control of the price, fearing that the producers had no protection when the diamond trade turned down. Few believed the Kimberley boom would last. Economic recessions – in which diamonds were the first hit – fed a constant terror that the diamond industry would be crushed.

One of the diamond-buying firms was Dunkelsbuhlers, which had an office in Kimberley and another in Holborn Viaduct, London. On its staff was a young man, the fifth son of a German cigar merchant, who had joined the firm in 1896 at the age of 16, on a salary of £1 a week. His name was Ernest Oppenheimer.

Those who lost out against Rhodes and Beit moved their wagons on. They drifted north to the little Boer republic across the Vaal. From there had come reports of gold discoveries. And there began to glow a new light: the golden arc of the Witwatersrand, a string of gold discoveries on the rim of a gigantic primeval saucer. Cecil Rhodes and Charles Rudd established their claims and formed their own company, called Gold Fields of South Africa, which would later change its name to Consolidated Gold Fields.

Oppenheimer arrived in Kimberley in 1902, shortly after Rhodes' death, but to a scene still dominated by him. He was a shy and diffident loner; few rated him highly. But from his position as Dunkelsbuhler's chief representative in Kimberley, he watched, waited, and noted. These were formative years.

Histroy has accorded to the rise of the Oppenheimers the creation of the diamond monopoly: this was not, however, quite the case. Dominant control of all major diamond mining at Kimberley by De Beers was already firmly established, as were nearly all the sales, through a unified sales organization, by the time Oppenheimer arrived. The production and selling of diamonds was interlocked from these early days. The economist Sir Theodore Gregory, in his account of the rise of Ernest Oppenheimer,[1] argues that this outcome was not the result of *a priori* thinking, but of the experiences of the diamond world between 1870 and 1890: 'Of weak producers with no staying power, selling at any price they could, and of weak buyers unable to hold stocks when market conditions were unfavourable'.

The structure had been shaped, too, by the *geographic* monopoly of diamonds which Kimberley at that time appeared to enjoy. From the beginning, one ever-present fear haunted Rhodes and his colleagues: new discoveries and new sources of supply beyond their power, which would send prices crashing. This fear came true, with the discovery of the Premier Mine, near Pretoria. Between 1904 and 1907, diamond production at the Premier rocketed. Then, just as Rhodes had predicted, there came the slump. The syndicate was forced to go back to its pledge to buy an agreed amount of stock each year. De Beers was forced to cut production at all five of its mines to 35 per cent of normal. In 1908, the company's records contained a laconic report from the Diamond Syndicate that sales 'were less than negligible'. Even directors' fees had to be cut. It was the year that Ernest's son, Harry Oppenheimer, was born.

Ernest, Mayor of Kimberley between 1912 and 1915, moved to Johannesburg towards the end of the First World War to look after

[1]   Gregory, Sir Theodore, *Ernest Oppenheimer and the Economic Development of Southern Africa*, Oxford University Press, 1962.

Dunkelsbuhler's interest in Consolidated Mines Selection, a moribund company in need of a shake-up.

He had been impressed by the theories of a young American mining engineer, William Honnold, who believed that there was one continuous gold reef stretching from Johannesburg to the Far East Rand. Oppenheimer negotiated a deal under which he would go 50/50 in financing any new mining venture. How best to exploit the opening? Oppenheimer began to think of a mining house of his own.

From the beginning, the development of the Witwatersrand reef was straddled by competing groups or constellations of companies that came to be known as mining finance houses. They were a unique response to the financial and technological challenges of South African gold mining. They enabled the mining groups to spread their risk across a number of prospects. Non-gold investments were undertaken in industry or property, thus protecting the finance house from the full effects of a downturn in the gold market, or the failure – or exhaustion – of a mining prospect.

This was the kind of grouping Ernest Oppenheimer, backed by Anton Dunkelsbuhler, now had in mind, with an initial capital of £1 million. American finance for the new company came from bankers J P Morgan and an enterprising mining company in America called Newmont Mining. Oppenheimer would be chairman and managing director; other directors would include Newmont's William Thompson. Anglo American Corporation of South Africa was registered on 25 September 1917.

Its timing was golden: within a year a mining boom was underway on the Rand with the CMS mines going into production. Oppenheimer could now embark on the building of what was to become a huge corporate edifice; a web of crossholdings in gold, diamond and industrial companies with control exercised from a tiny centre: the Oppenheimer pyramid. Over the years the pyramid would come to baffle financial analysts and commentators with its byzantine complexity: literally hundreds of companies would be caught up in a cobweb of direct and indirect shareholdings.

Oppenheimer, knighted in 1921, did not 'create' the diamond syndicate. But he was to solve the huge financial and logistical problems that the need for the protection of the diamond market involved. Step by step, he set out to bring it under his control. What unfolded was a complex series of deals, amalgamations and, finally, vertical integration and total dominance of a market. The scale of that achievement was breathtaking.

To the two existing impulses – control over production and control over sales through a single channel – Oppenheimer was to add a third: ownership of the selling operation *by the producers.*

If the magnitude of the achievement was colossal, so too was the manner of it. When Oppenheimer set out, he was neither a partner in Dunkelsbuhler nor a director in De Beers, the dominant producer. Nor was Anglo American at the start a member of the Diamond Syndicate. He had no personal, tangible power base to speak of. Yet he created, out of the splits, personal rivalries and in-fighting, an agreed and unifying order. It required the skilful deployment of friends, wealth and power.

He employed an 'indirect approach': where he could not persuade, he would bargain. Oppenheimer's strength derived from an uncanny ability to lever himself up between the interests of Anglo American, the diamond producers and his connections in the Syndicate, like a climber in a crevice. His power derived, not from formal and public positions of office, but from a triangular influence he created from the inside, an elliptical and discreet manipulation of alliances and interests. To do business with Oppenheimer in this era was an eerie experience, perhaps something akin to playing chess, against a ghost.

All along, Oppenheimer's enemies had underestimated him, and each, it seemed, was to be made to see the error of their ways. But then came shattering diamond discoveries: huge alluvial deposits at Lichtenburg in the Western Transvaal, and by the mouth of the Orange River in Namaqualand's Alexander Bay. Surely the new syndicate could not survive the challenge!

At Lichtenburg, 6,000 diggers were formed up in a line and at a starter's signal raced off to peg their claims. This, however, was dwarfed by the discoveries in the oyster beds of Alexander Bay. In just two years production soared to 1.2 million carats. As they flooded on to the world market and threatened the price, the Syndicate stood to be smashed – and Oppenheimer ruined. He was urged to buy the diamonds, all the diamonds – and keep on buying. He acquired these through Anglo American, and in 1925 Anglo American bought 45 per cent of the London Diamond Syndicate.

By uniting such huge forces in diamond mining, it enabled him to launch an assault at the heart of De Beers itself where he became a director in 1926. A fierce rearguard action was fought against

Oppenheimer. But the Oppenheimer Syndicate now held huge stocks of alluvial diamonds with the power to break De Beers. On 20 December 1929, the De Beers board finally caved in and elected Oppenheimer chairman.

In a month he got board backing for a new De Beers subsidiary – the Diamond Corporation to become known as the Central Selling Organisation based in London. It was to run one of the biggest commodity buffer pools in the world. He was elected chairman, thus putting him at the pinnacle of the diamond trade: producer, distributor and price controller.

In just 13 years, Sir Ernest Oppenheimer had 'outCeciled' Rhodes. He was not just the Jack of Diamonds. He was the King.

Any celebrations were shortlived. In the Depression years, diamonds tumbled from the thinning fingers of the world. Production in South and South West Africa collapsed from 4.3 million carats in 1929 to just 0.4 million by 1934. De Beers' cash crisis was so severe, 'it seemed', Harry Oppenheimer laconically remarked, 'the company's only asset was the unexpired portion of its overdraft'. De Beers was forced to suspend production and most South African diamond mines were closed. South Africa's share of world production crashed from 58.4 per cent to just 6.5 per cent.

But the price was held.

During the period up to the Second World War, and particularly during it, Oppenheimer's grip faced many challenges. All were beaten off.

Concerned by the sharp rises in unemployment triggered by mine closures, the South African Government set up a commission to investigate the industry. De Beers declined to give evidence and the commission fizzled out.

The United States fared no better. Declassified intelligence material accused the cartel of unwillingness to relinquish control of the diamond stockpile to aid the war effort. The Americans were worried by what they saw as an acute shortage of industrial diamonds, a shortage which Oppenheimer denied. The Americans were fearful of the Axis powers gaining control of Africa – and the mines. Oppenheimer, ever the imperialist, suggested a compromise solution under which diamonds would be stockpiled – in Canada. For the record, sales of industrial diamonds were supervised throughout by the British Government and that London was not by-passed. Prices were frozen throughout the War.

But the Americans were furious. The row sowed the seeds of suspicion and animosity towards the Oppenheimer empire that persists to this day. American regulators saw no reason to view a cartel in diamonds differently from any other: the monopoly should be broken, competition encouraged and the diamond price arrived at through the openness and transparency of the free-market system. The American Justice Department filed anti-trust actions against the cartel in 1945, and again in 1957 and 1974. These De Beers 'let lie' fearing, with some cause, that New York corporate attorneys would savage the cartel arrangements in the courts – during a period when De Beers was spending millions of dollars in a famous global advertising campaign to convince a new post-war generation that 'diamonds are forever'.

The campaign was the brainchild of Harry Oppenheimer, and it helped bring a new lease of life to the diamond industry: annual sales by De Beers, which had been running at some $15 million in the 1930s, had climbed to $700 million by the late sixties.

Harry Oppenheimer was appointed chairman of Anglo American in 1957 on the death of Sir Ernest. He had inherited an extraordinary legacy: the Anglo–De Beers group had risen to become the world's largest gold producer, the world's largest diamond source, controlling some 80 per cent of sales, and was producing half of South Africa's coal and over 15 per cent of the world's copper. It was a terrific concentration of power.

The Oppenheimer drive was to keep control in the family. Harry Oppenheimer's first love has always been diamonds, a business he once described as 'half-way between mining and selling works of art'.

Early in his chairmanship he proved his ability to defend the cartel in the extraordinary affair of the Williamson Mine. In Tanganyika an eccentric Canadian geologist, John Williamson, had stumbled across the richest diamond pipe in the world, a huge lake of diamonds. After signing an agreement to come in with the Producers' Association, he decided to go his own way. He stockpiled the diamonds, keeping the brightly coloured ones in jam jars as decoration. He threatened to hire planes and have the diamonds flown to America for sale. The CSO would be smashed.

Williamson, who would sit knitting for long periods, was a loner increasingly given to drink and depression. In rows with his secretary he would pelt her with diamonds out of the jam jars. In 1958 Harry Oppenheimer went to negotiate with him, a process which began with one of Williamson's tortuous long silences. Oppenheimer was determined not to say the first word. But finally, after 20 minutes during which Williamson had stared sullenly at the floor, Harry's resolution broke. The meeting ended with a deal whereby Oppenheimer bought a 50 per cent stake in Williamson. The threat to the diamond market was contained.

But Oppenheimer's problems did not end there. Continual challenges beset monopolies: placating governments, buying or knocking out new entrants to the industry and sustaining consumer confidence in the teeth of economic downturns and recession. The South African Government was a particular problem: it was both tax gatherer *and* historically a producer. It saw in the cartel a means by which to maximize the export price of a product that had a tiny domestic market. For the monopoly to continue it required, at best, government acquiescence.

In Namibia, where De Beers controlled local production through Consolidated Diamond Mines, a commission of inquiry was set up to investigate allegations of over-mining and transfer pricing. The report, published in 1986, backed allegations of over-mining and tax evasion. But a subsequent Government White Paper exonerated CDM of both over-mining and transfer pricing.

Even the Soviet Union, reckoned to be the world's biggest diamond producer by value, with exports of around $850 million a year, sells indirectly through the De Beers-controlled Central Selling Organisation headquartered in London. It must rank as one of the world's most spectacular marketing coups.

There are reckoned to be some 450 pipes in the Siberian platform where diamonds are mined in appalling conditions with winter temperatures 80 degrees below zero and with permafrost reaching 5,000 feet deep. Despite these conditions the Soviet Union produces some 12 million carats annually. The links with De Beers were established in 1959 and operated at the highest levels. Today, the Soviet Union sells its diamonds under CSO supervision through a third party. The Soviet Union continues to sell its polished diamonds (it is estimated to have some 6,000 to 8,000 diamond cutters) in the open market, occasionally demonstrating a veneer of independence by selling 'in uneven amounts' – i.e. dumping. In 1984, for example, it dumped a large amount of diamonds on the open market. The all-powerful CSO rode the bump.

Botswana proved to be a treasure trove of diamonds. The country,

80 per cent covered by the Kalahari desert, was destined to be one of the poorest nations until the discoveries. The diamond pipes were buried under 150 feet of sand and prospectors were led to them – by ants. The ants brought pyrope garnets and ilemites, which could only be found in kimberlite rock, to the surface for their nests. From three alluvials and in the host pits Botswana now produces 15 million carats a year. A prosperous and stable diamond market is crucial for Botswana: diamonds account for 80 per cent of the country's gross national product and more than half of government revenue. The industry is controlled by Debswana, a company jointly owned by De Beers and the Botswana Government.

How is this astonishing global control effected? At 9.30am, in the second floor reception room at 17 Charterhouse Street off Holborn Viaduct, London, a group of approved diamond buyers or 'sightholders' gather for one of ten annual sights. They are escorted to individual showing rooms. A broker from one of five recognized brokerage firms will appear, with a box filled with parcels of diamonds, which have been graded by some 600 sorters. The content of the boxes is tailored by the CSO's reading of the supply–demand balance.

Diamond sights are also held in Luzern and Kimberley where the Koffiefontein mine has been re-opened. At the Kimberley treatment and recovery plant, 17,000 tons of rock goes in, 600 tons come out. Out of every 100 tons, the plant will recover just 20 carats of diamonds. At the final stage the rough diamonds are delivered, in steel milkchurns, across a courtyard encircled by guards bristling with guns. In total, the De Beers mines produce around 24 million carats – 25 per cent of world production and about 42 per cent of the world's gem diamonds.

The fastest-growing market in recent years has been the Far East, Japan in particular. It has leapt to become the largest diamond market after the United States. Worldwide sales by the CSO are now running at more than $4 billion a year. This is an astonishing recovery from a slump in the early 1980s when CSO diamond sales were barely a quarter of this total. But that is the nature of the diamond market: it is subject to huge swings in consumer confidence.

It is because of the need to protect the industry from these downturns that De Beers makes no apology for operating the monopoly, and for doing so successfully: other cartels, like OPEC and the International Tin Council, have collapsed. It fears that a diamond market that did not have constancy would operate to the detriment of the product. But critics baulk at the implications of price fixing and supply control. Competition in production and distribution would classically act to secure less volatility, not more. Monopoly, by contrast, is open to vast abuse.

The cartel has to ride the switchback of a highly volatile world market. This volatility can be seen in the bottom-line earnings per share performance at De Beers. In 1980 the figure was 305 (SA) cents a share. By 1984 it had plunged to just 90 cents. The recovery to 1988 took it back to 327 cents, just seven per cent higher than the 1980 level. Thus, massive though the balance sheet figures are, they belie a problematic earnings quality. The cyclicity of the business means it requires a strong balance sheet to absorb the strain. And this is a key reason why shares in De Beers, despite the earnings burst in the late 1980s, remain among the most underrated in the world with a price earnings multiple of around six.

But when times are good, they are very good. In 1988 the CSO was confident enough to raise diamond prices by 15.5 per cent on average with a consequent further surge expected in De Beers' profits. The importance of the De Beers–CSO machine to the greater group was underlined by the recent appointment of CSO executive Peter Leyden to the main Anglo American board.

Critics keep up constant pressure. A secret, blistering complaint to the British Office of Fair Trading by Consolidated Gold Fields claimed that through the CSO, De Beers operated a price-fixing cartel that defied the laws of economic gravity. Not once has the CSO ever reduced the price of diamonds. The confidential research calculated that diamond prices are 15 per cent higher than they would be in an uncartelized market (this was before the recent price increase) and the full cost of this inflated price to the world jewellery trade across 54 million pieces of jewellery sold each year is thus reckoned at some $800 million on total sales of $39 billion. But the OFT declined to mount an investigation.

Nowhere is the De Beers diamond cartel more vocal than in its justification to the consumer. It has never promoted diamonds as an investment store of value *per se*. But it dances upon the pin of the psychological perception of value. People buying diamonds, says De Beers, have to be confident that the price will not collapse and their diamonds rendered worthless. The CSO has played to the hilt, through its $130 million-a-year consumer advertising, the psychological notion that diamonds are 'forever'.

Consumer confidence would evaporate if prices were allowed to plunge. Diamonds are, both by scarcity (a total of 350 tons is reckoned to have been mined in recorded history) and by intrinsic appeal, a luxury item. It is an iron law of marketing, whether of cars or Scotch whisky, that luxury items are killed by commodity pricing. 'Reassuringly expensive' is the implicit slogan used by market departments in order to maintain perceptions of product exclusivity and value. In the case of diamonds, the entire industry rests on a perception of product uniqueness, romance and beauty. They are signal senders, and people attach great importance to the signals they send – and receive.

Diamonds are, in the end, psychological: a 2000-year-old mystique, a true myth. Gem diamonds have no functional or investment value; they are, in Randolph Churchill's scathing words, 'all for the vanity of women', and, in the tart riposte, 'for the depravity of men'. Once cut, they have far greater brilliance than any other mineral. Freud would have fully understood: why else do people punch holes 3,000 feet into the earth?

This is the astonishing empire bequeathed by Harry Oppenheimer to his son Nicholas, now chairman of the CSO, deputy chairman of De Beers and a member of the Anglo American executive inner circle. A major decision taken in December 1989 was to develop the gigantic Venetia mine in the northern Transvaal. Capital spending of £300 million is required on a project involving the extraction of 3.3 million tons of ore a year, yielding more than four million carats of diamonds. The decision, important for South Africa, comes at a time when global consumer demand is slowing. Figures from the CSO in January 1990 revealed a consolidation of sales at around $4 billion. Can the market, headed for recession, take more diamonds? 'Dealing with a non-essential', says Nicholas Oppenheimer, 'is a constraint on us to think carefully about what we are going to do.'

The chairman of De Beers, Julian Ogilvie Thompson, enjoys a corporate power base that is unique. It is one driven by the necessity of stability and control. It is this culture which imbues the whole Anglo American empire. Across the crucial bridge of crossholdings – De Beers owning 38 per cent of Anglo American, Anglo American owning 34 per cent of De Beers – he enjoys a commanding pre-eminence. The history and culture of De Beers informs the need for such a grip.

This sense of protecting an inheritance, of making sure that control persists, is his central concern. He is a man sandwiched in a unique dynastic inheritance, who has had to beat off both financial and regulatory threats and challenges to the diamond empire.

Those threats and challenges do not lessen with the years. But the Oppenheimers have the benefit of experience. They have successfully beaten down every one for half a century.

2

Deepest Mines, Finest Wines

■

The Chinese word for crisis is made up of two other words: opportunity and danger. This definition more subtly allows for a sense of adaptive response to a deteriorating condition. It also more precisely captures the condition in which South Africa's largest company is now in.

This state of crisis has a number of facets: historical, cultural and political, and has arisen through the unique size and complexity of Anglo American. How does the company operate? And how have its problems arisen?

At the centre of Anglo American is its inner boardroom on the first floor of its headquarters in 44 Main Street, Johannesburg. It is a large room dominated by a sweeping oval table. Anglo American's 11-strong executive meets here twice a week.

The sense of quiet power emanates from the paintings in the room. Here are the paintings by Thomas Baines of great ships at anchor in the shelter of Table Bay in the Cape of Good Hope. Baines has caught them in the idle peace of a summer evening. 44 Main is the Table Bay of a hundred ships. Anglo American is one of the world's biggest and most complex industrial and financial empires, spread across South Africa and beyond, employing 200,000 people over a range of activities spanning gold mining, banking, life assurance, farming, brewing, car assembly, paper, coal, steel, platinum, diamonds, property development – and wine. It is a span from deepest mines to finest wines.

All told, the Anglo–De Beers quoted companies constitute some 60 per cent of the capitalization of the Johannesburg Stock Exchange. Anglo American's net assets alone stand at £4.6 billion. In 1988 its equity-accounted earnings totalled some £600 million. It is the Western world's largest gold producer with significant interests in mines, producing 20 per cent of total world gold output. But in the late 1980s gold was on the decline. In 1988 it accounted for less than a quarter of Anglo American's investment earnings.

The headquarters building, designed in 1937, is one of the most powerful in the world. Sir Ernest Oppenheimer said he wanted a building that was a marriage of a gold mine and a cathedral. He ended up with what can be best described as a police station designed by Mussolini. In an elegant reception room on the first floor, dominated by a grandfather clock, a receptionist picks up the phone and betrays the private company at the heart of the public one: 'E Oppenheimer and Sons. Can I help you?'

In a private suite, leased from the public company, Harry Oppenheimer works in a large long room, his desk at the far end. On the facing wall is a painting of his father; on the opposite wall a portrait of his son Nicholas.

There is a private Oppenheimer dining room at 44 Main, reached through an ante-room. All the furniture is black lacquer, but the most striking feature is the hand-painted French wallpaper. Under a swathe of turquoise sky are fantasies of the Orient, with golden temples and domes. In this opulent setting, even the cigar cutter is diamond encrusted.

The Oppenheimer family's direct shareholding in Anglo American of 8.3 per cent belies the enormous influence that it wields. It is hard to conceive that such a huge empire is under the control of a single family. But it is dominated by the Oppenheimer culture – Anglo American is a vast patriarchy. Sons and son-in-laws and godsons and cousins pepper the hierarchy.

Such a culture can be a source of great stability. But Anglo American is an uneasy, and at times unstable, balance between a private company and a public one; collegiate management and proprietorial; patriarchy and meritocracy. It craves understanding on the international stage, but its concerns can often seem those of a private club with its exclusive rules and personal enthusiasms.

'My father formed Anglo American,' Oppenheimer once declared, 'primarily of course for the good reason of making money. But from the beginning there was more to it than that.

'I've often said that a major job for the chairman of Anglo American is to keep a proper balance between what I call the monkeys and the do-gooders. Because without the monkeys the do-gooders never succeed. And without the do-gooders any success the monkeys bring about tends to be a bit second rate. Of course, the ideal man for the Anglo American Corporation is the idealist monkey.'

Seldom can such a playful remark have hit upon an inner truth at the heart of one of the world's most enigmatic empires. Oppenheimer has bequeathed not only a formidable intellectual tradition at Anglo American – the Rhodes scholar set must rank as one of the most intellectually powerful in any corporation anywhere – but one imbued with a distinctive liberal ethos. It is a culture that takes its social and moral obligations seriously. But that brings considerable problems in its train.

Maintaining this dual system has not been easy. Some feel that too much time is spent on social issues that the group by itself is not in a position to address; others feel that the company has failed to press home the corporate attack on Apartheid sufficiently. But the need to tackle the many corporate problems, and the political and financial isolation of South Africa, has become so acute as to be not just the concern of the idealists but of the entire corporation.

So how does it manage its primary concern of making money? Gold may be on the wane, but gold is at the heart of Anglo American; it is its central expertise.

*   *

Six thousand feet into the earth, half-way down the Western Deep Levels, 70 kilometres west of Johannesburg, in the deepest gold mine in the world, Fallang Mobe drills 80 holes a day into gold-bearing rock. He is 40 years old and comes from Lesotho. He is married with five children, four sons and a daughter. He earns R28.85 a shift. He works in what Sir Ernest Oppenheimer described as 'the most important enterprise ever started in South Africa'. Anglo American has spent tens of millions of rand on its development. It is one of the most technologically-advanced mines in the world; and arguably the Corporation's greatest feat.

A four-deck cage plunges 160 miners at a time down the most expensive shaft in the world. It travels through the hardest rock towards the centre of the earth at 15.3 metres a second. Fallang

Mobe starts to sweat long before his work begins. At the bottom of the Western Deeps, the rocks are hot: the temperature can reach 55 °C, hot enough to cause burns. The air needs to be cooled by 50,000 tons of ice produced every day.

The greatest hazard is 'rockburst'. Western Deeps suffers high levels of seismicity, some occurrences exceeding 3.0 on the Richter scale. In the area of Western Deeps are vast underground lakes. Once, the rockface burst and water flooded in to a depth of 550 metres. When the rival West Driefontein was flooded, Western Deeps tried to help by siphoning off the water. The intensity of the pressure was phenomenal: 'As the steel drill rods encountered the water, they were fired like bullets and buckled into what looked like spaghetti against the rock face of the drill gallery.'[1]

The journey time to the gold-bearing ore face, or stope, is half an hour. After walking along a tunnel there is a crawl through a maze of gulleys before reaching the stope. The rock is pinned by pontoons of logs, coated with fire-resistant paint. In this tiny bubble of air, the heat is intense and the smell of gelignite almost overwhelming.

This is where Fallang Mobe works. He has been tested for physical fitness, but the main occupational hazard at Western Deeps is mental breakdown: there is a high incidence of psychological illness, and no known cure for working at the Western Deeps.

Out of the darkness there suddenly comes a loud creak. Fallang Mobe stops drilling: every sound brings a sense of entrapment, but this one especially. *'Die Rotse praat,'* he explains. *'The rocks are talking.'* The creaks are reassuring for the miners. The time to get out is not when the rocks are talking, but when they cease to talk.

The reef he is drilling, tilted at an angle of 22 degrees, is like a tiny layer in an epic geological sandwich. The gold in the rock is microscopic: for every ton of rock that he blasts out of his gulley, the gold produced is equivalent to the sprinkle of salt on a boiled egg. In 1988 Western Deeps drilled six and a half million tons of ore. It produced 39 tons of gold.

In this black reef thousands of feet underground and subject to fire, flood and rockburst, Fallang Mobe makes gold possible. No one who has seen what he does thinks casually about a piece of gold

[1] Oxley, John, *Down Where No Lion Walked: The Story of Western Deep Levels*, Southern Book Publishers, 1989.

jewellery again. He, too, is at the heart of Anglo American. He is also a shareholder in the company.

*   *

The head of the gold division until recently, Peter Gush, a 51-year-old mining engineer and Rhodes scholar, ran an empire accounting for some 37 per cent of Anglo American's investments by value. Anglo American has a 49 per cent interest in Amgold – South Africa's premier gold mining company. In 1988–89 it earned R330.3 million (£75 million) on investments valued at over R6 billion (£1.3 billion).

The principal gold mining companies are Free State Consolidated, Vaal Reefs, Western Deep Levels, Elandsrand Gold, South African Land and Exploration, Afrikander Lease, South Vaal and East Rand Gold. Together, these companies produce almost 250 tons of gold, 40 per cent of South Africa's total output.

This core business is faced with crisis on three sides: pressures to improve black miners' pay; severe cost-inflation which is hitting profits; and a decline in gold reserves. A central concern of Anglo American in recent years has been to close the wage gap between black and white miners. Its gold division employs over 215,000 and is the largest of the six gold producing members of the Chamber of Mines. Some 38 per cent of the total workforce on Chamber-member gold mines is employed on Anglo American serviced mines. Anglo American thus sets the pace of mining pay and conditions. The black National Union of Mineworkers, which is granted office accommodation at Anglo American's mines and hostel sites, has some 111,000 members in Anglo American mines. Its nearest rival – Gold Fields of South Africa – has 24,000. Minimum wages in the lowest job categories at Anglo American mines are up to 20 per cent higher than at GFSA. Real wages in these categories have increased four-fold since the early 1970s.

The dilemma faced by Peter Gush's successor, Clem Sunter, is in raising pay scales against a background of ever-increasing depth, complexity and cost of mining operations (cost-inflation in South Africa is rampant: between 1984 and 1988 the working costs per kilogram of gold produced by the Chamber of Mines rose by 126 per cent). The hard realities of economics sit upon the social engineer.

'The whole industry was the last to be de-regulated,' Gush explains. 'Under the Scheduled Persons Act only whites could get a blasting certificate. The whole mining hierarchy is based on that. We fought it tooth and nail and finally got rid of it in 1988.

'In real terms the whole wage structure has been tilted. There has been a major redistribution of wealth.'

Lower profits seriously threaten the future of the industry on two fronts: first, less profit can be retained to keep existing mines in operation; second, lower dividends reduce investor confidence.

One of Anglo American's central dilemmas is having to confront mine development costs of R2 billion with a payback time of over ten years in a country whose political stability and commitment to a market economy is, at best, problematic. It is further compelled to this investment crisis by the fact that the majority of its mines are middle-aged and their reserves are being depleted at a rate faster than that at which new discoveries are being made.

Overall, gold production is on the wane. South African output has declined from 683 tons in 1984 to 619 tons in 1988. In contrast, other major free-market producers – Canada, the United States and Australia – have shown significant production increases on a cost base that is significantly lower. South Africa's share of non-Communist production has fallen from almost 60 per cent to less than 40 per cent in the 1980s.

Gold as a source of profit has been in both absolute and relative decline at Anglo American. Investment earnings from gold have fallen from 40 per cent to 22 per cent of the group total in the five years 1985–89. This is the crisis at the core.

There are other ships in the sweep of Table Bay. Anglo Farms is also at the heart of Anglo American. It is one of the biggest livestock, vegetable, fruit and wine companies in South Africa. Every day a fleet of 25 trucks delivers fruit and vegetables to Anglo American's mines. Anglo Farms feeds some 250,000 employees. The group owns half of the company, which has a turnover of R180 million. It provides fruit juice concentrate that the world will deny comes from South Africa. Anglo Farms' figures tell a different story: some 60 per cent of output is exported. The products are discreetly shipped to Europe. After an initial drop from sanctions, profits are bounding to R12 million. The company is also a leading producer of premium wines. It owns the Boschendal vineyard, one of the oldest in South Africa.

In 1985, the company was exporting R2 million of produce, almost all of it to the US. Now it exports R30 million to non-US markets.

Another ship is anchored in Table Bay: Highveld Steel and Vanadium. It is one of the most important steel companies in the world, producing one million tons a year. Its key product is high-grade vanadium spinel (vanadium enhances the durability and strength of steel required at extremes of stress and temperature). Highveld dominates the world vanadium market, of which it accounts for some 40 per cent. An important customer of Highveld is the Soviet Union: Highveld steel can be found in the trans-Siberian oil pipeline. Another important customer is the United States. It also serves the European car industry.

Highveld, a greenfield project in the Transvaal, is enjoying an earnings surge, and in the six months to end-June 1989 it turned in pre-tax profits 400 per cent ahead at R304 million. It is 52 per cent-owned by Anglo American Industrial Corporation, which has assets of R6.2 billion (£1.4 billion) and a turnover of almost R5 billion, spanning textiles, pulp, paper, car assembly, electronics, freight and travel, explosives and chemicals. The Mondi Paper Company alone employs 15,500 people.

The head of AMIC is Graham Boustred. He enjoys very little press exposure, but he is one of the most powerful figures in Anglo American and a key member of its inner circle. Within the Corporation he is viewed with affection – at a distance of a hundred yards. He has a way of cutting through the inessential, tilting his chair back and bringing a fist crashing down on the table, saying 'What bloody garbage is this!' Oppenheimer says of him: 'He is the most impossible man. But he is the greatest industrialist in South Africa.'

Boustred, a chemist by training, is best summed up by his bridge. It is impossible to miss his bridge. It spans one of the arterial motorways of Johannesburg and links the buildings of West Witwatersrand University. It is a solid steel bridge, an engineer's bridge, defiant with its huge bolts and girders and rivets.

A story is told (best treated as apocryphal, though some swear it to be true) that Oppenheimer wanted to soften the appearance of the bridge, with rococo motifs of famous poets on one side and scenes of early mining endeavour on the other. But he was apprehensive of Boustred and slipped in the plans anonymously. Crashing down on the plans came Boustred's great fist: 'What bloody garbage is this!'

Boustred's empire is one of the biggest in South Africa and its contribution to Anglo American's profits has shot from 11.8 per cent to almost 19 per cent in three years. Highveld and Mondi are two principal examples of 'self-started' Anglo American projects. 'We like', says Boustred, 'to germinate projects, starting from greenfield. People say we are not entrepreneurial. But they overlook the fact that some 30 per cent of companies on the Johannesburg Stock Exchange were started by Anglo American from the grass roots.'

There are more huge galleons in this Table Bay. Anglo American is a major force in car manufacture and distribution through the 76 per cent-owned South African Motor Corporation. Amcoal, with 12 collieries, is one of the largest private sector coal mining groups in the world. Anglo American has a 51.4 per cent interest. It also has a 22.5 per cent interest in First National Bank, which bought Barclays' South African subsidiary. Anglo American has a 40 per cent stake in Southern Life, one of the biggest life assurance companies.

There is also a near-40 per cent interest in Johannesburg Consolidated Investments, with substantial holdings in gold, platinum, diamonds, coal, copper and other minerals. Anglo American has a direct 23.8 per cent interest in Rustenburg Platinum Mines, the world's largest platinum producer; JCI has a 32.6 per cent interest. The Corporation therefore effectively blocks the encroachment of Afrikaner interests by JCI's holdings in diamonds and platinum. At the same time, JCI has a keen sense of independence from Anglo American, and has a distinctive approach to Anglo American in mining operations – one characterized by labour-saving capital equipment and participative management: group policy is to draw everyone into decision-making, regardless of colour or rank. In 1988, JCI's attributable earnings came to R324 million (£74 million).

JCI's group economic adviser, Dr Ronnie Bethlehem, sums up the mining industry's dilemma thus: 'South Africa is a schizophrenic country. It has conflicting economic requirements. Because of high black population growth there is an urgent need to create jobs. But there is a need, because of sanctions, to be super-competitive. This necessitates very efficient mining operations and this is best achieved by labour-saving technology. That is the paradox we are up against.'

Overseas, there is Minorco where Anglo American has a 39.1 per cent interest (De Beers an additional 20.9 per cent). Minorco, based in Luxemburg, holds dominant shareholdings in Johnson Matthey (through 36 per cent-owned Charter Consolidated) and Engelhard Minerals in the United States (30 per cent).

Anglo American has seldom been successful in exporting itself, or building a substantial assets and earnings base outside South Africa as, for example, Rembrandt has done. But sanctions and monopoly constraints in its home base, together with political uncertainties, have made successful international expansion critically important to the future of the group. Unless it gets Minorco right, Anglo American will slip very quickly down the global mining ladder.

The biggest and most important ship in this Table Bay is De Beers. Anglo American holds 32.6 per cent of the world's diamond supplier. Through its Diamond Services Division, it provides technical consulting and other services to De Beers. The diamond giant accounts for more than a quarter of Anglo American's equity-accounted earnings, and 20 per cent of its net asset value. This owes much to the strong resurgence in the diamond trade in recent years, but it remains arguably the most volatile and least stable source of Anglo American's earnings. Sustaining this percentage contribution should not be counted on.

De Beers' chairman, Julian Ogilvie Thompson ('JOT'), the leading Rhodes scholar in a corporate structure peppered with them, is arguably now the most powerful man in the greater group and one of the most financially astute; he is also chairman of Minorco and a deputy chairman of Anglo American.

A former personal assistant to Oppenheimer, he worked for merchant banking house Lazard Brothers before joining Anglo American where he quickly rose to head its finance division. He has been an executive director since 1971, playing a key role in central policy. He has climbed his way up through a blend of intellect, merit, guile, an uncanny ability to outmanoeuvre rivals – and an unswerving loyalty to Oppenheimer. Whichever room Oppenheimer was in, JOT would be at the door.

JOT is also one of the most cultured men in the Anglo American firmament and a respected corporate ambassador. A diplomat by instinct, with a shrewd way of reading men (if not always handling them too well) he has been for years one of the group's chief ambassadors to the Government in Pretoria, and a member of the President's Economic Council.

Although he has little time for the absurdities of Apartheid, he has not always seen eye-to-eye with the new generation of 'idealist monkeys' – the earnest young Anglo American Corporation liberals who have parachuted in from university to personal-assistant-to-director level and who have been urging the board to step up the pressure on the Nationalists. Not for him the white angst of a night with playwright Athol Fugard at Johannesburg's Market Theatre – a favourite haunt of the group's Young Turks. JOT has never lost sight of the fact that there is a business to be run, realities that have to be accepted – and living with Pretoria is one of them.

His concern at De Beers is to keep its single mindedness intact. It has a R10 billion portfolio of investments outside the diamond business, but these underpin those of Anglo American itself. De Beers is a major shareholder in companies such as Minorco, JCI, AMIC and First National Bank. These holdings buttress Anglo American's interest and further act to freeze out rivals and predators.

JOT works closely with Nicholas Oppenheimer who stands at the gateway to one of the greatest corporate inheritances in the world. Unassuming and diffident in manner, he is proving to be, like his father, a late developer. That should fool no one. He is a deputy chairman of Anglo American and has ruled the CSO with firmness. He is already a director of some 90 companies.

This inner quartet of Anglo American is completed by the chairman Gavin Relly, 63, who joined the Corporation in 1949 as private secretary to the Oppenheimers. He played a crucial role in the launch of Highveld Steel and Vanadium, and at 32 was appointed a manager of the Corporation. He took charge of Anglo American's copper operations in Zambia and the group's North American operations based in Toronto. He has a grasp of Anglo American's problem in the political theatre of the United States. Has Anglo American got to the limits of its growth? 'I don't think that at all,' says Relly. 'You have got to see Anglo in a longer perspective than one finds on the Stock Exchange where analysts concentrate on half-yearly or even quarterly results. Anglo's concern is much longer-term and it has to do with the development of Southern Africa. The general thrust can't respond to short-term demands. We are dealing with developmental issues which provide long-term business.

'We have a capital spending programme of R8 billion (£1.8 billion) and almost all of that will be spent in South Africa. We are moving into a political phase that will be extremely bumpy, but which will create the base for a multi-racial constitution.'

Relly's management has been collegiate in style. He presides over a formidable bureaucracy: a total of some 2,500 people are employed at the head office complex in Johannesburg. It spills over to 45 Main

Street and into the Unitas building in Fox Street. At its core is a Praetorian Guard of 350 employed in the finance office under Mike King: the state within the state at Anglo American.

In Table Bay, all the ships form part of a fleet. And the sense of a fleet adds greatly to Anglo American's formidable aura of strength.

Overall, the profit record looks impressive: between 1980 and 1989 equity-accounted earnings have risen from R525 million to R2.6 billion, a compound growth rate of 20 per cent. Net asset value has shot from R4.9 billion to R28.5 billion, a compound growth rate of 22 per cent. Dividends per share have risen at an annual rate of 16 per cent.

However, the figures should be seen in the context of an inflation rate now running at some 15 per cent a year. Moreover, even though the earnings rate has been accelerating, it counts for little on the world's stock markets. A particularly worrying phenomenon for Anglo American is not only the huge discount at which its shares stand to the assets of the business, but the relentless contraction in the number of outside shareholders. There has been a notable decline in the percentage of shares held by non-South Africans, from 25 per cent to 11 per cent during the 1980s, largely the result of sanctions and disinvestment. The percentage held by UK and Continental European residents is only 8.7 per cent; that by Americans just 2.1 per cent.

For the company to have any global pretensions this trend has to be stopped and ideally reversed. It is a colossal task, and not altogether within Anglo American's power to achieve. But it is one which the group appears to have wearied. Its chairman, Gavin Relly, puts it vividly: 'People have been bullied out of Anglo American stock in the US. We could spend 50 million rand a year on investor relations and it wouldn't make a twitch in people's enthusiasm.'

Despite protests that outsiders do not make a proper attempt to understand it, the group gives the appearance of having retreated into itself. It does not communicate well with the investment world. One leading stock market analyst in Johannesburg remarks: 'The Anglo people are very ivory towerish. They don't mix with the financial community at all. Its people are much more concerned about getting invited for Friday night dinners at Brenthurst than whether their division makes a profit. It has got super assets. But there is no entrepreneurship at the top. Anglo American is not really bottom-line orientated.' Says another: 'They are proud of their greenfield projects. But there has not been a major new venture since the Elandsrand mine in 1977. Now that De Beers has weathered the severe recession of the early- and mid-1980s and is generating enormous cash flow, the pressure is building up to find new projects for the greater group to invest in.' One analyst, reckoned to be the top Anglo American watcher in South Africa, still waits to be invited to lunch at the Corporation.

Like South Africa generally, Anglo American has to contend with a formidable brain drain: a fear-inspired exodus of white entre-preneurial and management talent, known locally as the 'chicken run'. But it seeks to attract the brightest with a system of fast-track promotion through 44 Main, one feature of which is the personal-assistant system: nearly all the key actors in Anglo American, includ-ing its chairman, Gavin Relly, have, at one time or another, been personal assistants to Harry Oppenheimer.

Arguably two of the brightest now in Anglo American are Bobby Godsell and Clem Sunter. They are the Young Turks of 44 Main. Godsell, 37, is a director of Anglo American and the man in charge of industrial relations and public affairs. He is plugged into a web of powerful contacts. He is a member of the state President's Economic Advisory Council and has served on the Buthelezi Commission. Together with Professor Peter Berger, he edited *South Africa Beyond Apartheid*:[1] one of the most seminal books written about the country and its problems.

Says Godsell: 'The company has a liberal culture in the old sense. It is run by highly individualistic people, not a politbureau. We like to think of Anglo as a wealth-creating exercise, not a job-creating one. We have got to produce the goods and services in the most effective way and we have got to look at optimal efficiency. The greatest investment we can make here is increasing the skill base. That is what increases the wealth potential of the black population.'

One of Godsell's central concerns is to hive off and 'privatize' central functions, such as transport and catering, to fledgling black firms. 'The challenge for Anglo American is to see how we can develop commercially beneficial relationships with small companies. We are not doing this philanthropically. We are doing it to save money. The development of small business is one of the challenges of Anglo's survival.'

[1] *South Africa Beyond Apartheid*, Human and Rousseau Tafelberg, 1988.

The official soothsayer of Anglo American is Clem Sunter. Until his recent appointment as head of the gold and uranium divisions, he was part of the chairman's office reporting on scenario planning. In his acclaimed book, *The World and South Africa in the 1990s*,[2] he set out the range of possibilities for a post-Apartheid South Africa.

The themes of black entrepreneurship, empowerment and power transference increasingly preoccupy Anglo American. Critics see this as evidence of an intellectual and moral escapism at Anglo American, claiming that in all this long range theorizing, it is evading the problems and requirements of the here and now. The company has acquiesced in political repression and has not, for example, been as outspoken as it might have been on press censorship. Anglo American, say its critics, is high on theory, low on the immediate redress of black grievances.

Similar criticism is made of its corporate responsibility role. To dismiss it as veneer would be wrong, but there are doubts over its effectiveness, and indeed, whether it can create anything like a 'critical mass' effect to be notable at all.

The Chairman's Fund, managed by Michael O'Dowd, with an annual revenue of R50 million, concentrates its central spending on education and housing. Anglo American also gives support to the state-backed Small Business Development Corporation which has lent R461 million to 19,000 entrepreneurs, creating some 200,000 jobs. In the West Orlando district of Soweto can be found some 19,000 square feet of industrial space for black businesses, where Anglo American has contracted-out activities ranging from sign-writing to the manufacture of catering uniforms. Says Gareth Penny, head of Anglo American's small business unit: 'Our target is to contract out work to the value of R90 million to small business. It is a great equalizer.'

Anglo American is a major corporate sponsor of the Urban Foundation, which provides housing finance for blacks. Some 6,500 sites are serviced by the Foundation. In October 1989, Oppenheimer was instrumental in getting the British Government to contribute towards a R20 million loan scheme which will trigger R1 billion of housing for low-income black families. The most recent innovation is an employee share ownership scheme. It required explanatory leaflets

[2] *The World and South Africa in the 1990s*, Human and Rousseau Tafelberg, 1987.

in 11 languages explaining alien concepts such as 'final dividend'. Of the 195,000 employees eligible, 141,000 (72 per cent) have taken up the offer.

But is the wealth spreading deeply enough, widely enough? Says Ronnie Bethlehem at JCI: 'Employee share schemes don't address the problem of redistribution of ownership in South Africa and the great inequalities. The focus should be on black economic empowerment, but at present in the entrepreneurial sector black participation is minimal.'

Anglo American is also up against time and the need to heed black aspirations of change *now*. One of the senior figures within Anglo American who despaired at the slow pace of change was former executive director Gordon Waddell who is still spoken of in awe at JCI where he was chief executive. At one electrifying board meeting at JCI, Waddell, in shirtsleeves, rammed home the way that history can cruelly judge the role of a too-compliant corporate sector. 'Well, gentlemen,' he concluded, his Scots rugby-player fist landing on the boardroom table, 'which one of you wants this company to be remembered as the I G Farben of Apartheid?'

For the Rhodes scholar set at Anglo American, the Waddell fist struck uncomfortably close, and it jangles the nerves to this day.

Such are the problems that face Anglo American's 'idealist monkeys'. It is a corporation whose intellectual calibre ranks among the highest in the world, but one troubled by the dangers inherent in its own management succession; a declining earnings base at its core; monopoly constraints at home; failures abroad; an exodus of overseas investors; and a political system that has brought increasing isolation. At each point, opportunity and danger press hard against each other.

3

At the Windows of Africa

■

From the crisis of the library, from the bureaucratic Hall of Mirrors that is Anglo American's headquarters at 44 Main, where does Oppenheimer escape to?

Lying deep in the semi-arid bush of the lower veld of the eastern Transvaal, bordering the Kruger National Park and snuggling into a fold of the Olifants River, is Harry Oppenheimer's private retreat. Called Ntoma, it is his personal game reserve, reached by private plane which lands on a makeshift clearing in the bush. From the sky it looks as if a finger has scratched the earth.

On visits, Oppenheimer's plane is talked down by one of the most makeshift and haphazard control towers in international air travel: a two-way radio in the front seat of a Land Rover driven by ranger John Robinson. There is a 20-minute drive by jeep across the bush. Its deep red earth is parched and on the makeshift track the soil is dusty grey: drought here is a long visitor, and little habitation presents itself. But the veld teems with life. Through the dust and baked scrubland there comes into view a small group of thatched huts, encircled by a pool of luscious green and manicured grass. Lawn sprinklers lazily keep the African heat at bay.

At all times this compound – so surreal it could have been painted on the scrub by Dali – is kept ready. In front of the main hut is a long veranda overlooking the veld and its wildlife across the dried-up bed of the Klaserie river. Ntoma, too, encapsulates the nature of its owner: a blend of understatement and the spectacular. It is here that some of the world's most powerful men have been entertained by the Oppenheimers.

The veranda is Oppenheimer's window on Africa. And power on

the veranda looks on power without: in Ntoma's carefully kept register of visitors can be found the names of Agnelli, Kennedy, Kissinger, Rothschild and Rockefeller. There are also the names of close family and senior executives of the Anglo American empire: Harry's son-in-law Hank Slack; his godson Roger Phillimore and his wife Virginia; Minorco's finance director Tony Lea and his wife Clare. Cousin Sir Philip Oppenheimer is a frequent visitor. Earlier visitors include Harry Oppenheimer's former finance chief Neil Clarke and his author-wife Sonia. Then there are the names of friends and associates: Max Borkum, one of the most powerful figures on the Johannesburg Stock Exchange; Conservative MP Tim Kitson and his wife Sally.

Here Oppenheimer has entertained the most powerful figures of 44 Main, the knights of Anglo American's Monsalvat. And it is here that Minorco's Young Turks met in secret during the battle for Consolidated Gold Fields. Here, away from Sir Michael Edwardes, young Anglo American discussed its moves.

In the centre of the compound is Oppenheimer's swimming pool, oddly shaped and curiously sloped. There is a reason for its shape: one night there came upon the camp a most disturbing series of bellows followed by an almighty splash. A hippo had wandered through the compound and tumbled into the pool. It took two days to manoeuvre the hippo out. Now the pool has a wide, gently-sloping ramp leading to the centre, enabling the hippos to wallow their way out with a little more decorum than they tumble in. Even for hippos, this is a five-star stay.

Lying some ten miles west of Ntoma, on the northern bank of the Klaserie and situated on a commanding ridge is the bush retreat of Julian Ogilvie Thompson. Here in the early 1980s he brought Consolidated Gold Fields chairman Rudolph Agnew.

JOT is married to Tessa Brand, daughter of Viscount Hampden. She has much to do at the Klaserie retreat, looking after the British visitors who are invited for weekend stays. On Sunday mornings, they often drive over to Ntoma and John Robinson will be the first whose eyes will narrow at the tell-tale dust of an alien Nissan jeep. JOT's British visitors are easily recognized, with their mint-new colonial hats, *Out of Africa* designer khaki and Royal Opera House field glasses.

Ntoma's first owner was the American platinum king, Charles Engelhard, on whom the novelist Ian Fleming based his book *Goldfinger*. The relationship between Engelhard and Oppenheimer was one of the deepest and most remarkable in the history of the natural resources industry. The basic understanding of that relationship was that Engelhard would look after Harry Oppenheimer's businesses in the United States; Oppenheimer would look after Engelhard in South Africa.

Oppenheimer was not only to take a major, and subsequently controlling share in Engelhard's platinum empire in the United States, but he was to cultivate and promote Charlie Engelhard's corporate adopted son, Hank Slack, to one of the most powerful positions in Anglo American. Slack sits on its 30-strong board and is head of offshoot Minorco's investments in America. Long-serving, hard-nosed career men in Anglo American fume at Hank's effortless elevation.

Although an anti-Apartheid activist as a first year student, and set for a business-school course at Harvard, Slack's encounter with South Africa was one of immediate fascination, followed swiftly by both personal and corporate involvement.

Engelhard bought Ntoma, with its hundreds of acres of bush, some 30 kilometres south of the Palabora copper mine, as a surprise gift for his wife Jane. The narrow clearing in the bush that now serves as a landing strip for Oppenheimer's private plane is still nicknamed 'Charlie Engelhard Boulevard'.

After Jane Engelhard suffered a heart attack at Jan Smuts airport, it was Slack who visited her in hospital and who kept an anxious Oppenheimer constantly briefed on her health. That is how Slack and Oppenheimer were to form a strong, unique and personal bond, consolidated when Slack married Mary, Oppenheimer's daughter.

The couple live at White Hills, a 60-acre estate in northern Johannesburg. It is policed by uniformed armed guards with gold capbands bearing the estate name. Mary Slack is now official art buyer for Anglo American. The spacious hallway between lounge and dining room serves as a showpiece, with large canvasses of modern African art. The paintings are bold and wide, with a vibrancy of colour and an intensity of space that is uniquely African. These are her windows on Africa.

The purchase price of Ntoma was just R250,000 (£57,000 at current exchange rates). Now, of course, it takes many times that figure in upkeep and maintenance alone. The sprinkler hoses maintain an oasis of lush green lawn and the impala lily in constant bloom.

In the evening, over open-air dinner by a fire of glowing logs, conversations have unfolded about the state of both Anglo American and South Africa.

It is a state of many windows. At them, Oppenheimer has cause to contemplate not only his successes, but his setbacks. Why has the head of so vast a mining, industrial and financial empire, failed to make any political impression on South Africa? Why (when one looks through one window) does Oppenheimer not throw the expected shadows across the political stage? Why has he never got near to the levers of political power? The answers are complex and multi-faceted. And the shape of truth changes depending on the angle from which one looks.

The United States has applied increasing economic pressure on South Africa and its corporate sector. Not only is there fierce political opposition to an extension of Anglo American's operations in the United States, but there is not a single federal agency or pension fund that holds Anglo American stock. According to Relly, they have been 'bullied out' by the anti-Apartheid lobby that has failed to recognize what Anglo American, over a sustained period of many years, has sought to do. The lobby sees an Anglo American that has prospered on an enormous supply of cheap black labour; central to its success has been Apartheid, surely the expression of the dominant economic interests in South Africa? Is not Anglo American a prime beneficiary, making its operations and ambitions legitimate for challenge?

In reality, it is not that simple. For many years Anglo American – and the Oppenheimers personally – have helped finance first the opposition Progressive Federal Party, and now the Democratic Party. Its senior directors have been prominent anti-Nationalist MPs. These have included Gordon Waddell, Zach de Beer (now co-leader of the Democratic Party) and, not least, Harry Oppenheimer himself. Anglo American was the first company to recognize the black National Union of Mineworkers, has banished racial segregation within the group and operates an equal opportunity programme.

The Corporation's window on South Africa is one less lit by moral conscience than by a fusion of an early imperial idealism and a hard-headed and increasingly urgent belief that Apartheid is throttling economic growth and the development of a high wage-earning, economically-powerful black entrepreneurial consumer class. Without this growth neither Anglo American nor the white tribe stands a chance of survival.

'Rhodes', Harry Oppenheimer declared, 'was in the habit of saying that his chartered company offered imperialism, which I think one could translate in modern terms into patriotism, patriotism plus five per cent . . . what my father derived from the doctrine of Rhodes was that making money, while extremely important in itself, should be looked upon as a by-product of the development of southern Africa.' His father believed 'that the process of economic development would inevitably, by its own internal imperatives, produce African advancement and an end to racial discrimination'.

Harry Oppenheimer updated the theme: free enterprise is 'the only economic system compatible with economic freedom, with freedom of choice'. It is incompatible with Apartheid.

Oppenheimer read politics, philosophy and economics at Christ Church, Oxford and was elected Member of Parliament for Kimberley in 1948, his father's seat, on the United Party ticket. The Afrikaners distrusted him from the outset. The Verwoerd and Vorster regimes saw in Anglo American a fickle and disloyal Jewish capitalist élite. In the Afrikaner press Oppenheimer was caricatured as 'Hoggenheimer': it wanted Anglo American nationalized.

They saw in the Corporation a centre of power greater than the state itself, and opposed to the state; and in any political order it is the will of the state that must prevail. Many has been the occasion when state president, P W Botha would leer and wag his finger in the faces of Gavin Relly and Julian Ogilvie Thompson: 'We, my friend, have over a million votes. How many votes has Anglo American?'

The Oppenheimers have been shut out from political power by instinctive Afrikaner mistrust. Two events in particular shaped this suspicion. The first was in 1922 when Jan Smuts brought in the army, and then the air force, to smash a white miners' rebellion sparked by fears that the mineowners were replacing them with cheap black labour. Some 230 were killed in the repression.

The second was the anti-Nationalist Party 'Torch Commando' movement in the 1950s, when English opinion in South Africa was mobilized against Afrikaner moves to create a white constitution and a break from Britain. The Torch Commando was soon dubbed a tool of 'Oppenheimer Ltd' and the fury of the Nationalist Party burst into the open over the discovery of a secret businessmen's fund of

£1 million. It was seen as an attempt to overthrow the Government, and the man behind it all was 'the honourable mining magnate on that side of the House' – Oppenheimer.

The caricature of the cigar-puffing 'Hoggenheimer' with its anti-semitic associations of 'money power' burst out again in the Afrikaner Press. Oppenheimer was forced to confess that, yes, the fund had been set up by businessmen 'worried about the way things are going in South Africa' and, yes, he was its chairman. Its objectives were similar to those of the United Party: to promote racial tolerance, uphold democracy and defend the constitution.

But the Nationalists saw the fund as something more sinister: an attempt by big business to subvert the Government. Oppenheimer and the Torch Commandos were, claimed the Nationalists, planning another Jameson Raid aimed at the overthrow of Afrikaner interests. The United Party, proclaimed Prime Minister Dr Loock, was 'now altogether controlled by Oppenheimer Ltd. What we have against us is money power, principally under the leadership of Oppenheimer . . . Oppenheimer with his millions exercises a greater influence than, I think, any man in South Africa has ever had.'

However influential Oppenheimer may have overtly or discreetly been, 'money power' was unable to dislodge the Afrikaner Right and block the rise of Dr Verwoerd, who ushered in Grand Apartheid and a rule by the Nationalist Party unbroken for more than 40 years. The suspicion that 'Oppenheimer Inc' was out to subvert the Afrikaner nation was a constant and recurring theme of the Verwoerd era. Secret Broederbond investigations sought to chart the Oppenheimer grip on South African life.

But the fact remains that, for all the economic and financial power of Oppenheimer, the will of Apartheid triumphed – and that raised an ambiguity over Anglo American's position. As the *Johannesburg Sunday Times* commented on the Verwoerd attacks: 'Don't worry, Mr Oppenheimer. They cannot do without you. They know it and you know it . . . The fact, of course, is that it is Mr Oppenheimer and men like him who make the wheels go round in South Africa, who provide it with the sinews of war and enable it to withstand the assaults of the world. Basically, it is they who keep the Government in power – and the Government knows it.'

In reality, the flow of power from 44 Main was not so simple. First, it could make little impact on the monolithic strength and ideological certitude of Afrikaner nationalism. Second, for all the spider's cobweb charts showing Anglo American reaching into hundreds of companies, the dynamics of the web often ran counter to the image suggested. Anglo American dare not push its weight around in many cases for fear of reprisals against its corporate power. And the ultimate sanction, that of being taken over by the state, was not one to be brushed aside as bluff.

Oppenheimer continued to speak out, and is regarded by most South Africans as an opposition figure of great stature. But, as Gordon Waddell, Oppenheimer's former son-in-law and ex-chief executive of Johannesburg Consolidated Investments recalls: 'The chairman of Anglo American cannot declare war on South Africa. There are limits to how he can oppose.'

There were limits, too, to what Anglo American and Oppenheimer personally could do on their own. Despite public expressions of support for the Progressive Federal Party by other major companies, little by way of financial support was forthcoming: Oppenheimer remained the largest single private donor. Recalls Waddell, himself a former PFP MP: 'Where business really let the future down was in its failure to provide the money required to finance a proper opposition. The amounts given were pitifully inadequate in relation to the donors' overall wealth. It was extraordinarily pathetic and they will live to rue the day.'

Waddell, an executive director of Anglo American for seven years, returned to Britain in 1987 disillusioned with the pace of change. He does not exclude Anglo American itself from criticism: 'What I felt very depressing was that really fundamental change was required to avoid bloodshed. But these views were held by a very small minority in the corporate hierarchy. Business has been a force for change in South Africa, but has it done all that it should have done? My answer is "no".'

Under Relly, Anglo American has tended to concentrate on an applied and pragmatic opposition rather than relying exclusively on the political front: it has forced the pace on raising minimum wages for black miners and devotes substantial time and resources to raising educational and technical training standards, enabling blacks to rise into the higher-skilled and better-paid jobs. The Urban Foundation, heavily sponsored by Anglo American, has mounted articulate and constructive lobbying campaigns for changes in policy and the law.

Meanwhile in public, Relly has denounced racial segregation in residence, schools, job categories and land ownership, and restrictions on free movement about the country as being incompatible with a modernizing, industrializing society: 'A society socially engineered on a race basis is not economically viable.'

Dr Ronnie Bethlehem, group economic adviser to JCI, joined Relly in warning that the need to expand secondary and tertiary industries in the economy 'cannot be reconciled with Apartheid any longer. The needs of a modern, Western-type industrial state have become inconsistent with a system which does not permit the development of black skills when the white population is not large enough to provide the skills required. Nor can such needs be satisfied if artificial restrictions are imposed on the development of the domestic consumer market.'

But there was a deeper worry: the longer Apartheid dragged on, the greater the polarization in South Africa and the likelihood of its violent replacement by black radical socialism. From the window of the banned African National Congress, exiled in Lusaka, the more the Nationalist Government criminalized its existence the stronger the mythology of the ANC became.

The ANC sees South Africa as the last outlaw state, denying one of the most universal rights. According to a survey by American political analyst Tom Karis, 'in a free election in South Africa, the outlawed ANC could possibly win three-quarters of the black vote as well as some white votes'.

Such a conclusion would be challenged by Mangosuthu Buthelezi, head of the predominantly Zulu Inkatha movement which claims a mass membership of 1.3 million organized in 3,000 branches. There has been close contact between Anglo American and Buthelezi, in a search for middle ground. But here, too, Anglo American has to confront the legacy of its past and the perception of little space between white big business and Afrikanerdom.

Faced with this utter lack of dialogue between white and black, Relly, though traditionally thought to be more conservative than Oppenheimer, led a group of businessmen in an extraordinary flight to Zambia in 1985 to talk to the ANC. Harry Oppenheimer was reported to be 'twitchy' about it, but Relly clearly felt dialogue had to start. Discussions with ANC leader Oliver Tambo and senior ANC officials went on for some six hours. That meeting more than anything distanced Anglo American from Pretoria in the public eye. Later, in his book,[1] Anglo American director and economic soothsayer, Clem Sunter, spelt out the need for South Africans to negotiate their political future on an open agenda and to restructure the economy in an equal opportunity multi-racial state.

The Afrikaner Right went wild. Nothing more confirmed its suspicions about Anglo American and its readiness to barter away other people's interests for its own survival.

And here we come to the Afrikaner window, perhaps the most misunderstood of all. Outside South Africa there is a prevalent view that treats Afrikanerdom as a sort of aberration, a condition like alcoholism or drug abuse that will pass if only the patient could pull himself together. It is a profound misreading.

However deep the Oppenheimer mines can drill, they will never penetrate the depths of the Afrikaner sense of landhood and belonging. Afrikaners, like the Zulu and the Xhosa, are a tribe. Greater than the value of gold is the Afrikaner value of earth. Splintered though its voice is across a range of organizations, there are common themes: the importance of home, family, common language, culture, history, religion and tradition. These bond into nationhood. The Afrikaners sense that their nationhood is undergoing a profound crises, and cannot approach the future without a sense of deepest foreboding.

Apartheid was born, not out of a gut will for racial subjugation, but from the universities as a theoretician's address to the irreconcilable dilemmas of white poverty and political rights. It sought to legitimize, in a black continent, the belief that the Boerevolk, by history and by commitment, were entitled to a *volkstaat* (*nation state*), ratified by a Calvinist Protestantism, which colours Afrikaner belief with a divine sanction.

Apartheid, the idea of separate homeland and nationhood based on the recognition of ethnicity and cultural differences, was on a demographic ebb tide from the start. But, as the Afrikaner sees it, if he loses, he has nowhere to go.

Although originally agrarian (Afrikaners initially had no wish to be urbanized any more than they wanted blacks to be) the bulk of the Nationalist Party's support today is drawn from urban middle- and lower middle-class workers, many of them in the public sector. It

---

[1]   *The World and South Africa in the 1990s*, Human and Rousseau Tafelberg, 1987.

has been consistently voted into power by the white population for more than 40 years. The NP lost votes to the Right in the mid-1980s, partly through fear of the Rhodesia experience. 'Reform, not surrender' was the slogan of the NP. The Conservatives damningly sloganned back: 'Look at Rhodesia: it reformed – and surrendered'. Now, under De Klerk, the Nationalists are seeking to ride the tiger of reform.

Looking out of their window on Africa, what makes the Afrikaners so fearful? In 51 independent African states there have been 72 violent changes of leadership, by coups, purges and military interventions; there have been 21 assassinations and executions of presidents and prime ministers; out of 53 countries 16 countries, or 28 per cent, are radical socialist states, and just ten have a multi-party system.

Twenty-one countries have suffered a decline in real gross national product per capita between 1973 and 1985; of 22 economically advanced African countries only two – Mauritius and Tunisia – have achieved an employment rate higher than South Africa; 41 countries have a gnp per head per annum of under $1,000 (less than half the figure for South Africa); South Africa has the highest rates of literacy and life expectancy. Across the entire continent, radical black politics has failed to deliver an economic success story. A World Bank survey in 1989 revealed an appalling picture of debt, stagnation, inefficiency and corruption.

In South Africa, Anglo American is caught between the survivalist politics of the white tribe and the inexorable march of demography. Afrikanerdom can hold out little further against black urbanization – a point now made dramatically every Saturday morning in the Carlton shopping centre in central Johannesburg: blacks form the vast majority of shoppers.

The compelling logic of change lies in the fact that the total urban population of South Africa is currently around 17 million, of which whites comprise about 4.5 million (26.5 per cent), blacks more than 9 million (53 per cent) and coloureds and Asians together about 2.5 million (just over 20 per cent). In the urban areas of the country, there is already an approximate balance between whites, coloureds and Asians taken together and blacks.

Says Ronnie Bethlehem: 'By the year 2000 the number of whites, coloureds and Asians will have increased to around 10.5 million, while urbanized blacks in the cities and towns of the country are likely to outnumber all other races by nearly three to one. And the imbalance between other major population groups and whites will, in all probability, be close to eight to one.'

To meet the demands imposed by an overall rate of population growth of 2.5 per cent a year, the economy must grow by more than that (i.e. in inflation-adjusted terms) if it is not to be caught in a downward spiral of poverty. Ironically, sanctions are having just that effect: they will, Bethlehem calculates, increase unemployment (most of it black) by two million to 9.8 million by the year 2000. Bearing in mind that every breadwinner supports a family of four to five, the overall effect is even more severe.

The arrival of De Klerk has now brought arguably the most significant change in climate by an Afrikaner government. Says Relly: 'F W's first 100 days have been dramatic not so much because of what he has done, but because he has put a seal on an entirely different style of leadership – and convinced whites that the process now in train cannot be reversed.'

And here is a final window: the one through which Americans look. Of all the windows that Anglo American and the Oppenheimers have needed to keep clear for corporate reasons, this is the one that has been the most clouded and confused. The Americans have sought to put pressure on Apartheid through the Comprehensive Anti-Apartheid Act of 1986, limits on South African investment by corporations, corporate disinvestment and bank loan and finance barriers.

This policy is now a shambles. More than 160 US firms have pulled out, with the effect of phasing out the liberal black-advancement programmes which many of these companies promoted, and pushing up the level of black unemployment. As pointed out in *International Currency Review*:[2] 'In cases where outright closure has taken place, the black population has suffered through increased unemployment and the wastage of skilled labour. In instances where various arrangements have been made, the sanctions have simply been by-passed. Some American firms which had provided social or educational facilities for the black community . . . have since made no new financial commitments – to the detriment of the black community.'

Research by the US General Accounting Office in 1988 found that many circuitous ways round sanctions legislation had been perfected. These ranged from comprehensive relationships with successor com-

[2]   *International Currency Review*, June–July 1989.

panies and royalty fees for the use of trade marks and consultancy services. More often than not, the same people provide the same services for the US company as prior to the withdrawal – though they now work for an intermediate firm. A major beneficiary has been Anglo American itself, or its affiliates, which acquired the South African arm of Barclays at a knockdown price.

Even if President F W De Klerk pushes forward with constitutional reform, there is a widespread view in South Africa that most American financial investment is unlikely to come back and that many of the giant US industrial and financial corporations have gone forever.

Both the US Government and the corporate sector have been able to legitimize a massive industrial, service and financial pull-out by reference to a moral crusade against Apartheid. In effect, the 'crusade' may have come to disguise a deeper racism. Disinvestment tended to be most marked in those periods following civil unrest in South Africa when the white minority regime looked especially vulnerable and close to collapse.

Disinvestment and disengagement by major US corporations has in fact contributed little to the process of black empowerment. On the contrary: according to a study by Bethlehem, by the end of the decade the growth in the blacks' share of income distribution would be 35.1 per cent without sanctions and 25 per cent with, due to the brake applied on gnp growth. Sanctions, vehemently opposed by Inkatha for the social damage they have done, have also allowed key economic inequalities to persist.

Forcing South Africa, through debt repayment schedules, to become a capital exporter at a time when the economy needs capital to provide growth and employment for the swelling numbers of urban blacks, further loads the dice against the black empowerment process. Yet some of America's most senior representatives appear innocent of the fluidity and complexities of what is involved. A recent example was a pronouncement by the former CIA chief, Stansfield Turner, that Anglo American itself was under the control of the South African Government. Such perceptions are naturally the laughing stock of Johannesburg.

Meanwhile, the US Department of Congress has continued to promote exports to South Africa, 'particularly where US manufacturers maintain a technological advantage'. Most important of all has been exemption from sanctions of any product or mineral which the US Government believes to be of 'strategic' value. These include andalusite, antimony, chromium, cobalt, industrial diamonds (natural), manganese, platinum group metals, rutile (including titanium) and vanadium. In most of these, Anglo American is a major supplier.

Were supplies of six of the ten 'certified minerals' to be suspended from South Africa, the US Bureau of Mines has calculated that the cost to the United States would be $9.25 billion over a five-year period. The United States could reasonably be said to be more in need of Anglo American than its regulators would comfortably admit.

Such are the windows of Africa. Looking out of them, neither the contours nor the habitat are simple. The net effect has been a profound boxing in of Anglo American. It has been squeezed on four sides: Afrikanerdom, the revolutionary ANC, international sanctions – particularly American disinvestment – and the limitations of an economy denied the growth it vitally needs. These are the exterior pressures of Anglo American's crisis of letting go.

It is one now heightened by the expectancy of political change and the gathering pressure to test whether De Klerk's 'bottom line' extends to the hand-over of power to the black majority. Until the last few weeks of 1989, Relly and the Anglo American liberal élite frequently likened South Africa's mood of change to *Perestroika* in Eastern Europe, largely to trigger a more positive and sympathetic attitude among the international financial community. Similarities there may well be, but not ones totally comfortable for Pretoria. In many ways the most difficult period for Anglo American has still to come.

4

The Escape That Failed

■

Polished brightly on the fifth floor of a magnificently-sited office in the heart of London is an eye-catching bronze figurine. It is a statuette of Cecil Rhodes, originally presented to the HMS *Diamond*. Here, in this story, it is also a haunting, disconcerting ghost.

Number 40 Holborn Viaduct – one of the most imposing office sites in the world – is a corner of London made for Rhodes. The rounded nine-floor building commands the bottom of Holborn like the superstructure of an ocean liner. Looking out of the boardroom window on the seventh floor is to catch a postcard view of London.

Hugging close to Number 40, on its right flank and straddling Charterhouse Street, is the centre of the diamond trade – the Central Selling Organisation. Running off to the right are the genteel terraced houses of Ely Place, a tiny island of Cambridgeshire in the middle of London. Here is where the boundaries of the old City of London ended. It was to Ely Place that the thieves and vagabonds ran to escape their police pursuers, and beyond it, across the rooftops towards Farringdon, Charles Dickens was to locate the infamous Fagan's hideaway in *Oliver Twist*, where the scamps of London returned with their stolen trove.

In Ely Place can be found the demure London representative office of one of the most important overseas companies of Anglo American: Mineral and Resources Corporation – Minorco.

But before, Minorco was 40 Holborn Viaduct. It was to be the London eyrie of Harry Oppenheimer. It still remains the head office of what was to be his empire out of Africa: Charter Consolidated.

But no second empire was achieved. All that remains is the

building, whose grandeur belies the disasters that unfolded. Charter was to become the corporate Ulster of the Anglo American empire.

Originally known as the British South Africa Company, it was chosen by Anglo American to be the agency for a corporate second coming. Charter was to be Anglo American's vehicle to build, finance and lead a worldwide mining and natural resource empire outside of South Africa. As Francis Howard, Harry Oppenheimer's personal assistant at the time, recalls: 'The concept of Charter was to be a company outside of South African exchange controls which would have the financial and technological clout to undertake major mining business around the world.' From its international ambitions to the hands-on, active management style, Charter was Anglo American's Minorco Mark One. In the way that we may have premonitions about ourselves, Minorco was Charter's premonition; and Charter, Minorco's *déjà vu*: everything that it was set up to be, Charter had already been – 20 years earlier.

Charter made its debut on the London Stock Exchange in 1965 with a founding board comprised of the greatest names in international mining: Harry Oppenheimer, Chester Beatty and the American platinum king, Charles Engelhard. But behind the great ambition to establish a British-based mining finance house pressed a compelling corporate problem: Anglo American, like so many great empires before it, was running out of time and space.

Oppenheimer was finding himself increasingly cramped in South Africa, and Anglo American needed to diversify and spread geographically. It needed both to lessen its reliance on South Africa and to rejuvenate. Without new areas of exploration activity – new mines with cash pouring from them – it was headed for attrition.

South Africa was also becoming increasingly isolated politically: it was missing out on the international banking and finance explosion. And the Johannesburg banks could not provide the foreign exchange on anything like the scale, or with the flexibility, that Anglo American needed. A London-based finance house which would raise money in the City's capital markets to nurture and feed Anglo American's new empire was a priority. Charter was it.

Charter also played a vital role in enabling Anglo American to operate elsewhere in Africa, in a different guise, without the post-Sharpeville political stigma that prevented it from operating on its own account. The most elaborate procedures were undertaken to get

Anglo American engineers camouflaged as Charter employees, with UK passports and papers that belied their South African links.

Charter was to embark on three major mining projects: Cleveland Potash; copper mining in Mauretania; and later a joint venture to mine copper at Fungurumu in the heart of the Belgian Congo. They came to be the three great landmarks in the history of Charter. They were landmarks of catastrophe.

In 1966, the Government of Mauretania awarded Charter the rights to mine a copper deposit at Akjoujt. A separate company, Société Minière de Mauretanie (Somima), was formed to develop the mine, backed by loan capital from the World Bank. Charter was the major shareholder and managing partner with a 33.5 per cent stake. Initial capital spending of $56 million was authorized. Akjoujt was in a bleak, desolate Sahara-desert landscape with barely any habitation. It was, however, confidently expected to be producing 30,000 tons of copper within four years. Central to its success was a very promising new copper-smelting process called 'Torco' developed by Anglo American.

Nearer home, and in a landscape Charter's shareholders could more readily identify, was Cleveland potash. Charter went into a joint venture with chemicals giant ICI to establish a major potash mine near Staithes in North Yorkshire. Surveys indicated an annual output of between one and one and a half million tons of potash, sufficient to meet the UK's entire potash requirements. Initial cost was put at £25 million. Planning permission was given in 1968. Not only was ICI a heavyweight joint partner, but it would also be a customer for the mine's potash – truly an ideal situation for Charter.

As the bold Charter experiment took off, in came two of Anglo American's most formidable people: the flamboyant Sidney Spiro, who became managing director in 1969 (and who later took over as chairman), and Murray Hofmeyr.

Spiro, then an Anglo American Corporation director who had joined from Anglovaal and went on to found Union Acceptances, South Africa's first merchant bank, had struck an immediate rapport with Ernest Oppenheimer when they had first met at dinner years before. As Ernest said at the time: 'There are only two people in the world who understand what I'm talking about. One's Harry. And this is the second.' Spiro's appointment at Charter was to expose a profound conflict at the heart of the company: was it to be a hands-on mining company? Or a new London financial house, generating for

Anglo American outside of South Africa what Spiro, with Union Acceptances, had so brilliantly achieved within?

During his stewardship a number of young aspiring mining-finance tycoons were to start their careers. Two in particular were to learn valuable lessons: Anthony William Lea and John Roger Broughton Phillimore, a godson of Harry's.

To the company's two promising mining ventures was now to be added a third. In 1970, an international consortium led by Charter and the Congolese Government formed Société Minière de Tenke-Fungurume (SMTF) in which Charter had a 28 per cent stake. The most ambitious of Charter's ventures to date, the project had copper reserves of 51 million tons. Estimated total cost of developing the project came to $660 million.

But the first ominous crack now appeared: Somima had hit trouble. The Torco smelting process literally fell apart in the heat and dust of Mauretania. For Anglo American, at the peak of its technical and financial prowess, it was a devastating blow. A further $24 million had to be injected to meet extra costs and delays in start-up. Torco simply could not work in the high temperatures and constant dust of the Mauretanian desert. In 1973, the Somima venture was written off in full, with a cumulative loss of $31 million. As a final kicker, the following year's accounts revealed additional spending of $5.5 million to wind-up Somima.

Then the Fungurumu project collapsed in disaster. The fall in copper prices, the war in Angola and runaway inflation tore apart the project's economics and forced up cost projections to $800 million. Charter axed the project. But some $230 million had already been spent.

By now Cleveland, too, was coming to its point of crisis. By 1977, it required a further £7.5 million boost from Charter because of start-up delays. It had run into horrific problems. Although the deposit was carefully drilled, it was enormously variable, the potash seam suddenly lurching left and right. The miners would have no sooner got the cutting gear into position at the rock face than the machinery was suddenly drilling salt. 'Where's the ****ing seam now?' was a constant cry at Cleveland.

Logistical problems compounded an already formidable challenge. Charter was finally forced to throw in the towel. 1978 was the year of reckoning: low production levels and weak prices had led to heavy losses. By the end of 1978, Cleveland had absorbed £117 million, of which the partners had provided some £76 million. Charter's tab was reckoned at £22 million. Pull-out costs in the following year added another £5 million to the total. Anglo American, with a 12.5 per cent interest, finally took Charter's share off its hands.

These individual setbacks effectively broke Charter. Income from the group's passive investments in RTZ and Selection Trust, and its portfolio of investments, helped mask the full extent of the damage to shareholders. But across the three projects, Charter suffered losses of more than £100 million. Says Francis Howard, who was later to become Charter's finance director: 'It was a chapter of accidents. And they decimated the company over that period. There was bad luck, certainly. But there was bad management, all over the place.'

Longer term for Anglo American, the failure of the Charter adventure delivered a profound shock. The significance of Charter is that it broke the myth of Anglo American – a myth of invincibility, managerial prowess, technological expertise and the financial clout to bulldoze its way through adversity. Charter shattered that. Charter was a vine of self-knowledge for Anglo American. From it fell a seed of self-doubt. Where the firm hand of 44 Main had once confidently settled itself, a tremor had set in.

Charter's analyses of its failures tended to focus on factors outside its control. But was it *all* the truth? Doubts began to creep in. What if there was a problem that lay, not with the *technical* competence of Anglo American, but with its *managerial* ability to assess and handle projects outside of the South African milieu where it was used to being top dog? Was it imposing financial targets and operational demands that were smothering, if not cutting out altogether, more appropriate local solutions?

At a mature stage of development the prime concern of a corporate empire ceases to be success, and becomes security. In the need to protect the centre, always paramount, the entrepreneurial currents of wealth-creation become switched: instead of resources running from the centre out, they come to be drawn inwards from the periphery. And Anglo American's entire culture was one now informed by an all-powerful centrifugal force: Anglo American was driven from the centre, and it tolerated no countervailing powers to it.

What it wanted, it often seemed, was not so much success, but stability. Control had become the corporate obsession. And to ensure it, hands-on management came to mean less an entrepreneurial propulsion than a method of effecting control in ways that would more often than not frustrate the re-enervation it was supposed to achieve.

One critic was John Du Cane, former chairman and chief executive of the mining finance group, Selection Trust (in which Charter held a 25.7 per cent stake), and a former Anglo American man. 'Mining ventures need a gut feeling about mining. The trouble with Anglo people is that they did not understand the countries they were operating in. They were always sending out South Africans, rather than local people who knew better what was going on. On the Mauretania project the Anglo managers would take their instructions from Johannesburg. And with Charter's people on the board of Selection Trust it was a constant referral back.

'Anglo is not really a mining company at heart. It is a financial management company. It's a company that wants to manage and control investments rather than run mines.'

Not really a mining company *at heart*? Extraordinary though Du Cane's point must seem, it hit exactly the dilemma highlighted by Sidney Spiro's appointment at Charter: he was to take much of the blame for what went wrong, and the subsequent closures and redundancies involved gave rise to the alliterative sobriquet, 'Cyanide Sid'. But the three mining ventures were commissioned before he took over, and behind the scenes he advocated a different course, urging that it should get out of distant mining projects and build up a UK earnings base in corporate finance and financial services. That would have been a most prescient move given what was to unfold in the City ahead of Big Bang deregulation. Recalls Spiro: 'The line we were going down was never clearly defined. No one knew what Charter stood for. How could we run a sophisticated mining operation in places like Mauretania? It was a difficult and hazardous route. I always hoped Charter would evolve into a major financial institution. But that view was not shared.'

Charter forced Anglo American to reappraise the way it looked at the world. Important questions surfaced. First, why was Charter getting bogged down in two colossal mining ventures in Africa when the whole idea was to build a non-African mining empire? Second, how exportable was mining expertise from one country to another, and particularly from a culture in which Anglo American was a dominant corporate player to ones where this was not so? Had not Anglo American overestimated the exportability of its gifts? And third, given the challenges of different climates, temperatures, political circumstances, local economics and operational requirements, was greenfield start-up overseas really an appropriate route for Anglo American?

These doubts were to lead the Corporation to a fundamental shift in strategy. In 1979, Charter was restructured and Phase Two began. The immediate impact was one of a cutting corporate demotion in the grand hierarchy of the Anglo American fiefdoms. There was a capital reduction. Its South African investments were taken from it and returned to Anglo American, and so too were interests in other Anglo American companies.

Not only did this mark the effective running down of Charter Consolidated, it also dusted down and brought to the fore a pre-viously barely-known Anglo American company. This was registered at 43 Church Street, Bermuda. Its only corporate *raison d'être* to date had been as a conveniently tax-sheltered parking place for Anglo American's $155 million investment in platinum concern Engelhard Minerals and Chemicals. Now it was to hold Anglo American's 36 per cent interest in Charter. The name on the brass plate in Church Street was Minerals and Resources Corporation Limited – a name so rarely used no one had thought to shorten it to Minorco.

Charter Mark Two set out to build a base of industrial companies in Britain. The man who was to play a key role, not only in Charter's affairs at this time but also in Anglo American, was John Neil Clarke. He had impressed Harry Oppenheimer by an acute attention to financial minutiae and grasp of corporate mechanics. He had joined Charter in 1969 as an accountant and was promoted to finance direc-tor in 1973. He became finance director of Anglo American in late 1976 and was appointed chief executive of Charter in 1980. But while he may have been the best man for Anglo American, was he the best man for Charter?

Clarke had read law, and was now a fully-fledged accountant – qualities that held an entrepreneurial spirit in check. By training and experience he had grown to be a man who knew the dangers of everything and the certainty of nothing. John Du Cane had a vivid memory of him at Selection Trust: 'He used to get terribly interested in small esoteric things. He would light up at board meetings on the minutiae of pensions. He would hold forth on subjects that numbed the rest of us with boredom.'

The push into British industrial management by Charter could scarcely have been worse timed: Britain was heading for recession.

Barely had Clarke time to scan the market for acquisitions then across the heartland of manufacturing Britain business turned dramatically down.

How was Charter going to be better than, or different from, the likes of Hanson Trust and BTR that were proving so adept at industrial company acquisition and turnaround? Plunging into such a new area, what expertise could the Anglo American-trained people at Charter call upon? Disturbing answers tumbled out in the wake of a hostile takeover bid in 1982 for mining equipment concern, Anderson Strathclyde.

When Charter launched the bid, there was an outcry from the mining industry and from the Scottish industrial and labour lobby. The bid was referred to the Monopolies and Mergers Commission. It was concerned to establish how Charter was run. Had it really changed its spots and did its managers have the space and the autonomy to run the show? Who really ran the company? And to what end? Charter insisted that it had the management experience and that, far from seeing Anderson Strathclyde as a milch-cow, it would feed the cow. But Anderson's men did not see a contented cow at all: they saw a tethered one. And they could not see what benefits it could bring.

Concluded the MMC: 'Judging by the financial record of its mining and industrial subsidiaries, and disturbing incidences of its attitude towards the management of acquisitions, little confidence should be placed in the suitability of Charter for the control of Anderson Strathclyde.

'Charter's very different nature, and the different characters, attitudes and motivations of its managers would be likely to reduce entrepreneurial and innovative drive. We conclude that ... acquisition would be likely to lead to a diminution in the effectiveness of the former company's management.'

Charter was outraged by the verdict, which had drawn a note of dissent from Sir Godfray Le Quesne, chairman of the MMC itself. The MMC's recommendation that the bid be vetoed was overturned. Charter went on to acquire Anderson, for £95 million. But how prophetic the MMC's judgments on the bid proved to be.

By 1986, profits of Anderson Strathclyde had slumped to £7.2 million against a forecast of £15 million. By 1988, in the wake of the miners' strike and a slump in orders from British Coal, they were down to £5.6 million. By 1988-89, the group was more than £3 million in the red. Charter's acquisition of Anderson Strathclyde proved an abysmal failure.

But Charter's problems were not confined to Anderson: it was struggling to make any headway at all. Its performance as a group was dismal. Group profits started to slide. Even, it seemed, when the gods brought a gilded chalice in the form of extraordinary profits from share sales, the wine poured out through invisible holes.

A new crisis soon broke upon Charter: the collapse of Johnson Matthey Bank. Charter was hit through its 27.9 per cent shareholding in the bank's parent company, platinum refining and marketing group, Johnson Matthey.

In the year to March 1985, Charter suffered a net loss on trading. Extraordinary item debits, mainly relating to JMB, totalled £53 million. It was to be five years before profits would recover to their pre-JMB débâcle level. As for Charter shares, they were almost universally thumbed down by analysts.

The great Charter experiment Mark Two lay in ruins. It had set out in 1979 to grow and add value by being an industrial holding company. In the years 1980–88, pre-tax profits went from £50.7 million to £55.4 million. Over the same period, profits of BTR went from £70 million to £819 million. At Hanson, profits soared from £39 million to £880 million. RTZ, the corporate animal with closest resemblance to Charter during this period, saw pre-tax profits climb from £507 million to £879 million.

Neither Charter's management nor its culture fitted the role marked out. To build quickly by acquisition required opportunism, bravura and *élan*, and Anglo American had none of these in any measure.

Neil Clarke soldiered on until a sudden and quite unexpected coup in November 1988 when Sir Michael Edwardes and the Young Turks at Minorco sought to speed up change – ironically just when profits were recovering sharply. He was replaced as chief executive by a 43-year-old accountant, Richard Wakeling. Now at last the axe fell on the trappings of delusion: the cooks and the butlers and the chauffeurs have gone; the number of people employed at 40 Holborn has been slashed from 180 to just 45; and most of the cavernous 80,000 square feet office was sublet. The dining room silverware on the seventh floor and the marble fire places have been valued for disposal.

The task has been to build some coherence out of what is left of

Charter: bits and bobs of businesses extending from beer-cooling equipment and spirit measures to loss-making civil engineering, Portugese tungsten mining and industrial rail fasteners. Much management breath is spent trying to coax these embers into roaring fires.

Little by way of cultural inheritance or continuity survives. Charter is a company that does not wish to know its past and is uncertain of its future. Concluded stockbroker Shearson Lehman Hutton in a damning research note on the company in August 1989: 'As an entity, Charter seems to have outlived its role and has not yet succeeded in finding a new one.' The annual reports have been kept, but as for the company's records, everything bar the necessary five-year period has been thrown out.

Only the little statue of Rhodes endures. And all the ghosts.

5

Winter of the Six Grey Squirrels

∎

It was the year Harry Oppenheimer could not believe his eyes. But then, no one in South Africa could. It was 1979 – and the price of gold was to climb its Everest.

Throughout the 1970s, as the gold price broke from the official mooring of $35 an ounce, both the rise in value and the volatility of behaviour startled everyone. As the American budget deficit, monetary expansion and the oil price shocks began to shake investor confidence, the price responded with a violent series of convulsions, like a comatose body to electric shock. Gold had become a barometric measure of the world's confidence in itself. As the price swung violently, it appeared to be tracking a neurosis.

After rising to almost $200 an ounce in the mid-1970s, it fell back over 20 months to $103. But in 1979 it went wild.

Throughout that summer, as the epic climb in the price gathered pace, Oppenheimer was having the financial contours of his empire rewritten by this inhuman hand. Mining prospects in South Africa were being transformed as investors across the world stampeded into gold. Gold had started the year at around $200 an ounce – within a few weeks it had shot to $225. By the spring it had smashed to a new high of $250. Then the price broke back. Surely it had now peaked?

But the price launched itself on a new rally that continued without a break through the summer – back through $250, on to $260, up to $280. In an extraordinary series of leaps, uninterrupted by any downward reaction, the price swept through $300 an ounce, then $350, and in September pierced the $400 level.

That year, total net private purchases of gold hit 1,765 tons, 70 per cent up on the 1970 figure and almost twice the amount of non-communist gold being mined. Nowhere was the momentum gaining faster than in sales of Krugerrands. Among the most frenzied buyers were the Americans. There seemed to be no stopping the Krugerrand boom. Not only had gold been rediscovered as an investment, but there was a rapidly growing view that it was here to stay as a feature of any long-term asset-diversified portfolio. For Anglo American, it heralded a surge in dividend income from its myriad of holdings in gold mining companies. Moreover, the prospect of a new wave of exciting mine exploration seemed possible as the price of gold pushed hitherto 'dead duck' prospects well over the barrier of viability.

But while the economics of Rand mining seemed to be transformed by the gold price explosion, this masked an unpalatable truth: that Anglo American, and the entire South African gold mining industry, was being boxed into a declining world market share.

Gold production from the Republic was falling, both in absolute and relative terms. Between 1969 and 1978, South African production had declined by 27 per cent, from 973 tons to 706 tons. According to forecasts by the Chamber of Mines, even a gold price of $534 by 1984 would not stop South African gold production halving by the end of the century. As for the price improvement, it masked a development that had increasingly been troubling the directorate of Anglo American: mining costs were soaring. Equally worrying from where Oppenheimer was sitting, the South African hegemony in the world gold market was slipping. All over the world, and particularly in the United States, new supply would come forward to meet demand: gold always had this unerring capacity to appear from a thousand new pores in the earth's skin each time the price went up. This slow, creeping attrition carried the most ominous portents for Anglo American.

Into this global view, but for quite local reasons, came Consolidated Gold Fields. Gold Fields was Anglo American's nearest rival, the world's second largest gold producer. Founded in 1887 by Cecil Rhodes and Charles Rudd, it had pioneered the development of the fabulous Witwatersrand Reef and was the largest shareholder in the world's most profitable mine, West Driefontein, the first mine in the world to make a working profit of £1 million a month. Gold Fields retained a vital 49 per cent stake in the holding group for these gold mining investments in the Republic – Gold Fields of South Africa

(GFSA), a separately quoted company. But throughout the 1960s, Gold Fields had sought to reduce its dependence on South Africa.

The trigger point for Anglo American's interest in Gold Fields was not its global pretensions, but its vulnerability to a bid; and its particular concern lay very close to home with the true engine of Gold Fields' profits: GFSA.

GFSA was providing the profits that kept Gold Fields alive. In 1979, Gold Fields reported profits before interest and tax of £113.8 million. Of this total, just over £40 million, or 36 per cent, came from South Africa. Not only were GFSA's mines working at substantially lower costs to those of Anglo American, but it was a critical player in the South African mining industry, accounting for ten per cent of world gold production.

Oppenheimer, himself sitting on a direct 11 per cent holding in GFSA, had watched Gold Fields' diversification attempts with increasing unease and was particularly worried that it was planning to sell its GFSA stake. The buyer would almost certainly be a rival Afrikaner-controlled South African mining group, General Mining, closer by ties of blood, culture and politics to the ruling Nationalists in Pretoria. Between GM and Anglo American, GFSA was a critical swing producer, control of which neither side would dare to allow the other.

In the complex mining politics of South Africa, Anglo American, undisputed leader, had 12 mines out of 39 altogether; GFSA and Union Corporation had seven each; Barlow Rand five; and General Mining four. Anglo American itself had encouraged the Afrikaners to get into mining, partly to balance its own position and also to compensate for repulsing Afrikaner attentions uncomfortably close to its own earnings base. To satisfy the Afrikaner ambitions, Anglo American helped them to take over General Mining, and later supported the merger of General Mining and Union Corporation in which it retained a substantial minority interest.

Now there loomed the possibility of GM acquiring GFSA. There was much that Anglo American was prepared to concede to the Afrikaners. But not that much. First, there was the threat posed to Anglo American's pre-eminence. As Oppenheimer recalled later: 'We are substantially the biggest mining group in South Africa and a lot of business comes to us because of our size. Obviously our position would be affected if another group was as big.' Second, and even more serious for Anglo American, the sale to GM would profoundly upset the critical balance of power in the South African Chamber of Mines where Anglo American ruled the roost, controlling output, wage rates and, most crucially, the level of sales to the South African Reserve Bank. Any change here would threaten Anglo American's most vital power base in the Republic.

Thus it was that the internal politics of the South African gold mining industry came to spark one of the most far reaching and bitter corporate battles ever. Like a Sicilian family feud, it flared out from the confines of the Johannesburg Chamber of Mines to legal and regulatory battles across the world.

How, then, could Anglo American block General Mining and neutralize the threat? A move on Gold Fields would be the most effective way. Anglo American could acquire 20 per cent and block the path of a predator – while at the same time getting boardroom seats. The objective, as Anglo American saw it, was not to put Gold Fields into play but to get it *out* of play. Handled skilfully, Oppenheimer could get everything he wanted without having to launch a hostile bid or pay a bid premium. It was a strategem that would later be cited as evidence of a theory of corporate power that made the Oppenheimer style notorious the world over. Oppenheimer summed this view up: 'Who needs takeovers when you can control with a minority stake?'

In Britain, the Conservatives had won a sweeping election victory in May under Margaret Thatcher. This opened up the distinct possibility of easier access to Gold Fields. For it was enjoying the benefit of an invisible protecting hand: UK Exchange Controls. These were a formidable tripwire for Anglo American. Any overseas buyer who acquired ten per cent or more of the equity of a UK company would have to notify the Bank of England. This would have effectively put paid to Oppenheimer's pounce-by-stealth approach, but a free-market Conservative administration was expected to lift the controls soon. And that would clear the way for Anglo American.

But Oppenheimer now had further cause to worry. Around the third week in September a troubling telex was delivered to his desk. It came from Anglo American's London stockbroker, Rowe & Pitman. It warned him that their market scouts had spotted something odd: someone appeared to be building up a stake in Consolidated Gold Fields; what, please, were Harry's instructions?

Oppenheimer believed the stake was being built by General Mining. Even if he was wrong, he could not afford the luxury of doing nothing. No time could be lost: a pre-emptive strike at Gold

Fields was now a priority. He called an immediate inner-cabinet meeting of colleagues, which discussed the outline of a complex plan, prepared by Clarke's team in Anglo American's finance department, to acquire, from under the noses of the British regulatory authorities and without anyone in the stock market suspecting, 20 million shares in Consolidated Gold Fields.

Those taking part could scarcely have imagined the consequences. Not only was it breathtaking in its audacity, it was also to mark the beginning of a nine-year battle for control of one of Britain's biggest and most prestigious companies. That battle would see three British Government investigations, changes in UK company law and legal and regulatory battles on three continents.

'The plan was', Gold Fields' chief executive Rudolph Agnew was to claim later, 'to build up in secret, and almost certainly illegally, a major shareholding in Consolidated Gold Fields in defiance of all the known rules.' The Anglo American share purchase scheme captured in miniature the Oppenheimer style: it was detailed, thorough, efficient and, above all, clandestine. But how exactly was the famed Anglo–De Beers machine to work under the secret cloak? In what way did this secrecy add potency to its formidable financial clout?

De Beers was to begin an orchestrated but stealthy purchase of a major block of Gold Fields shares. Secrecy was the vital ingredient of the operation. On no account was the market to be alerted (thus adversely moving the price) and, above all, on no account was anyone to discover the identity of the buying parties. In Johannesburg, not only was secrecy the hallmark of every move made. Somehow, it had to delay and frustrate all official attempts at disclosure, up to the highest levels of the Stock Exchange Council.

This was the scheme in outline: from within 44 Main, five nominee companies would be activated in a controlled 'slow release' strategy; each would be given funds to build up a 4.9 per cent holding in Gold Fields. When the 4.9 per cent level was reached, it would go to ground and another company would come into play. The companies were to be, in effect, Oppenheimer's grey squirrels in the night: five companies let loose to pounce on a target number of Gold Fields shares and disappear as quickly as they had come; all the discerning ear could ever catch would be the faint rustle of a Luxemburg telex and the click of a numbered account.

The squirrels would be set loose from different points in the Anglo American empire, each acting independently of the other. Later, De

Beers would announce that it would purchase two of these companies through option agreements, putting further distance between itself and the manner in which the Gold Fields shares had been acquired.

But hidden even from senior executives was the existence of a sixth squirrel which would play a critical role.

The UK announced, on 24 October, the lifting of Exchange Controls. That, for Anglo American, was the final green light: it made the entire secret share purchase scheme legitimate. Or did it?

Two days later, on 26 October, the first of the five grey squirrels was let loose and the share purchases began. By 1 November, De Beers Holdings (a wholly-owned subsidiary of De Beers) had acquired a toehold 330,000 shares, bought on the Johannesburg Exchange through brokers Davis, Borkum, Hare & Co.

Out then popped grey squirrel number two: Central Selling Organisation (Proprietary), an offshoot of Debhold. It bought 7.1 million Gold Fields shares through Rowe & Pitman in London, financed by an interest-free loan. The two holdings together added up to 7.43 million shares, equivalent to 4.99 per cent of Gold Fields. Squirrel Debhold then went to ground.

Next squirrel was Chajo Properties, a wholly-owned subsidiary of Rosmic which was in turn an offshoot of E Oppenheimer & Son. Chajo bought a further 4.9 per cent. The money to finance these purchases came from Debhold. The authorizing letters were countersigned by Neil Clarke.

Then, in early January, came Squirrels four and five: Debhold lent money to Eastdale Investments, a 30 per cent-owned offshoot of Johannesburg Consolidated Investments, to buy up to 7.43 million shares. Eastdale activated two subsidiaries, Welsburg and FEW Properties, to buy 5.22 million and 1.3 million Gold Fields shares respectively. Eastdale then granted Debhold an option to buy all the equity of Welsburg and the right of first refusal on the equity of FEW.

Were these companies specifically formed to acquire shares in Gold Fields? The answer provided intriguing evidence of the extent to which the master planners of the six grey squirrels had gone to cover their tracks: Chajo had been incorporated on 10 June 1966; Welsburg in February 1937; and FEW on 8 May 1918! *Grey* squirrels? These were nearly white.

But for this elaborate scheme to work at all, the same secrecy and thoroughness had to govern the buying operation in London. The purchase of some 20 million shares in one of Britain's most prominent companies in the space of ten weeks had somehow to be concealed. And that meant that two of the biggest firms on the London Stock Exchange – Akroyds and Rowe & Pitman – would have to be knowing participants in the secret. In addition, the Stock Exchange surveillance system itself would have to be 'squared'. But how?

The genesis of the London operation can be traced to a meeting in Johannesburg on 25 October between Anglo American's local broker, Davis Borkum Hare, and a director of Akroyd, London's biggest firm of stock jobbers (share wholesalers). The DBH partner asked if it was possible to cut out a stockbroker intermediary altogether and deal direct with Akroyd's. This, it was explained, was against the rules of the Exchange. But, Akroyd added, there was no reason why a broker could not be asked to deal with a particular jobber.

On 26 October, DBH's senior partner, Max Borkum, phoned Rowe & Pitman and placed the first order for Gold Fields shares. Instructions were given solely by telephone throughout. Nor did R & P need the comfort of written instructions: it knew from the beginning who the ultimate buyers were. And, so, too, did Akroyd, if only because Anglo American's Neil Clarke was to phone on a number of occasions asking about the state of the market in Gold Fields shares.

Central to the operation were two of the most prominent figures on the London Stock Exchange: Peter Wilmot-Sitwell, senior partner of Rowe & Pitman, and David Henry LeRoy-Lewis, chairman of Akroyds. Wilmot-Sitwell was instructed to buy the shares as secretly as possible. He thus dealt only with Akroyd. But he was then asked by Max Borkum to meet two strange and quite unprecedented requirements: first, Akroyd must deliver the stock by transfers with the buyer's name in blank (and upon which stamp duty had not been paid); and second, the share transfers should not be delivered to Gold Fields' registrars. In this, LeRoy-Lewis was to play a central role.

Never before had Wilmot-Sitwell, or anyone at Rowe & Pitman, been given such instructions, and from an early stage he was uneasy about them. But he was also unsettled by a matter much more fundamental: that Anglo American may have resolved to pursue a massive share purchase plan oblivious to the legal requirement to disclose to Gold Fields when it had bought five per cent or more of the equity. This would be in breach of Section 33 of the Companies

Act – an offence punishable by fine and/or a prison term of up to two years.

At Akroyds, LeRoy-Lewis had even more cause for concern: it was his firm that was to amass shares without disturbing the market and supply the blank stock transfers. But under the new computerized Talisman settlement system such blank transfers were impossible. Somehow, Lewis had to keep dealings in Gold Fields shares well clear of Talisman. But meanwhile, what about the little matter of the five per cent rule? He phoned Wilmot-Sitwell and told him that while the disclosure rule 'was not a matter for us as jobbers, we did look to them as the brokers acting on behalf of the clients to make certain we were not involved in any contravention of the statute'.

On 15 November, Wilmot-Sitwell met with Anglo American's deputy chairman Gavin Relly and Neil Clarke in London. He politely drew Relly's attention to the five per cent disclosure rule. Relly replied that there was nothing to worry about: Anglo American was acting within the Companies Act and was breaking no rule. Then he announced an idea that gave Relly and Clarke much to think about: why not launch a 'dawn raid'?

He told them, with some pride, of recent daring Rowe & Pitman raids that had stunned the market: a swift and effective means by which a corporate predator could gain up to 29 per cent of a target company – often as a prelude to a full scale bid. And it was all within the law. First, Rowe & Pitman would raise the price of the target share appreciably above the market price; sellers would flock to the Rowe & Pitman pitch and offload their stock. When Rowe & Pitman had bought the required percentage of shares, it would cut the price back down to the market level and withdraw. The whole operation, from start to finish, could be done in 20 minutes. Surprise was the key.

Relly and Clarke listened carefully. Their main preoccupation had been to acquire a large percentage of Gold Fields *without* disturbing the market and raising the price. But at the very same time that they were assuring Rowe & Pitman they were fully aware of the five per cent rule, Anglo American's finance department and grey squirrel number six was sweeping De Beers' holding in Gold Fields over 6.3 per cent, putting it in breach of the Companies Act.

It was swept there by the purchase of 1.9 million Gold Fields shares by Rowe & Pitman, on instructions from David Borkum Hare. Problems in obtaining sufficient financial rand had required De Beers to settle in another currency. On the instructions of Neil Clarke, the purchases were booked to Central Holdings a/c Brent Limited. Central, registered in Luxemburg, was known to Rowe & Pitman as a key private company in the vast Anglo–De Beers web. But of Brent Limited, it knew nothing.

Brent, registered in Liberia, belonged to Charter Consolidated, where Clarke had been finance director prior to his transfer to Johannesburg. It was bought by Anglo American on 19 November, and lent money to acquire Gold Fields shares by a Liberian-registered Anglo American offshoot. De Beers' subsequent explanation was that this was a simple 'parking' arrangement which would be unwound once the financial rand problems had eased.

De Beers subsequently admitted it had breached the five per cent limit. But it claimed that no one had told it of the Brent arrangement. In the empire of a thousand far reaching arms, one hand, it seemed, did not know what the other was doing. It was a damning oversight.

At Consolidated Gold Fields' head office, such subtleties could hardly be appreciated. But a massive developing problem certainly was. Almost as soon as the De Beers buying plan began, the group's stockbroker, Cazenove, had spotted not only heavy dealings in the shares, but also that they were being bought by a single jobber and going to a single broker. Similar unusually heavy activity was reported by the registrars.

But Oppenheimer's six grey squirrels were not yet ready to break cover.

6

The Swoop of the Korhaan

■

About a mile from the centre of the Oppenheimer game reserve at Ntoma, close to its approach road, can be found a nest of the Red Crested Korhaan. Its most spectacular and startling feature is the way it attracts attention: it soars into the air, pauses, somersaults, and then swoops down to within inches of the ground. Oppenheimer was now about to embark on his own swoop of the Korhaan.

For Gold Fields, it was to mark a turning point. It was to be swept to a new definition of the world, a reskewering in which all its relations would be fundamentally and irretrievably altered. For the company's senior officers, what now unfolded was the start of a transition equivalent to shooting the rapids: a traumatic and bruising rite of passage.

Once share-dealing irregularities had been discovered, Gold Fields had to move fast. Its merchant bank, Schroders, wrote to the Bank of England setting out its suspicions that the lifting of Exchange Controls was being exploited. Protests were made to the Stock Exchange deputy chief executive, Jeffrey Knight, urging him to alert his surveillance department to its suspicions. If a foreign buyer was prepared to flaunt a Companies Act requirement, what chance did the voluntary Take Over Code stand? One of its provisions obliged companies to make an outright bid when they acquired 30 per cent of the target company's equity.

By 12 December, it was clear at the Gold Fields registrar office that something very definitely was afoot – and the klaxons were blaring. The registrars had spotted a sharp increase in the volume of outstanding 'certified transfers'. While they were receiving transfer forms for parts of registered holdings, forms for the outstanding shares were not being delivered. Continuing checks showed the number of these shares was growing sharply – way above the average level of 500,000. In November the number had shot to 3.8 million. By December it had reached 5.3 million. By mid-January it had climbed to 6.3 million. For Gold Fields, action was now vital. Its patience with the Stock Exchange was running out. Why wouldn't it investigate?

The Stock Exchange assured Gold Fields' chairman, Lord Erroll, that its shares would soon be going on the Talisman system. No more blank transfer forms and matching delays as under the old system. The outstanding certificates would flood in – flushing the buyer out. On 16 January 1980, the Exchange announced Gold Fields was going on Talisman. But then, to Cazenove's astonishment – and Erroll's fury – the announcement was revoked two days later, with no explanation.

Erroll fired a letter to the Stock Exchange chairman, Nicholas Goodison, demanding an immediate meeting. It was held on 24 January. Erroll was accompanied by his company secretary Peter Roe and Robin Lyster of Cazenove. Flanking Goodison were the Exchange chief executive Robert Fell and his deputy chairman Jeffrey Knight. Erroll urged the Exchange to investigate the share build-up. Goodison promised his people would look into it.

The Exchange officials tracked the problem down to Akroyd. No detailed explanation was ever furnished by LeRoy-Lewis to Robert Fell as to why Akroyd could not adopt Talisman for these deals: Fell, an executive brought in from outside the Stock Exchange, was helpless against Lewis, a lifer with Akroyd, and a powerful member of the Stock Exchange Council. He insisted on the need for 'market secrecy' and left Fell with an impression of some awkward 'technical' problem.

Meanwhile, Fell's mystified officials within the Exchange were getting little further, though their suspicions were aroused: they had established that no other jobber had a problem with Talisman and Gold Fields. An Akroyd statement, on 16 January, said it was the result 'of an unforeseen problem with these securities': words devoid of meaning but which served to mask the truth at Akroyd. As for Erroll's request to the Stock Exchange for an investigation, the response, several days later, was as predictable as it was brief: it was declined.

By 5 February, Gold Fields had calculated that some 12 million shares were unaccounted for, and feared that purchases of a further 16 million shares might not have been registered. It put out a statement, saying it had drawn matters to the attention of the Exchange (though not, diplomatically, indicating the Exchange's response). The market sensed something was afoot: shares in Gold Fields jumped 23p to a peak of £5.06.

Six days later, on 11 February, the avenues of self-regulation now, so to speak, exhausted, Erroll made a formal request to the Department of Trade for inspectors to be appointed under Section 172 of the Companies Act, and informed the Press. The game was up, and the six grey squirrels could rest.

Oppenheimer's problem now was how best to break the news to Erroll that he had acquired, well, a number of shares in his company. 'And how many is that Mr Oppenheimer?', Erroll would ask. Practise as he might to keep his voice steady over the next few words, Oppenheimer found it impossible to speak them without a tremor of emotion: '20 million, sir.'

*   *

At the break of dawn in Johannesburg, there is a deep, rich golden light, as if the sun is drawing the light of the gold from below the earth. It is like a giant paintbrush of gold, running down the sides of all the buildings: Johannesburg painted in its natural colour.

On the morning of 12 February, Oppenheimer was up and doing early. He had not one surprise to give to the London Stock Exchange, but two. The second was to be *very* big, and there was much to be done. Shortly before 9am Johannesburg time (around 7.45am in London), Oppenheimer put a call through to Lord Erroll's office at 49 Moorgate.

It was to be a frequent joke at the dinner tables of top Anglo American men for years that they literally woke up Gold Fields. Erroll was not in his office; Oppenheimer's call had to be transferred to the executive director, David Lloyd-Jacob. Oppenheimer told him that De Beers was the mystery buyer of shares and that it would be seeking to increase its holding in the open market that morning to 25 per cent. Oppenheimer, polite to a fault, made it sound almost like a gesture of contrition. In fact, it was to be the dawn raid to beat them all.

The raid was executed by Rowe & Pitman and made stock market history. Confirmation came from Johannesburg at 8.30am with a phone call from Clarke confirming that 16.5 million shares were to be bought. The price agreed was £6.16 – some 70p above the previous night's closing price of £5.35. The total sum involved was over £100 million.

The price was marked up on the 'pitch' and fed to the computer screen market price display system. Within Rowe & Pitman itself, near bedlam had broken out: 30 staff were briefed and ordered to hit the phones to buy stock from 200 clients. There was no time to go through the share register and select holders of large blocks; each member of staff went through his own client list asking them if they held Gold Fields shares and telling them of the bid.

By 9.50am, Rowe & Pitman had received more offers of stock from clients than were needed and scaling down was necessary. By 9.55am, the operation was complete. At 11.30am, De Beers announced it held 23.4 per cent of Gold Fields – 20 million shares, or 13.4 per cent through the exercise of options to acquire companies with large holdings, and 16.5 million or 10 per cent through the raid. Adding in the right of first refusal over the 1.3 million shares held by FEW, the grand percentage total came to 25 per cent of Consolidated Gold Fields. De Beers had been sitting on 4.73 million shares (4.99 per cent) on its own account. It had 'bought a company' owning a further 7.43 million shares, and bought another, holding further options on 5.22 million shares.

At Moorgate, numbed shock soon gave way to anger. Had it been a group of predators outside the mining industry such blatant corporate rape might have been understandable. But Oppenheimer! Not just one of the club, but head of the world's largest gold mining company!

The clandestine accounts, the elaborate nominee holdings, the furtive buying over the months, the embarrassed telephone call when it was all done trying vainly to make light of it – to Gold Fields the very methods offended as much as the fact. It was a corporate dagger in the back, the blade carefully blackened lest a sudden flash give it away, plunged in by a man with whom Erroll had frequently shaken hands.

It was hard to believe of the diffident, liberal, respected Oppenheimer. But then, that was Harry: for as much as he was the man of thought and culture, corporate correctness, fastidious good manners and diplomacy, he was also the son of his father; and that thoughtfulness of expression masked the second inner man – acquisitive, instantly alert to his self-interest, and capable of acting ruthlessly to win advantage. The twin-sided personality was seldom more starkly in evidence: visionary and yet schemer; graceful but grasping; light and dark; yin and yang.

As for the ethics of it all, here, too, Oppenheimer had made a shrewd calculation. He cares a great deal about his reputation and his name in the City. The concert party and the dawn raid were not launched without some consideration of possible adverse publicity and the impact of that on the standing of Anglo American. But Oppenheimer surmised that such damage, if any, would be slight. As John Du Cane, former chairman and chief executive of Selection Trust, and himself an ex-Anglo American man, put it: 'He calculated the concert party very well. He would have said to himself, "They won't like me for a bit, but they'll get over it". And of course, he was absolutely right.'

But was he? For Erroll, it was even harder to acknowledge, that such a knife had been aimed at a company of Gold Fields' eminence and pedigree. Minutes later, as if to shake Moorgate fully awake to the nightmare of what was happening, came an unprecedented plunge into the market, adding blatancy of aggression to the earlier crime of acquisition by deceit: insult to injury. How could Harry have done it? And how was he allowed to get away with it?

The answer came with the sound of two stable doors clicking gently shut. The first came later that day as the Department of Trade announced it was appointing inspectors to investigate the share purchases. Then, two days later, on 14 February, came a second. Erroll had good cause to greet it with a withering smile. Only now, after more than a quarter of his company had changed hands, did it bring news that an inquiry would be held into recent dealings in Gold Fields shares. It was from the Stock Exchange.

The Department of Trade report was published six months later. 'De Beers', it concluded, 'formulated its scheme with the express intention of avoiding the disclosure requirements of the Companies Acts'. Brent, the Liberian-registered company being used by De Beers, had allowed its holding to spill over the five per cent limit for a month. De Beers argued that this had been inadvertent. The report also concluded with a recommendation that any shareholder in a UK company who breached the disclosure provisions could be deprived 'of the fruits of his enterprise' or ordered to sell the shares.

All told, this was not one of Oppenheimer's golden moments. For some, it merely confirmed what they had suspected all along about Anglo American's business methods: a private club with its exclusive rules, it was seen to care little for other people's. Anglo American would bend any rule, push aside any regulation, twist any arm in the pursuit of its interests, said its critics: no gentleman's club, this, at the heart.

And the heart was what Gold Fields feared. From this moment on, it was to remain deeply suspicious of every move Anglo American made, for it feared that more lay behind its pounce than concern to protect the 'controlled' independence of GFSA by ensuring the independence of Gold Fields. 'Anglo,' Gold Fields' managing director, Antony Hichens, subsequently recalled, 'has a reputation for emasculating previously great companies by trying to interfere too much.'

But for the moment, victory was Oppenheimer's. As he saw it, he had inadvertently, and quite regrettably, temporarily infringed a disclosure rule. But nothing else De Beers or Anglo American had done had wilfully broken a law. And there was no regulation then in force in the London market obliging a dawn raider to make an offer for shares at above the market price widely available. (There is now.)

Above all, he had, or thought he had, acted in the best interests of Gold Fields itself. Other, alien predators may have struck. GFSA was, after all, a crucial factor in the South African mining industry and Gold Fields did appear to be ambivalent about it. But that uncertainty was now resolved; the two could move forward in partnership.

Just two months after the dawn raid, in the last week of April, Oppenheimer came to London with a gift for Lord Erroll: it was a handsome statuette of Cecil Rhodes, founder of both Gold Fields and De Beers, and a companion of the figurine at the headquarters of Charter Consolidated. Oppenheimer had this one specially engraved for the occasion.

If there was any warmth in the discussions it did not show through in the joint announcement made to the Stock Exchange. Its three terse paragraphs, hacked out of a deep freeze of lawyers' distrust and icy redrafting, provided the context for seats on the board for the new shareholders. The words, and their meanings, had to be precisely correct and fully understood. Above all, the announcement had to be true if it was to form the basis of trust.

It read: 'De Beers and AAC have made it clear that there is no immediate intention on their behalf or of any of their associates to increase their existing holding and that in any case it would not be their intention to increase their combined holding in CGF beyond 29.9 per cent in the future.

'De Beers and AAC have repeated the assurance given at the time the acquisition of the holding was announced that there is no intention to use the holding to bring about any change in the control or management of CGF.

'De Beers, AAC and CGF believe it is in their interests to maintain a fully-competitive situation in the mining industry in the Republic of South Africa and elsewhere. However, they will, where appropriate, seek to co-operate to the mutual advantage of all shareholders.'

Eight years later, Rudolph Agnew was reciting these paragraphs by rote. For, over these years, he had come to a different, and very forceful, view about the truth of them. And the truth he had encountered much angered him: each paragraph had enshrined a lie. But for Anglo American, to have waited eight years made it seem very paragon of patience.

7

Fatal Attractions

■

Rudolph Agnew, then 45 and chief executive of Consolidated Gold Fields for just a year, came to love and hate that statuette of Rhodes in turn. It reminded him of everything that Gold Fields once was – and everything he did not want it to be. It reminded him, too, of what attracted Oppenheimer to Consolidated Gold Fields – and what repelled Agnew by that attraction.

Oppenheimer's pounce was one less sprung by an ambition to control Consolidated Gold Fields than to ensure a Balkan neutrality for a force much greater and nearer home: Gold Fields of South Africa, pioneer of the fabulous Witwatersrand and the world's most profitable gold mines, West Driefontein and Kloof. Gold Fields was to become a hapless battleground for a much more intense war, which had less to do with control of the British company than the South African one.

The company of which Agnew had taken command in 1978 must have seemed a gilded inheritance for one so young. Agnew, on the inside, had cause to know better. Gold Fields, under a veneer of financial strength, had major problems.

West Driefontein and the development of the West Witwatersrand Line had given Consolidated Gold Fields a terrific thrust. It was by far the Republic's lowest-cost mine: in the development of the Witwatersrand, GFSA had concentrated on the shallower mines while Anglo American went for the deep-level operations. Western Ultra Deep Levels, for example, involved sub-shafts sinking into the Carbon Leader Reef at depths of between 10,000 and 13,500 feet and heavy investment, while Gold Fields limited itself to depths of around 8,500 feet. The mines pioneered by GFSA were accounting for almost a fifth of the gold output of South Africa, and was the largest single source of the parent group's profits. Sharpeville and South Africa's break from Britain was to begin the breaking of control of GFSA from the London parent, which was under increasing political pressure because of its South African interests. Ironically, the break came just as terrific financial pressures forced the gold price off the fixed price of $35 an ounce.

The formal merger of GFSA and West Witwatersrand Areas took effect in 1971, with the holding of Consolidated Gold Fields in the joint company reduced to 49 per cent. No longer could London simply send barking telexes to Johannesburg for the remittance of yet more dividends.

But ironically, the profits from GFSA were to assume greater importance than ever in London. Indeed, some 40 per cent of Gold Fields' profits were coming from GFSA, a proportion that was rising rather than falling – and this in the teeth of a major effort by previous Consolidated Gold Fields chairman, Sir George Harvie-Watt, to diversify from South Africa. After ten years of heavy and questionable investment overseas and a huge expenditure of management time, Gold Fields seemed as dependent as ever on South African gold.

The story goes that Gold Fields' future chairman, Rudolph Agnew, was playing golf with a fellow director who pointed out that the market value of Consolidated Gold Fields was less than that of its shareholding in GFSA, so GFSA could buy Gold Fields and get all its assets for next to nothing. Agnew paled: 'I hope,' he replied, steadying himself on the tee, 'GFSA doesn't find out.'

Consolidated Gold Fields now had to find a separate style and function. Few men were more qualified – one might say destined – to lead it than Rudolph Agnew. His family links with the company dated back to his grandfather, John Agnew, an Irish military man sent to New Zealand during the Maori wars. He joined the board of Gold Fields of South Africa in 1922. Rudolph's father, a mining engineer, also worked for the company during the 1930s.

Rudolph Agnew, born in Perth, Western Australia, joined Gold Fields as a management trainee in 1957 after schooling at Downside and a spell as captain with the 8th King's Royal Irish Hussars. He worked in the United States, South Africa and Western Australia and returned to the UK in 1972. He was a lively character with a reputation for being a firebrand – at times literally so: in the sepulchral gloom of 49 Moorgate, Agnew would set fire to his waste-paper basket to see how long it would take before anyone would notice. The record was 18 minutes. He was duly despatched to run the group's newly acquired quarrying interests, a business which expanded rapidly with the acquisition of Amey Roadstone (ARC).

It proved to be one of Gold Fields' few successful diversifications. The Gold Fields search took it into Australia where it made a major investment in the copper giant, Mount Lyell Mining. In the United States, it bought the American Zinc, Lead and Smelting Company. It proved a disaster. Overall, Harvie-Watt had bought some 20 companies at a cost of £20 million. But the programme brought little in the way of profits. Gold Fields went on to build a portfolio of US industrial businesses principally in oilfield servicing and energy equipment.

Meanwhile, the Australian mineral sands operations ran into losses. Now the surge in the gold price had driven up GFSA's profits to the point where it was yet again the undisputed flywheel of the business. How, then, in 1978 did Agnew see the way forward?

'The policy of redeployment had not been successful. In the UK, we had a range of interests – Close Brothers merchant bank, scrap metal merchants, all sorts of things.

'I wanted to reduce our dependence on South Africa, but in my view this did not include being ambivalent: I wanted to stay there because the assets were so good.

'When I came back to 49 Moorgate [after running ARC] it was into an atmosphere I had left ten years previously: a state of conflict between the centre and the operations, where the centre was allowed to believe that it controlled operations but did not have the mechanism or the intelligence to do so. So I set out on a policy whereby the centre should be a "think tank" for the operations and would look after the investments. What the centre could not do was tell Bill Brown, head of our mining operations in the United States, where to explore. We worked hard at the machinery of federalism.'

Because of the dawn raid, the relationship with Anglo American had got off to a terrible start: Agnew did not accept Oppenheimer's 'protection' story – that it had moved in to prevent a bid for GFSA. 'There were dissenting voices on the Gold Fields board', he recalls, 'who said you couldn't trust Anglo; that it had designs stretching back to the 1940s and that the takeover of Gold Fields was its long-term plan.'

Meanwhile, Gold Fields' build-up of energy-related services

proved a deadly snare. In 1980, it made one of its biggest investments ever: in Skytop Brewster, for $60 million.

It looked a bargain. Skytop operated by buying in parts of its rigs from other manufacturers and then selling on the completed rigs to a range of small exploration companies. It had a colossal $250 million of orders when suddenly they stopped, followed by a flood of cancellations. The collapse was as severe as it was sudden and Gold Fields had to write off $151 million (£87 million at the exchange rate of the time). Group profits collapsed 39 per cent. It was a humiliating lesson for Agnew and the City would not quickly forgive. Skytop marked the end of Gold Fields' excursion into industrial businesses. From now on it would concentrate on mining and natural resources.

Gold exploration in the United States was stepped up under Bill Brown, head of Gold Fields Mining Corporation (GFMC). It had discovered the Ortiz Mine, 7,000 feet up in the desert at Cerillos, New Mexico. Most of it is submicroscopic gold: each ton of ore extracted contained less than one-twentieth of an ounce of gold. It yielded little more than ten tons altogether.

Then came two exciting discoveries. The first was the Mesquite Mine at the foot of the Chocolate Mountains in the California desert. Production began in 1986. Total gold production over its 20-year life is estimated at 2.4 million ounces. But to get at it, more than a quarter of a billion tons of ore have to be moved. The second discovery was Chimney Creek in Nevada. The mine, commissioned in 1987, should produce 126,000 ounces of gold in its first year at an average cost of just $86 per ounce, less than a third of the cost of Anglo American's Western Deeps.

But these were on nothing like the scale Agnew needed to catapult Gold Fields into the big league of North American mining. He resolved that Gold Fields would have to buy its way into an established copper producer, and in 1981 he found his target: Newmont Mining – the co-founder of Anglo American.

Newmont, one of the oldest and biggest mining companies in the United States, had been quoted on Wall Street since 1925. It had grown from a market capitalization of $8 million to $2 billion. It was the creation of two of the most legendary figures in international mining: Colonel William Thompson, who founded the business, and Plato Malozemoff, who built it into one of the leading American mining companies.

Through the extended family network that is international mining,

Gold Fields had come full circle in meeting Newmont. Not only had the company been a founder shareholder in Anglo American in 1917, but some ten years later Newmont had helped defeat Chester Beatty in the Rhodesian copper belt by taking a 25 per cent stake in Rhodesian Anglo American – the company that became Minorco.

The first Malozemoff knew of Gold Fields' interest was in late 1981, when Gold Fields acquired a seven per cent holding. It paid an average $59 a share for its stake, and had simultaneously filed with the Federal Trade Commission saying it wished to go up to 49 per cent. For Agnew, this was a massive commitment, involving more than £350 million.

Malozemoff was furious and wanted to see the stake limited to 25 per cent. Agnew pressed on. Battle ensued. The FTC, whose appetite for paper is insatiable, wilted under the Gold Fields onslaught: according to one report, 80,000 documents, weighing half a ton, were delivered by truck to its headquarters. Newmont's objection was that a company buying control should pay a premium. Malozemoff also went to court alleging anti-trust injury and won a 'standstill' agreement: a 32 per cent maximum limit on the equity holding of Gold Fields. Malozemoff, who was now reluctantly retiring in favour of Gordon Parker, made no secret of his unhappiness over his new partner.

And the new partner, which had raised its stake to 26 per cent, soon had cause to be unhappy about its investment. In 1983, Newmont's copper interests suffered losses of more than $35 million. Had Agnew bided his time, he could have bought his shareholding at half the cost. Certainly, the immediate implications for Gold Fields' profits were not encouraging.

This was the background which set the tone of the relationship between Agnew and his new dominant shareholder, Anglo American. It came to view the problematic earnings per share performance and the standstill dividend record with an understandable apprehension – it had paid £6.16 a share to build up its holding in the dawn raid. By the time of the Newmont investment in 1981, that was down to £4.85. By 1985, the shares had dropped to £3.97. Net assets, far from rising on these overseas investments, were falling. When, if at all, would the Agnew strategy deliver?

From the moment Harry Oppenheimer's two representatives joined the Gold Fields board in 1980, relations were, at best, polite; for the most part they were guarded. But as time wore on – and with little sign of an earnings breakthrough in sight – they grew increasingly strained.

The two representatives were Julian Ogilvie Thompson, chairman of Minorco (to which the Anglo–De Beers holding had been transferred); and the quiet and diffident Neil Clarke. Agnew had never forgotten that it was Clarke who was involved in the secret share build-up and the dawn raid; Clarke's neat, fastidious signature that had appeared at the bottom of an innocent-looking letter forming part of the clandestine share purchase system. Clarke, Agnew suspected, had not just fired the bullet but had polished the gun. Clarke also knew the City better than JOT did, and he would brief Oppenheimer. Not always, however, did Oppenheimer listen.

These were the two personalities involved in what Agnew was to describe as 'the corporate equivalent of an exchange of prisoners': in return for JOT and Clarke joining the board of Gold Fields, Agnew was to join the board of Anglo American.

In Johannesburg, such an appointment was regarded as a prestigious mark of recognition in business, but Agnew was soon to develop quite different ideas: 'I joined the board in the mistaken belief that it was a significant body. I soon discovered it was a total waste of time. All the decisions that mattered were taken elsewhere.' Initially in 1980, and for some time, Gold Fields and its people were treated as the favoured sons. Generous invitations were extended to Agnew to come to Johannesburg and stay with the Anglo High Command. On a personal level, the Johannesburg charm was as flattering as it was genuine.

But within a year, the strains in the Anglo–Gold Fields relationship started to show. In 1981, Gold Fields made an £185 million rights issue cash call on shareholders. The financial call on Minorco was just £30 million: hardly a strain for the satellite of the great Anglo American group. But as so often in business, a small, niggling matter became a flashpoint. At stake was a sum much smaller than £30 million: it was just £45,000. Minorco suggested it should get this as a commission for 'underwriting' its share of the rights. For an empire capitalized at £5 billion, it seemed a trivial pursuit. And the basis of the claim offended Agnew: it was that Gold Fields was an Anglo American group company, and that as it was group policy to pay the same underwriting fees offered to outside institutions, Gold Fields should stump up. But Gold Fields did not consider itself within 'the group' at all. It refused to pay commission.

The cash was to help pay for an increased shareholding in Newmont. Here a second, more serious note crept in. According to Agnew, news of the intention to go for Newmont was disclosed to JOT the night before the board meeting called to approve the purchase. At the time, JOT expressed surprise, but said nothing. But when Gold Fields representatives went to see Newmont, they discovered to their astonishment that Oppenheimer was in the room next door. Agnew was appalled. JOT had to call his people in Johannesburg – and Anglo American backed off.

Increasingly concerned at the lacklustre earnings and assets performance of the company, Anglo American began to press for a seat on Gold Fields' inner strategy committee. It argued that if such 'embarrassing clashes' such as Newmont were not to recur it was wholly sensible. And it had, after all, paid its ticket – both in the original share purchase and subsequent support for the rights issue.

But Agnew and his fellow directors would have none of it. A key reason was that when Gold Fields took its holding in Newmont it had to file with the regulatory authorities in Washington. One of the reasons why the deal was allowed to proceed was, in Agnew's view, that Gold Fields was able to satisfy them that Anglo American did not sit on its executive committee. The Americans, openly hostile to Oppenheimer interests since they outlawed the De Beers diamond cartel, had no favours to grant to Anglo American.

But the concern was not confined to Washington. Gold Fields' then finance chief, Antony Hichens, later recalled: 'We felt if we started to give access to our inner cabinet meetings then control would be in danger of passing to Anglo American. They could say their piece as directors. But we could not encourage them to encroach on our discretion operationally.'

Hichens, who had joined Gold Fields in 1981 at the age of 44 as finance director, found himself in an eerie atmosphere, caught in the middle of a hidden but all-encompassing feud: 'The mistrust was extraordinary. If Anglo did X, we would do Y. I couldn't understand the attitude of my colleagues towards Anglo. I came to the company free of all the hang-ups about Anglo American and the religion of gold. I couldn't see what the other directors were getting at, when they kept warning me about Anglo. Before too long I did.'

Within 18 months, Gold Fields' exploration programme was proving a cash drain and Agnew was soon considering a second cash call on shareholders. This notion was vigorously opposed by JOT and

Clarke. For Anglo American, any further issue of shares meant that unless it stumped up the cash, its percentage holding would be diluted. And it felt it deserved to have a say in how the money was being spent. What were Gold Fields' real motives, it wondered?

Behind the scenes, pressure was mounting on JOT in Johannesburg to push his way into Gold Fields' inner sanctum. It came directly from Oppenheimer. Agnew suspected that JOT supported the Gold Fields board, but was under pressure from 44 Main which was increasingly frustrated at the failure to bring Agnew and Gold Fields to heel. Some even began to see JOT as a patsy 'secretly working for Agnew'. And Agnew, too, was apt to see him like a character out of a John Le Carré novel, whose ultimate loyalty had been 'turned' somewhere in the plot.

But the pressure on the Gold Fields board now stepped up as Anglo American's opposition to further cash-raising took a new turn. It developed into a suggestion – 'absurd' is how Agnew recalled it – that Oppenheimer would be happier if his holding in Gold Fields could go up to 35 per cent. That way, Agnew was told, 'he would feel more secure. He could afford dilution'. Gold Fields took advice from the legal advisers, Freshfields. But there was no way the board could connive at getting one shareholder over 30 per cent without getting the agreement of all the others – there had to be a bid. Neil Clarke understood this. JOT and Oppenheimer looked for loopholes.

It was to be a recurring issue between Gold Fields and Anglo American, and it bubbled and boiled for two and a half years. Says Hichens: 'By 1986, a powerful resentment had built up within Gold Fields that Anglo was holding them back. Anglo just did not want to put their hands in their pockets. We looked at a major acquisition in 1983 and they fought it like cats and dogs.

'They seemed obsessed with the 35 per cent control level. It was seen as the minimum. But 30 per cent was the level at which a full bid had to be made. They couldn't understand that. Neil Clarke did. But never JOT. But it was never a case of JOT saying: "I'm unhappy". It was always, "Oh, Harry would be unhappy".'

Recalls Agnew: 'There developed a fascinating series of conversations about Harry's ethos and methods. At after-dinner sessions at Anglo's flat in Eaton Square, JOT would start on at me: "You've got to realize", he'd say, "that Harry is the inspiration of the Anglo group. We look up to him and love him. He's infallible and all-wise, kind and considerate. He doesn't seek to dominate. He seeks to work *through* people. But he seeks also to be secure."

'It was during this that JOT disclosed that many of the executives of Anglo and De Beers were employed by Oppenheimer personally, and were paid out of Oppenheimer accounts in Switzerland, not out of Anglo coffers. So you can judge that Harry had also looked at the machinery of corporate government over the years.

'He had his senior executives by the balls. He paid their salaries. Anyone who co-operated with Harry, it was hinted, would be rewarded.'

Anglo American has never denied the salary system suggested to Agnew. But it explains the arrangements in a quite different way – as a necessary means of paying executives who were spending increasing amounts of time abroad or who were working for more than one Anglo American company. It also saw the relationship with Gold Fields and Agnew in a less personalized light. It had supported the company in reasonable cash-raising, had not once interfered in acquisitions, had stood back when the Newmont clash arose, and had rarely raised its voice against Agnew or any of the investments he had made – even though some, like Skytop, had been disasters. 'We were a model shareholder,' recalls Roger Phillimore.

Anglo American argued that its wish to step up its shareholding was hardly the action of one critical of strategy and overall direction. Thompson and Clarke had fully backed Gold Fields' management. So what was it that Agnew was frightened of? Says Agnew: 'In any study of the Oppenheimers, power and possession are the obsessions. Corporate performance comes second.' It was to be a familiar, if sinister, refrain.

Within the Anglo American group, holdings of around 35–40 per cent were common. By effectively making associate companies secure from outside takeover bids, it matched Oppenheimer's need for security through dominance while not himself having to pay a bid premium. As Gold Fields saw it, here was the old Oppenheimer maxim at work: why go for full ownership when you can get control?

Skytop, American Zinc and Newmont; GFSA and Consolidated Gold Fields; Julian Ogilvie Thompson and Rudolph Agnew; Oppenheimer and the inner board of Consolidated Gold Fields: such were the makings of fatal attractions. What crosscurrents of tensions and relationships, and what misunderstood relationships they were to become. The Gold Fields–Anglo American saga was now to turn into arguably the most fraught and misunderstood relationship in the international mining business.

It was to prove the fatal attraction of them all.

8

Wedding, What Wedding?

■

In London, three great financial stories were in full flow in mid-December 1986: the stock market float of British Gas, BTR's £1 billion hostile bid for glass giant Pilkington, and the Guinness link with disgraced Wall Street arbitrageur Ivan Boesky: the Guinness scandal was about to blow.

But one story got away: the £1.8 billion merger between Minorco and Consolidated Gold Fields. It would create the biggest mining and precious metals empire in the world.

The agreed merger was code-named 'Wedding of the Romans'. Everything was set up and ready, including a detailed draft press release on the terms and strategy. There was even a 15-page crib sheet to help directors of both boards deal with press questions. The plans had been drawn up in the tightest secrecy on 19 December with the code-names 'Mark' (for Minorco) and 'Caesar' (for Gold Fields).

But not a word appeared and the astonishing story of the Romans wedding never leaked. Looking back on the battleground that Gold Fields' relationship with Anglo American had become, the story would have met with blank incredulity. But that Anglo American had won Gold Fields' Rudolph Agnew close to the altar was in no doubt.

From where Agnew stood after the smoke had cleared in 1980, such a prospect would have been inconceivable. He had plenty of occasions that year, and subsequently, to recall to himself in more thoughtful moments the legend of the Limpopo river: it is held that if you stand long enough by the banks of the river, you will see the corpses of your enemies floating by. From where Agnew was standing, the Limpopo looked full of directors of Anglo American drifting like crocodiles – and all worryingly alive.

In the great battle that was to erupt, the point that was to raise astonishment with the investing public was not that the marriage of the Romans had been called off, but that it ever got as far as it did.

In the summer of 1986, Anglo American's formidable City intelligence had gathered something potentially alarming. A plan to break up Gold Fields had been drawn up by the American investment bankers, Merrill Lynch. Normally, this would have been worth little more than a wry smile and a speculative write-up in the Sunday papers: American corporate finance houses are forever drawing up break-up plans and such schemes existed for virtually every major company in the *Financial Times* 100 Share Index. In most cases, these are little more than speculative exercises tarted up with pie charts and computer graphics that some mistook for genuine analysis, or worse, actual business. They are normally only kept for next year's simulated corporate slaughter in the graduate induction courses.

This one was different. The Merril Lynch plan had been bought by rival mining giant RTZ where chairman Sir Alastair Frame and new chief executive Derek Birkin were considering it closely. Over a secret dinner the plan was discussed between Birkin and the three Young Turks from Minorco: Hank Slack, Roger Phillimore and its bright young finance man, Tony Lea. The scheme they hatched was called 'Operation Snakepit'.

RTZ and Minorco would get together and would bid for Consolidated Gold Fields. It was called 'Snakepit' because each would take various parts of Gold Fields once the victim was in the pit. Each part had a code-name.

Birkin wanted the aggregates business of ARC. He was not interested in owning minority shares in companies, such as Gold Fields had in GFSA and Renison. Birkin said he liked 100 per cent control and full cash flow. Tony Lea's eyes lit up at that: as a finance man this was the language he liked. Phillimore was less enchanted. Birkin was shrewd, but was he too shrewd to be trusted? Hank, in charge of Minorco's American operations, would take control of GFMC. He could barely keep still for the excitement. Gold Fields' stakes in Newmont, Renison and GFSA would pass to Minorco, to retain or sell as appropriate.

It was all go for the Snakepit. The Young Turks wanted to move straight away. But there was one problem: their chairman, Julian

Ogilvie Thompson, would have to be told. JOT accompanied Slack to a subsequent secret meeting with Birkin at an RTZ flat. JOT said it would only work if Rudolph Agnew was supportive and would go along with an agreed deal.

JOT picked up the phone to Agnew in mid-July. He had something important to talk over: could he come round for the weekend? Reluctantly, but also strangely flattered, Agnew agreed.

There, at ARC's headquarters at Mells, Somerset, which Agnew used as a weekend retreat, JOT told him what he had heard about RTZ, but delicately spared him the gorier details of the Snakepit. Agnew was not at all keen. But on one point both men were in no doubt: Gold Fields was vulnerable.

This was a problem they discussed frequently over a weekend that proved on a personal level to be a great success. For all that Agnew was suspicious of Oppenheimer, he looked up to JOT and was impressed with his political acumen and the knockabout, hair-raising stories he would tell of Botha's antics in the Pretoria cabinet.

Agnew had been having a series of clashes with his finance chief, Antony Hichens, a former Royal Navy officer who had come from Redland after starting his business career with RTZ. More than once Hichens had to cope with Agnew's stand-up rows. 'He's an intuitive thinker rather than an intellectual,' Hichens had once said of him, 'very quick at getting to grips with problems.' And, now and again, the people he held responsible for them.

What JOT found, however, was a personality quite at odds with the difficult, and at times tempestuous, public persona. He found a settled, highly-intelligent, well-read and literate man, head and shoulders above the corporate equivalent in Johannesburg and capable of the most incisive analysis of both Gold Fields' and Anglo American's problems.

JOT found a considerably more thoughtful and sensitive man than he had been led to expect. Agnew's persona had been changed profoundly by the tragic death of his only son in a car accident near Johannesburg. Despite humour on the surface, he battled with depression.

But in the outer layers, JOT found in Agnew an engaging and wickedly funny observer of the London corporate scene – full of spicy remarks about his Gold Fields colleagues. Agnew also let casually fall that his relationship with his second-in-command, Antony Hichens, was not of the best. And he made no secret of his tussles with him.

JOT soon realized there was little love lost between Agnew and some of his operational directors. These candid exchanges bonded them. Another weekend launched what both thought at the time to be a genuine and enduring friendship. Without doubt it launched the whole programme for the Wedding of the Romans: an agreed merger of the two companies.

JOT's dalliance with RTZ was not solely a devious ruse. Gold Fields' massive spending was turning a familiar wheel of attrition: pushing up borrowings which increased the interest charge which lowered profits, held back dividend growth and lowered the shares. Meanwhile, the rights issue route looked problematic. How long would investors go on forking out for more equity on a stock that was looking increasingly lacklustre? In a phrase that was to become chillingly familiar to Agnew two years later, Gold Fields was, financially, 'in a box'.

Meanwhile, mega-bids were becoming commonplace. Blue chip companies that looked to be impregnable were starting to tumble: Imperial had gone to Hanson; Distillers to Guinness; Debenhams to Burton; Dixons had fired at Woolworth. Now BTR was trying Pilkington. In such a climate, who dared count themselves safe? Certainly not Gold Fields. In the autumn of 1986 came evidence that someone was building up a shareholding. The buying was finally traced to the ambitious Canadian mining concern, American Barrick, which had amassed a 4.9 per cent stake through the stockbroker James Capel. The Gold Fields price was jumping all over the place. And who else might James Capel be buying for?

Gold Fields, which immediately called for a DTI inquiry, had reason to feel vulnerable. Profits for the year to June had fallen by just £4 million – to £111 million. The exploration programme, which would take years to bear fruit, had pushed up borrowings and with them the group interest charge which came to £45 million. Debt as a percentage of total funds had risen ten points in two years, to 45 per cent. Also, looking at the exploration programme to which the group was now committed, cash demands were going to push those borrowings higher still.

Exactly these worries had been exercising the group's merchant bank adviser, Warburgs. It saw this company, strategically seeking to do the right things, in danger of falling to a predator unless something was done, and quickly. Its solution, which it put to the Gold Fields board, delighted Oppenheimer. The plan was to create a new holding company, putting together a cash-hungry Gold Fields with its cash-rich 25 per cent shareholder, Minorco. The plan carried a secret code-name: 'Romans'.

Warburgs drafted a paper which it submitted to both Gold Fields and Minorco in September 1986. A new holding company would be created, based in Europe, into which Minorco and Gold Fields would be decanted. Not only did Minorco have substantial cash and a portfolio of investments in mining and natural resource, it also had, in its 60 per cent shareholder Anglo American and De Beers, a stout, sympathetic and, above all, financially formidable parent with funds that would enable Gold Fields not only to meet but to *accelerate* its gold exploration and production programme.

Accelerated development! It was hard to think of an operational manager of Gold Fields who would not jump at the prospect. The commercial and financial logic looked compelling. Agnew himself had drafted an outline business plan for the new company which had been accepted by Minorco. One of its proposals was the sale by Minorco of its Salomon Brothers holding.

On a personal level, JOT enthusiasm for the plan was gradually winning over Agnew. 'What a marvellous way this will be', he told Agnew at his London flat, 'for the Anglo family to learn the mining and natural resources business outside South Africa.' Agnew would be their teacher, their pathfinder; he would never have a greater or more fulfilling opportunity than the one now opening.

Others did not agree. Recalls Hichens: 'I was in the lead position on all the negotiations. We argued for three days to reach agreement and then put the paper to the Gold Fields board without any comment. I told them often during the talks that I didn't think it would stand a ghost's chance in Hell of getting through the board.'

There was outright hostility towards the financial implications – particularly the absence of a premium for Gold Fields shareholders and the extent of South African control. Directors had reason to look warily on the prospect. With the profound political problems in South Africa, increasing pressure on governments to step up sanctions and the accelerating exodus of multinational companies, any company where Anglo American had a significant shareholding would have a stock market rating problem. The shares would be automatically 'out of bounds' for a gathering number of institutions. In Johannesburg, shares in Anglo American were standing at a discount of more than 40 per cent to their true worth. That, they feared, would be the fate of the new enlarged Gold Fields. Behind all the rhetoric of corporate synergy and complementary benefits, it would be swapping a financial box for a political one.

Three distinct camps now emerged: those for a minimum 40 per cent holding by Minorco (Oppenheimer); the largest camp, urging that the South Africans should not be able to exercise more than 25 per cent of the votes except on special occasions; and a third, wanting the South Africans throttled down to below 20 per cent. 'But', as Hichens recalled, 'they would not concede South African control. And there was no way we would allow them more than 30 per cent. We wanted an independent board that could choose its next chairman and chief executive. But the whole thing was about them getting control.'

In December, Agnew flew out to Johannesburg with his personal assistant, Louise Du Boulay. There he met Oppenheimer and the Minorco Young Turks: Slack, Lea and Phillimore. Agnew told them that he was sorry but the scheme could not work because no one could solve either the premium or the South African problem. The tone of their reply troubled him as much as its content: 'They told me I was wet, wet because I was lacking in courage, wet because I could not control my non-executives. The meeting was pretty unsatisfactory and certainly not in keeping with the great compliments they had been paying me a week earlier. There were suggestions that I fire the opposition.'

But Anglo American was determined that he should press on. Recalls Oppenheimer: 'I had an hour-long meeting with Rudolph and he seemed very happy with it. I probably had about six weeks of enchantment with Rudolph. Later, I had the impression he was leading me up the garden path.'

Once Agnew was back in London, JOT invited him round to Eaton Square (where Slack was staying), on Monday, 14 December. A new secret plan popped out: Romans was dead; now came 'Friends'.

The proposals had been drawn up by Minorco's new merchant bank adviser, Morgan Grenfell. The plan involved a friendly merger with Gold Fields by means of a public offer which would give its shareholders a 29 per cent premium over the then market price (around £6.67). The outline business plan was as agreed with Agnew before. But this time, much greater emphasis was placed on the independence of the board, with substantial representation from

Gold Fields and, in particular, Agnew to remain as the chief executive of Gold Fields.

Negotiations on the plan went on all through that week. Agreement was reached on all key aspects of the offer ahead of a Minorco board meeting in Luxemburg on Saturday. The crucial Gold Fields board meeting had been called for the following Monday, 22 December.

Earlier that week, financial public relations consultant Lowe Bell was brought in to prepare a draft press release and background briefing. What resulted from the discussions by Friday was a 27-page dossier, bearing the code-names Mark and Caesar, setting out the agreed terms, reasons and conditions of the merger. The terms were three Minorco ordinaries, three Minorco convertibles and £51 cash for every ten Gold Fields shares. The offer priced each Gold Fields share at £8.66 (against a price of £6.67 in the market) and the whole of Gold Fields at £1.8 billion. Even the dividend had been worked out: there would be an income uplift of 32 per cent.

The new enlarged board would have some 20 directors, including seven from Gold Fields. Those 'invited to join' were: Rudolph Agnew, Campbell Anderson, Michael Beckett, Robin Herbert, Antony Hichens, Gordon Parker and Allen Sykes. JOT would remain as chairman of Minorco; Agnew would still be executive chairman of Gold Fields and would also become deputy chairman of Minorco. As for remuneration, 'it is', said the release, 'Minorco's intention to introduce appropriate incentive schemes in the enlarged group'.

But the reality behind the scenes was not as smooth as the prose. The phrase 'invited to join' papered over huge divisions within the Gold Fields board, now about to explode. Hichens had no intention of staying on. And recalls Slack: 'Part of the problem was that JOT wanted all this rushed through by Christmas. Rudolph wanted to be called chief executive officer and JOT was not going to be pushed aside as a non-executive chairman.

'Here were two good friends: each knew the other was powerful. When you are in a close relationship with someone, it implies a mistrust if you start pressing on being specific with titles. But we told Rudolph: "Look, Tony and Roger and I will be working with you. We will all recognize you as chief executive."

'Then there was pay. I think we were too gentlemanly about it. It was always understood Rudolph would get a generous salary, but the detail was never actually discussed. We should have given him a specific title and a big specific salary.'

The Anglo–De Beers holding in the enlarged company would fall to just under 40 per cent. Or not quite. As Hichens totted up the Charter holding and the personal Oppenheimer stake in Minorco, the reduced holding was nearer 50 per cent.

Although it was Minorco that was doing the takeover, the enlarged group would be known as Consolidated Gold Fields. Said the draft release: 'The transaction will create a major international natural resources group strongly orientated towards precious metals . . . The two boards believe that the transaction should lead to enhanced growth potential in earnings, both from further development of Gold Fields' core businesses and from an improvement in the returns from Minorco's resources.' Back-up quotes followed from both sides.

JOT: 'This merger will give shareholders of both companies an investment in the best spread of international mining assets in the world.'

Agnew: 'The new group will have substantial financial capacity to generate new natural resource business throughout the world. It is our intention to make the new group the largest, most profitable and best balanced international mining finance house.'

Agnew was to say later that he was a passive partner in this grand plan. Yet, it is hard to avoid the conclusion that Agnew, far from being some passive bystander, a cork bobbing on the in-tide of Minorco's relentless ambition, was on the contrary, an active and willing participant.

Others were less so, and, clearly, Agnew himself was not without considerable doubts. But the truth was barely visible beneath the merchant bankers' crib sheet for awkward questions, smoothed by the silk emulsion of the Lowe Bell prose.

It required careful reading. Donny Gordon, the South African financial magnate, has a way of reading documents and it is a method worthy of emulation. He would get one of his personal assistants to read a copy of a difficult passage out loud while he himself studied it with his eyes. Sometimes he would have the passage read aloud 40 times. In this way, Gordon wore out quite a number of personal assistants. He also became a very rich man.

The briefing notes skirted over two crucial points. First was who the chief executive of the enlarged company would be – if, in fact, there could be one? Under Luxemburg law, all material executive decisions had to be made within its boundaries. The moment corporate pronouncements were made outside of the Duchy, the authorities would prick up their ears. This was to prove a difficult point behind the scenes.

But much more so was the second. Under the proposals, Hichens and his co-managing director, Humphrey Wood, were to be discreetly fired from their executive positions. Meanwhile, Allen Sykes and Michael Beckett had no confidence in Slack and the Minorco team – and were angry with Agnew. Recalls Beckett: 'Agnew was not a great communicator. He did not discuss it with me until Friday when he called me in. We were excluded – and we were extremely unhappy.'

Hichens' job was to be given to the young Tony Lea. Recalls Hichens: 'Agnew told me, "I know that's not acceptable to you. But that's it". Those who were supposed to be running the company were not on the inner executive. The management structure was absurd and offensive. It was an extraordinary and insulting suggestion.' Hichens was not alone in this view: other Gold Fields directors bitterly resented Agnew's failure to keep them in touch. Hichens was certainly shut out. Agnew was about to be confronted with a revolt of his generals.

Says JOT: 'Rudolph initialled the business plan. It was not for me to tell him who he wanted on the executive committee. He came up with the names, and Antony Hichens and the others weren't on the list. That was his choice, not ours.'

Says Agnew; 'I never initialled anything. I received their plans on structure and passed them on without any agreement.'

Says Slack: 'There were long discussions with Rudolph into the night. He suggested I would go on the Newmont board. It was understood Antony Hichens would leave the company.'

Other problems surfaced. The document acknowledged that Gold Fields' paper was preferable to Minorco's. 'It should be possible', the crib sheet coyly prompted, 'for these shares to be quoted in sterling'. But that was the least of the difficulties with Minorco.

Finally, how would the political problem of such a large element of South African ownership be resolved in respect of Gold Fields' interests in Australia (Renison) and the United States (GFMC, Newmont)? On these points the draft release and crib sheet were silent.

But the wagons rolled on: what could possibly stop them? The full meeting of the Minorco board in Luxemburg that Saturday unanimously approved the scheme as the snow swirled outside the offices in Boulevard de la Petrusse. Oppenheimer and his entourage had flown from Johannesburg, the Young Turks from London, Jim Glan-ville of Lazard Freres and Robert Clare from the United States. JOT kept Agnew informed by phone throughout. When the meeting was over the party immediately left for the airport and their private plane.

Trouble awaited them in London. Later on Sunday afternoon, while Phillimore and Lea were working with Gold Fields' advisers on the draft, JOT and Slack went to Gold Fields' headquarters in Charles 11 Street, just off St James Square. They were taken straight to Agnew's elegant and spacious drawing room on the second floor. As they walked in something was definitely amiss. They noticed the tell-tale signs of crumpled cushions and heavy cigar smoke. It was like the three bears discovering that someone had got to the porridge before them.

Recalls Slack: 'I knew something was amiss when I saw the cushions hadn't been fluffed up. Rudolph looked a worried man. He had just had a session with Gordon Parker, the head of Newmont. And Parker was dead set against the merger.'

Parker was not the only one. Says Robin Plumbridge, head of GFSA and an implacable opponent of Anglo American: 'I had been in the United States for a meeting and was scheduled that weekend to stay overnight in London. When I got off the plane I was contacted and told there was going to be a merger. I had just the weekend to brief myself.'

Agnew, meanwhile, helped with advice on the final touches to JOT's speech to the Gold Fields board, scheduled to meet on Monday. Agnew, as JOT remembered, was deft and assiduous with his eve-of-meeting advice on how to overcome Parker: stress this aspect, don't go into that point. Do highlight this. Don't mention that. 'We went through the ground so carefully. He couldn't have been more helpful,' says JOT. Gold Fields' Michael Beckett recalls: 'I have no doubt Agnew went to bed that night thinking a deal was in the bag.'

Monday dawned. It was one of London's inhospitable days: a cold, sharp wind and snow flurries throughout the day – a far cry from the powerful heat of the Lower Veld and cooling drinks at JOT's eyrie at Klaserie. When JOT arrived with Neil Clarke at Charles 11 Street for the meeting, Agnew introduced them warmly, but at the same time was carefully neutral in his opening remarks. JOT was on his own. Agnew would not give a hint of approval until he had heard his board.

JOT began the well-rehearsed presentation. It was not long before he had a sense that the chill outside had settled within. The words and phrases that came so easily 24 hours ago sounded stumbling and hesitant now.

He stressed that all important decisions would have to be made in the tax haven, but that staff would be retained in London. However, care would have to be taken about what was said in London.

The presentation was falling apart. JOT looked for a reassuring sign from Agnew. None came. Stumbling, unconvincing and apologetic, he fell back on what some at the meeting recalled as arrogance: 'And, of course, you're being offered a fair price. We would really like to get agreement by this afternoon.'

Agnew stared ahead and slowly smoked a cigar. Neil Clarke barely looked up. Robin Plumbridge, who in Thompson's eyes would have voted against even if he had put on a performance that outshone Lord Olivier, spent most of the presentation staring out of the window. Parker gazed impassively into mid-air. Across Hichens' face could be seen a gathering thunder. JOT could never communicate with Hichens who saw in him a man who regressed to a child in Oppenheimer's company.

Half-way through a speech that was by now clearly rambling and out of control, a folded note was passed along the table to Agnew. He opened it and its five words made his heart sink. It came from one of the non-executive bankers on his board. It read: 'This one won't fly, Rudolph.'

As he came to the end of his presentation, JOT tried to rally the table with passionate words on a new international mining partnership that would never have to worry about lack of cash and that would be unbeatable worldwide. He sat down to silence. Agnew politely thanked him and said the meeting would now consider his remarks. Could he and Neil kindly withdraw for a period?

Barely had they left the silent room then the directors were clamouring to speak. But first there was a letter from Campbell Anderson in Australia who had been unable to attend. It was a powerfully-written piece, listing the formidable political problems that an Anglo American-controlled Gold Fields would face both in Australia and in Papua New Guinea. It would vote the company off the international mining map.

Gordon Parker then spoke. He saw a barrage of political objections in the United States: mining operations there would come under the most intense political pressure, he said. Michael Beckett also spoke against, pointing to the problems of the Anglo American link. Hichens spoke against. What would be the procedure when there was a conflict of interest between Anglo American and Gold Fields on, say, acquiring a new exploration prospect? What would be the arbitration machinery? And who really would pull the levers: Gold Fields – or Harry Oppenheimer? Plumbridge spoke quietly. He said such a merger, with the increased shareholding it would give Anglo American in GFSA, would imperil the company's independence and almost certainly create problems with the South African competition authorities.

When Agnew went round the table, there was not one director who had a kind word for Thompson's performance. If there was some way of reducing South African control with a better plan, the board would certainly consider it. But not this scheme.

Agnew, by tradition, spoke last, on behalf of ARC. Even he spoke against.

At 5.10pm, Agnew, accompanied by company president Lord Erroll, Robin Herbert and other non-executives, left the meeting and went to break the news to JOT and Clarke. Clarke sat writing down notes as a shattered JOT sought to piece together what had gone wrong. He could barely comprehend how, in the space of two hours, a great gulf had arisen between Agnew's evident attitude when the merger was being positively discussed to the reality now; from what he could hear, the merger had faltered not on technicalities but on basic principle. Bitter and inconclusive post-mortems would go on in the Anglo American camp for months. Gold Fields, according to Minorco, said that all options were still open, 'including a merger'. But meanwhile, this plan was off. Consultant Lowe Bell stood down, Anglo American's men returned to South Africa and the announcement of Britain's biggest ever merger was buried.

What really had gone wrong with this extraordinary relationship between Agnew and JOT? Had Agnew been outvoted? Or had he simply led JOT up the garden path? Says Plumbridge: 'I think on many occasions the two were talking past each other. Neither seemed to hear or understand what the other was saying.' Says Slack: 'We should have been more specific on Rudolph's title and salary.'

JOT says regretfully: 'Perhaps I should have spoken more with the independent directors. That is my one regret now. But I didn't want to do anything behind Rudolph's back.'

Hichens' view was that 'Anglo does not understand independent directors and board decisions. That was the problem. Behind the public company is the private family agenda. Rudolph had to be as crafty as they were. That's why he strung them along. He played a very subtle hand and in extraordinary difficult conditions'.

And Agnew? 'Both in Romans and Friends we bent over backwards to find a sensible solution. I was not stringing JOT along, but the only thing I agreed to was JOT calling the board meeting. I feel sorry for him now; very sad. He is trapped among the Bourbons at Anglo who have forgotten nothing and learnt nothing.'

Says Oppenheimer: 'It was a sad end. But you see, the perceptions people have of each other are always so much more important than the reality.'

Weeks later, in February 1987, Agnew flew to Johannesburg to take a final look at the South Africa control position. There was a plan to put ten or 15 per cent of the merged company in a trust fund to get round the control issue. But Anglo American insisted that in certain key circumstances it must be allowed voting access. Yet again, deadlock.

Recalls Agnew: 'They were very angry. And I think at that point they laid their plans for the hostile bid. They had one enormous problem: they had failed to deliver for Harry Oppenheimer. And Harry is not a man who takes failure well.'

Oppenheimer thought he had good cause to be angry – and for a new reason. In the immediate aftermath of the failed merger, there was now an extraordinary move within the Gold Fields camp: secretly, and without, it was claimed, the knowledge of Agnew who was on its board, GFSA stepped up its holding in Consolidated Gold Fields. The buying, by GFSA and Driefontein, started on 19 January. It took GFSA's shareholding in Gold Fields up from 4.9 per cent to 7.8 per cent. The significance of that precise holding was that it gave GFSA ten per cent of Consolidated Gold Fields' equity not owned by Minorco – a blocking percentage which, under company law, could frustrate a bidder from gaining full control.

Thompson was livid – and he was not the only one. The share purchase, seen as a means of insulating Gold Fields from further encroachment by Anglo American, was concealed from a number of senior GFSA directors, including Anglo American's representative on the board, Peter Gush.

GFSA's deputy chairman, Dru Gnodde, revealed that the decision to increase the holding had been taken by himself and two other GFSA directors. GFSA's chairman, Robin Plumbridge, said he took no part in the discussion. It was, he later said, 'considered to be a good portfolio investment'.

Both JOT and Neil Clarke had attended a Gold Fields board meeting on 23 January – right in the middle of the GFSA share purchases – and not a word had been mentioned. When Thompson found out the following weekend, he immediately called on Agnew to refer the purchases to the Department of Trade and Industry, already carrying out an investigation into how American Barrick had come to acquire a 4.9 per cent stake in Gold Fields the previous autumn. Both the implicit purpose of the increased holding – and the clandestine manner in which it had been carried out – appalled him.

To 44 Main, it undercut Anglo American's position, first as a direct major shareholder in GFSA, and second as a direct major shareholder in Gold Fields. It also made a mockery of Gold Fields' mollifying assurance that all options were still open, 'including merger'. The significance of the GFSA purchase was barely noticed as the outside world knew nothing of the merger plans just a few weeks previously.

A ferocious row now broke out. Tempers snapped and a slanging match erupted between Agnew and Phillimore in front of Oppenheimer. Anglo American could scarcely believe that Agnew could have led them to the point of an agreed merger at one moment and barricaded himself in behind an enhanced GFSA shareholding the next. The entire relationship between them now dissolved into suspicion and acrimony: Agnew saw jealousy, Anglo American betrayal.

Not only had the wedding ended in tears, but from this point on there could be no possibility of an agreed merger between the two. Says Agnew: 'We told them that there was no way we would voluntarily accept South African control because it was harmful to our business. We also told them, in clear and unambiguous terms, that if they ever tried to take control we would throw the book at them. Simon [Lord] Garmoyle of Warburgs also warned them. They were fully warned of what the dangers were.

'As for Plumbridge, he felt he had to protect himself. And as it turned out, he was proved right. In that move in 1987 he got 1988 right more than anyone.'

9

Carlin My Darlin'

■

Barely had Gold Fields time to recover from the Wedding That Never Was when it found itself in a Rescue of the Reluctant Bride – this time in the United States. It was to play a central role in the extraordinary events at Newmont Mining, by now America's largest gold mining company.

The episode came near to breaking Gold Fields. But at the same time it enhanced its attractions to the Oppenheimer empire more than ever. In personal life, so, too in business: nothing more kindles passion than a rival involvement. Gold Fields' relationship with Newmont as its 26 per cent shareholder had not got off to a good start, but that was nothing compared to the traumas that were to follow.

Newmont's encounter with destiny began with a magnifying glass and a piece of paper. The paper was a US Geological Survey aerial map of north-central Nevada. Scrutiny of the map back in 1960 revealed tell-tale bubbles in the thick sedementary and volcanic rocks. These created 'windows' revealing ore bodies containing mineral deposits. It led to the discovery of America's richest gold deposit – Nevada's Carlin Trend, in an area appropriately called Eureka County. By the end of the 1960s, it was the second most productive gold mining area in the United States.

But the Carlin pit was, literally, only scratching the surface. In September 1985, Newmont went public on a startling discovery: three miles away came drilling finds from a prospect called Genesis, suggesting a breathtaking five million ounces of gold. Altogether, Carlin, including the gold quarry Maggie Creek, Blue Star and Bootstrap, was now reckoned to have reserves containing 12 million ounces of gold.

For Newmont, the news could scarcely have been better timed. That year it reported its first net loss since the 1930s: $35 million. Magma Copper and the smaller sister copper operation had together lost more than $100 million. Carlin was thus to provide an early test for Newmont's new chief executive, Gordon Parker, who took up office in January 1986.

In physical appearance, Parker suggested to Agnew a man no more to be trifled with than Malozenoff: tall, with a firm, determined face, his formal corporate photo shows him looking down into the camera with a clenched fist grazing the side of his chin. Parker was a born and bred South African from a well-off and respectable family in Cape Town. He had started as a trainee with Newmont at 19. Now, as chief executive, he had to stamp his own mark on the business. Wall Street soon took a liking to him.

To reduce group debt, which had jumped by more than 50 per cent in two years, Parker placed the Carlin gold mining operations in a separate company, Newmont Gold, offering five million shares to the public, with Newmont itself retaining 90 per cent. The shares were offered in June 1986 at $9.50 apiece, backed by 1985 gold production of just over 218,600 ounces and pre-tax profits of $13 million. By 1986, gold production hit 591,000 ounces, with an average production cost of $170 and average sale price of $371.

At Gold Fields' headquarters in Charles 11 Street, initial dismay over the Newmont investment gave way to delight. Gold Fields' own profits were taking a dramatic turn for the better: results for the half year to December 1986 showed profits up 146 per cent, with US earnings accounting for 30 per cent of the total.

At Newmont, the figures now started to jump. With gold production climbing further to 786,000 ounces in 1987, Wall Street analysts were forecasting net income soaring to over $300 million. In the first half of that year, Newmont shares more than doubled to almost $50. It was, it seemed, just the beginning.

Then trouble struck. In August, Texas oilman T Boone Pickens raised his stake in Newmont to just under ten per cent. Pickens was a name that sent shivers down the corporate spine of America. He had a formidable reputation as a stock market raider, once even moving in on Boeing, the world's largest aircraft maker. Here was a man who played to the 'Wham, bham, thank you Ma'am' psychology of Wall Street.

Wall Street was not disappointed. Within weeks, he fired a $95 a share offer for Newmont, valuing it at $6 billion (£3.7 billion), saying he would break it up. But such was the magnitude of the Carlin discoveries, Newmont's assets were now reckoned to be worth between $100 and $105 a share.

Parker immediately rejected the Pickens bid, alleging violations of securities laws. At the same time, Newmont Gold announced it was going to double total capital spending to $400 million in a drive that would make it the United States' largest gold producer. Pickens responded by raising his bid to $105 a share.

Shares in Newmont Gold had now quintupled in value since the company was floated 15 months previously, putting a price tag on the operation of almost $5 billion.

Agnew now moved to counter-attack, declaring that he would increase Gold Fields' holding to 49 per cent to stop control going to Pickens. And Newmont itself announced its poison pill: a radical restructuring under which all of Newmont's non-mining interests would be sold to finance a special dividend of $33 a share. The scheme would cost the company a crippling $2.2 billion.

On 25 September, Gold Fields bought a further 23.6 per cent of Newmont, paying an average of $98 a share. The cost came to $1.5 billion. Then, three weeks later, came the October stock market Crash.

In the space of three days, the slate of assumptions about value was wiped clean and substituted by a new one: the wiper was computer-programme trading. Shares in Gold Fields tumbled by half to £7.70 As for Newmont, it experienced a stomach churning collapse to $33 – a third of the price that Gold Fields had paid, though it had the consolation of the special dividend. There was only one buyer of shares in Consolidated Gold Fields in the week that shook the world. That buyer was Harry Oppenheimer's Minorco. It took its stake to 28.4 per cent.

Agnew's gallant cavalry charge to the rescue of Carlin looked to be his most fatal attraction of all – and the most expensive mistake made on Wall Street for years. Gold Fields' debt, having risen from nothing in 1981 to more than £500 million in 1986, leapt to £638 million.

But this was nothing to the damage done to Newmont's corporate structure. After the special dividend payment, debt at Newmont stood at $1.75 billion. It was forced to sell all its oil and gas interests; its remaining equity in Magma Copper; most of its shares in Du

Pont; its South African interests; its Canadian copper company; and its interests in two other mining ventures. The sales realized $1.2 billion.

Newmont, now 49 per cent-owned by Gold Fields, was full of surprises, and soon came another one. In January 1988, it announced initial findings from a deep, long-drill hole at its Post property, Carlin, Nevada. It indicated mineralization of nearly one ounce of gold per ton of ore: 'The richest assay over such a long intersection', Parker declared, 'in the history of gold exploration'.

Newmont Gold announced an increase in its estimate of gold reserves, from 20 million ounces to 30.9 million ounces. The biggest increase, 6.5 million ounces, came at Gold Quarry, Newmont's largest mine. The entire Gold Quarry Deep West area was now estimated to hold 18 million ounces of gold. To bring this on stream required substantial capital spending. That meant that the debt pile, reduced by the asset sales to see off the junk bond raid, was forced back up again. Newmont's borrowings bounced back up to $1.2 billion.

Interest payments, now compounded by rising interest rates, shot from $16 million (pre-Pickens) to almost $62 million in 1987, and were to hit a crippling $123 million in 1988. This, Gordon Parker and his shareholders had good cause to reflect, was the ongoing damage inflicted by the Pickens assault.

Gold Fields, too, had been damaged. But Carlin effected a transformation of Gold Fields sufficient to make Anglo American lust after it more than ever. Analysts were now confidently predicting a jump in pre-tax profits to £315 million, earnings per share breaking through the £1.00 barrier for the first time.

Gold Fields was now the largest gold producer outside South Africa with a commanding stake in the spectacular Carlin Trend. All told, Gold Fields production totalled 4.9 million ounces a year, with a net attributable interest of 1.3 million ounces.

But most significant of all, the push into US gold mining – Newmont and the discoveries by GFMC at Mesquite and Chimney Creek – had reskewered the earnings base of the company: some 34 per cent of the group's gold mining profits now came from North America. South African earnings were down to 17 per cent of the total, against 47 per cent in 1984.

Such a change could not have come quickly enough: despite the very high grades which GFSA's winning mines like Kloof and Driefontein enjoyed, cash operating costs there were $175 an ounce against $160 at Carlin. (The average across the South African mining industry as a whole was $260.)

As for Anglo American, it was being pushed ever-further up the cost curve: the weighted average cash cost of production worldwide was $241 per ounce. Gold Fields' figure was $177 per ounce. Anglo American's was $302. And whatever happened to the gold price, Anglo American was set to be pushed further up the curve with its commitment to deep-level mining and wage rate pressures, while lower-cost capacity came on stream overseas. Anglo American thus faced a major competitor that was not only growing stronger but doing so at the effective expense of Anglo American. In a prescient piece of research that summer, Shearson's mining analyst, Robert Davies, wrote: 'What this means is that CGF's earnings from gold will rise relative to AAC in any price scenario, but the discrepancy will be even more marked at lower gold prices. CGF will therefore become stronger at the expense of AAC, unless AAC does something. Hence the bid rumours.'[1]

Overall, Davies argued, Gold Fields now had an asset value of £2.8 billion or £13.40 a share against a price in the market that struggled to make £10 a share that summer.

But how long would it stay so low? Agnew knew well the dangerous waters into which Gold Fields had now sailed: if there was a silence from his major shareholder that summer, he knew it to be a calm before the storm. One question now dogged him: when the storm broke loose, would Gold Fields be ready?

Hichens, a competent and forceful manager, had none of the extensive social distractions or ambassadorial commitments of his chairman, necessary as they were often tedious. By comparison with Agnew, he lacked the imagination and broad-brush approach of his chairman. But he had a formidable grasp of the detail of group operations, and in any other company would have emerged as natural leader: indeed, he held several outside directorships, among them the chairmanship of building products group, Caradon.

Hichens could be relied upon to deliver massive financial and statistical firepower in the event of any hostile bid, and Humphrey Wood had an organizational grasp to help co-ordinate any defence campaign, while Beckett ran the business. But who among Gold

[1] *Consolidated Gold Fields: North America's Unrecognized Gold Mining Giant*, June 1988.

Fields' outside financial advisers would mastermind the battle to mobilize support in the City? That role was indisputably reserved for Lord Garmoyle, one of the top corporate finance men at Warburg. But it was denied him – and the row over this tore at the heart of Warburg.

Agnew and Simon Garmoyle had been close friends for years. They had spent many shooting weekends together, and throughout the ups and downs of the Anglo American relationship in the 1980s it was Garmoyle to whom Agnew turned for advice. But earlier in the year, there had been a mighty row at Warburg over Garmoyle's support for Gold Fields – and it took him to the point of resignation and a showdown with the Warburg chairman, Sir David Scholey.

The problem was a deep conflict in Warburg between its corporate finance arm and the securities trading side acquired two years earlier, with the advent of Big Bang reforms in the London market that enabled bankers to acquire broking and jobbing firms.

Warburg had bought *inter alia* the stockbroker Rowe & Pitman, which had for years acted for Anglo American. One of its most senior people, Peter Wilmot-Sitwell, had been instrumental in the 1980 dawn raid. It was inconceivable to him that with such a prestigious client on its books Warburg could act for Gold Fields. But Garmoyle stuck to his guns. Gold Fields had for years been one of the bank's most valued corporate clients: and Gold Fields looked to Warburg to do the defending.

Scholey ruled against Garmoyle on the grounds that the bank's position had changed. Warburg could not in honour have both Anglo American and Consolidated Gold Fields as clients.

Garmoyle, in an impossible situation, now tendered his resignation and planned to defend Gold Fields by setting up a small team on his own, which would have been a devastating blow to Warburg. Scholey drew attention to clauses in Garmoyle's contract that such a course would leave him open to substantial legal claims from the company. The bank, in effect, would finish him.

Agnew, furious at Garmoyle's treatment but unable to assist, turned to Gold Fields' other merchant bank, Schroders, and its chief executive, Wyn Bishoff. The bank had recently shot to the top of the UK merchant bank league tables. Top flight clients included Hanson and BP, and the bank had gained a reputation for take over defences through David Challen.

Challen introduced Agnew to one of Schroder's most remarkable recruits and a man who was to play a striking part in Agnew's life. He was a cerebral, intense-looking 39-year-old former Treasury civil servant, called Gerry Grimstone. He was to become Agnew's confidante, personal manager, watchdog, probation officer and general minder.

Grimstone was not at all in the merchant banker mould, with his intense, intellectual, at times tortured air. He had been at Schroders less than two years. An Oxford graduate in chemistry, he had started as an administrative trainee in the Department of Health and Social Security, and eventually became private secretary to David Owen when the former Labour MP was Secretary of State for Health. Grimstone worked his way up, joining the Treasury where he became Assistant Secretary responsible for privatizations, of which he handled 20. He became, in effect, the Government's in-house merchant banker until Schroders beckoned.

As the summer of 1988 progressed, Schroders read all the signs of an impending bid and sought to put an organization structure in place. 'Preparing for a hypothetical bid', Grimstone recalled, 'is not nearly the same as coping with a real one.'

He would not have long to wait.

10

The Weaning of Minorco, Société Anonyme

■

From every angle in the northern financial sky, Minorco was a star that seemed to shine from nowhere.

Minorco? To the New Yorker, it suggested some fractious Italian restaurant with a noisy cappuccino-maker and steamy waitresses. To the Brits, it had the ring of a Peter Sellers pocket republic with a flag, a cacophonous brass band and a ten-minute national anthem. Only South Africans would have got close. Even a London fund manager who had heard of the name would struggle to form an opinion of what it did and when its shares last moved, or why.

As for those calibrated triumphs of hope over experience – stock-brokers' research circulars – few bothered about Minorco. It was a Gamma stock, Luxemburg-based, with 85 per cent of its shares held by just 35 people. In the year to September 1988, the total number of press releases issued by Minorco came to just two. That is why, when its record-breaking bid for Gold Fields was launched, Minorco seemed to come from nowhere. Not for the dumb observance of legal exactitude alone did Gold Fields entitle its first defence document with the full Luxemburg incorporated name of its assailant: Reject Minorco *Société Anonyme*.

But Minorco was not a new company. It had a past that reached back through the great dynastic saga that was Anglo American. It played a pivotal role for Anglo American in its first years. It was Sir Ernest Oppenheimer's imperial creation, established to fulfil an imperial mission: to guard the great copper belts of Africa for the British Empire.

The company that was to become Minorco was registered in England on 8 December 1928. It was called Rhodesian Anglo American. Sir Ernest Oppenheimer was its first chairman. And one of the biggest founding shareholders with Anglo American was the Newmont Mining Corporation of New York. It even had a man on the board.

The board was overwhelmingly British, taking in representatives of Anglo American and the British South Africa Company. In the complex politics of the African copper belt and against a background of booming demand, Rhodesian Anglo sought to keep the Americans, bent upon cartelization, from seizing control. Oppenheimer wanted to amalgamate and control all the copper interests in Rhodesia and achieve in copper what he had achieved in diamonds: control of supply and, through supply, price. It was a breathtaking ambition, with an immediate imperative: this copper belt, practically the only one in the British Empire, had to be maintained for, in the four most powerful words in the Ernest Oppenheimer lexicon, 'imperial and financial reasons'.

But Oppenheimer's dream was crushed by the Wall Street Crash. Between 1929 and 1932, the price of copper plunged from over 18 cents a pound to just 5.5 cents, and dreams of a new hegemony were shattered.

Anglo Rhodesia was involved in the African copper field until the mid-1960s, when Kenneth Kaunda, President of the newly independent Zambia, moved to nationalize the mines. In 1970, it moved out of Africa to one of the world's fast-growing brassplate canyons: Church Street, Hamilton, Bermuda. It was to have a new name: Minerals and Resources Corporation. Thus from mighty oaks did a little acorn grow.

In its second phase, lasting from 1970 to 1981, Minorco was an investment trust for Anglo American, holding sizeable shareholdings in mining and natural resource companies. In 1981, there was a second shake-up. It took over Anglo American's 36 per cent stake in Charter. Also transferred to Bermuda was the 28 per cent holding in Gold Fields. Minorco was now to be an active 'hands-on' manager of assets. Said Harry Oppenheimer: 'We want this company to be big enough, and powerful enough to . . . finance itself so that it isn't a question, when you want to do international business, of always having to export money from South Africa.'

But not having learnt from the mistakes of Charter, it was destined

(1)   Four faces of Harry Oppenheimer.

(2)   All smiles for shareholders, but tensions within. SEATED Anglo
American chairman Gavin Relly. STANDING, FROM LEFT deputy chairmen
Julian Ogilvie Thompson, Nicholas Oppenheimer and Graham Boustred.

Enemies of Anglo American,
home and abroad. (3)   ABOVE
Robin Plumbridge, chairman of
GFSA at Fox Street,
Johannesburg. (4)   RIGHT The
Denver Boot: Gordon Parker,
chairman of Newmont Mining
Corporation. Note the fist.

(5)   ABOVE Hands on for Gold Fields: Minorco's battering ram Sir Michael Edwardes. (6)   BELOW Minorco's finance brain Tony Lea. Relly called him 'Crackerjack'. Few disagreed. ABOVE RIGHT The godson: Roger Phillimore, Minorco's strategy director. BELOW RIGHT The son-in-law: Hank Slack, Minorco's high flyer.

MINORCO

SIR MICHAEL EDWARDES

Making points. (7) ABOVE Edwardes, flanked by Thompson (left) and Lea, at the press conference to launch the epic bid. (8) BELOW Gold Fields' chairman Rudolph Agnew on the attack, with finance director Antony Hichens (left) and Gerry Grimstone, the mastermind from Schroders. Note the furniture and 'opera house' curtains at the Gold Fields headquarters. Minorco dubbed it 'Versailles'.

(9) LEFT Judge Michael Mukasey: trust buster and George Orwell fan.
(10) BELOW Eight months of battle – and the strain shows: a moment of doubt for Agnew at Charles 11 Street.

(11) The son also rises: Nicholas Oppenheimer at the
headquarters of the Central Selling Organisation in
Charterhouse Street, London. At 44 years of age, a
diffident, soft-spoken king of diamonds – and an
enigma to most.

to repeat them. Minorco was given no autonomy or separate leadership. It was registered in Bermuda; it was run from the first floor of 44 Main. It lost Anglo American millions.

Around the periphery of the void where leadership should have been, three young men looked after Minorco. They were: Slack, Oppenheimer's son-in-law and personal assistant; Phillimore, Oppenheimer's godson and personal assistant to Anglo American chairman Gavin Relly; and Lea, appointed a main-board Anglo American director that July. They were keen to break from the bureaucracy and what they saw as a stifling atmosphere at 44 Main. The world would come to see them as the advance guard of a new generation at Anglo American – the pathfinders for the empire in its drive for fresh assets and earnings overseas.

Each had arrived at their positions in Minorco through the remarkable patriarchal culture. Tony Lea, born in Johannesburg, read economics at Witwatersrand University. His father was group financial planner for Anglo American and had worked closely with Sir Ernest Oppenheimer. After a spell at Charter in London, he returned to Johannesburg in 1974 as a management trainee, progressing up the finance ladder. Lea played a hand in the winter of the six grey squirrels and the subsequent dawn raid on Gold Fields. He was to be the financial architect of Minorco. Relly used one word to describe him: 'Crackerjack'.

Roger Phillimore's father, an officer in the Royal Navy, had gone to South Africa during the Depression and worked for Anglo American at the Springs Mine. Roger was a godson of Oppenheimer's, a point he would often play down: 'There's nothing special in being one. I think I am one of 96.' After reading economics at Witwatersrand University, he went to Europe, living hand to mouth and quite unsure of his future. 'But I was determined', he recalled, 'I was never going to work for Anglo American.' Oppenheimer urged him to join Charter's investment department in London. In 1974 Phillimore returned to Johannesburg, working in the gold division and, for a year, as marketing manager. He became secretary to Anglo American's executive committee and then personal assistant to Relly. Phillimore now looked after administration at Minorco.

Hank Slack's rise (see page 39) gave him a keen knowledge of Minorco's American investments – Engelhard and Inspiration in particular. Slack would think nothing of flying from New York to Johannesburg, then to London, on to Europe and back to New York in a week. Between these awesome peregrinations, colleagues would rib him mercilessly about needing two secretaries: one to fix his appointments; and another to unscramble them. In this frenetic global rush Hank, it seemed, was never late, only a continent behind.

The immediate and principal concern of these three men was to bring an asset-rich but languishing Minorco to life. But it was six years before the new hands-on, proactive Minorco emerged. One of its largest – and Anglo American's oldest – investments, Hudson Bay Mining and Smelting, fell into a corporate black hole.

Minorco bought Inspiration Resources, a United States natural resources, chemicals and copper operation which took over the Hudson Bay interest. But in the early 1980s, base metal prices collapsed. Minorco's net earnings plunged from $172 million in 1981 to $73 million in 1983. Recalls Lea: 'It was a hell of a setback. Minorco took a massive hit in extraordinary items, in the area of $500 million. It took five years to straighten out.' More trouble was to come. In 1986, Minorco took an additional $45.8 million hit on misfired deals stemming from a leasing business acquired by Inspiration.

Minorco, like Charter, was foundering. Between 1980 and 1985, earnings per share from operations stood still at 27 cents. Hands-on managerial success eluded it. Inspiration was not an apt name.

But the massive damage Inspiration inflicted was masked by a quite extraordinary success elsewhere. It was to provide Minorco with one of the biggest and most dramatic corporate killings in Wall Street: the taking of Salomon Brothers, New York's largest investment trading house.

Salomon became the biggest single investment in Minorco's portfolio, accounting for more than half of its assets: an astonishing state of affairs for a satellite of a South African mining house that had set out to build an empire in mining and natural resources. Minorco also came to play a major role in the power struggle that raged for control of Salomon.

Minorco, through 30 per cent-owned Phibro, acquired Salomon for $350 million in 1981. Salomon's fortunes soared on the back of the 1980s financial boom and Slack played a critical role in helping Salomon's John Gutfreund in his power battle against David Tendler. Minorco sold down its Phibro holding and, just ahead of the October 1987 stock market crash, sold its remaining 14 per cent stake in Salomon for $809 million. Barely had the deal been struck then Salomon's problems burst into the open. The bank had suffered an earnings collapse and would struggle to clear a third-quarter profit. Then came the 19 October stock market massacre, with shares in Salomon collapsing to $16. In the vast electronic caverns of the Salomon Nibelung, the hammers ceased to beat.

The amount raised by the brilliantly-timed September killing brought Minorco's total proceeds from Salomon to $1.4 billion – all of it profit. It was the profit from Salomon Brothers, not the proceeds of some Anglo American Apartheid mine in the Rand – a picture of darkness and evil lovingly painted by some – that provided the cash for the bid for Consolidated Gold Fields. Coincident with the deal, Minorco's chairman, Julian Ogilvie Thompson, announced the new policy of active management of investments, and a shift of corporate headquarters from Bermuda to Luxemburg.

Political pressures had been building up in Bermuda to tighten the tax concessions that had built the brassplate canyons of the fiscally discreet. Many companies moved to the less turbulent (if cocaine-brushed) shores of Grand Cayman. Minorco was also feeling the heat from those in Bermuda wanting a clampdown on South African companies. 'We had to get a special Act for the Scheme of Arrangement through the Bermuda Parliament,' recalls Lea. 'The whole thing was fraught with political difficulties.' More than Minorco cared to admit, moving to Luxemburg made a virtue of necessity.

Operationally, Luxemburg had nothing to offer Minorco as a head-quarters. It is in no sense a corporate centre. The only natural resource that Luxemburg could reasonably boast was the croissant. But it was tax efficient. James Capel calculated that if the company had moved to London and sold its portfolio, it would be liable to Capital Gains Tax of $500 million.

Minorco's cash resources now stood at just over $1 billion. The group's investments across five quoted companies on three continents stood at $1.8 billion. On top of this were unquoted investments with underlying net assets of $213 million. All told, Minorco was a $3 billion company. Its biggest asset was the 28 per cent holding in Consolidated Gold Fields. Next came a 30 per cent stake in the metal processor and refiner, Engelhard, worth around $340 million. Minorco had a mirror of Engelhard in Johnson Matthey, the world's largest platinum refining and marketing organization. Minorco owned 36 per cent of Charter which in turn owned 37.5 per cent of Johnson Matthey.

Johnson Matthey and Engelhard are the great platinum bonds that span the Anglo American empire. The two businesses receive their platinum from the same source: the Anglo Rustenburg platinum mine in South Africa – the world's biggest. Together, the three form a global tripod giving Anglo American a massive presence, not only in the production of platinum (Rustenburg produces around 1.3 million tonnes a year) but in its refining and processing for use in end-products, ranging from evening dress brooches, through autocatalysts, to applications in drugs being developed with Bristol-Myers Squibb to combat cancer. Matthey is also researching metal-based compounds to fight viral diseases such as AIDS.

For Minorco, in its new, born-again, hands-on mode, where better to start than with Johnson Matthey and seize 100 per cent control? But here Thompson knew just how far Anglo American could go – and that an extra inch could be ruinous. However much JOT would like to go hands-on with Charter, and through Charter to Johnson Matthey, he dare not move lest the closing of the distance between Minorco and Johnson Matthey spark anti-trust objections from the United States car lobby with Engelhard.

Between them, Johnson Matthey and Engelhard's domination of the United States autocatalyst market reached up to 80 per cent in some areas. Charter was a necessary dividing door between Minorco and Johnson Matthey and a limitation of access to the control levers of the platinum industry. Removing it could spark major problems for Anglo American.

Here was yet another example of how, in the Anglo American firmament, so much delicately rests on the perception of space between the various objects and the balancing of gravitational pulls, one to another. Any attempt to concertina this relationship would risk regulatory action. Hence the fraught petrification of the platinum *ménage à trois*.

A further problem for Minorco was that however canny the investments it made, the share price trailed these assets. In 1987, that discount was 35 per cent. Moreover, Minorco was not just suffering the discount problems of a conventional investment trust, but it was suffering them twice over: not only were Minorco's shares standing at a discount of 35 per cent to the value of its underlying shares, but these shares in turn were standing on discounts to *their* net assets. Closing the first discount alone would raise the value of Minorco's shares by $1.6 billion. Recalls Lea: 'Anglo and De Beers were moaning that the Minorco price was trailing. It was one of Anglo's most valuable foreign assets and their view was, "Look, nothing's happening to the price. We increased our net assets 150 per cent in five years but nothing happened to the shares".'

How to narrow this discount and realize the missing billion? By becoming an active, hands-on manager of its assets, running businesses directly, like RTZ or Hanson, so that underlying value would be released through to the Minorco share rating. And where Minorco could not effect hands-on management it would sell the investment.

This was the background to the last dance in Bermuda. Looked at from a distance, the 17 names on the Minorco directors list suggested a rest home for retired Anglo American executives, a silent row of Harry's spent volcanoes. They came from all corners: there were no less than eight Anglo American- or De Beers-linked directors on Minorco's board: JOT, Oppenheimer himself and Gavin Relly; then came Lea and others from Johannesburg: Phillimore and Slack. From London came Neil Clarke, the chairman and chief executive of Charter and chairman of Johnson Matthey. Also from London was the ubiquitous Sidney Spiro, a director of De Beers, Harry's confidante and an old Anglo American hand. Spiro had a knack of slipping across the back of the screen in Anglo American's big moments, like Alfred Hitchcock in his films. Non-executives included Bill Loomis of investment bank Lazard Freres, Sir Michael Edwardes and Bob Clare of legal adviser Shearman and Sterling.

But where was the *operational* leadership? The new, hands-on, activated Minorco would need a full-time executive of operational managers. But nothing changed: the old greybeards would carry on as before. The failure to give the Young Turks full executive command at this point was a lapse.

It was not the only one. None of the operational objections to Luxemburg that had arisen during the Wedding of the Romans had been resolved. Minorco still had no chief executive. All the awkward questions about how decisions were to be made, by whom, and where, were left hanging.

Minorco also needed some big British names to give it recognition and legitimacy in the London financial theatre. But under Luxemburg law, there was a restriction on the number of British resident directors it could have: a majority of the board had to be non-British. With Lea now planning to move from Johannesburg to London, that brought the total up to the maximum allowed. It was a barely noticeable omission in Bermuda. It was to become a chasm now.

Still no agreement had been reached on whether to go for a hostile bid for Gold Fields. JOT was reluctant. The Young Turks bridled at this. Indeed, as the world's stock markets crashed in October, they wanted to strike there and then. Hit first by the cost of its defence of Newmont against Pickens, and now by the stock market crash, Gold Fields was in disarray. Here, thought the Young Turks, was the moment to strike! On the stock market, Gold Fields' shares had halved, and dealers would jump at the chance to unload and cut their losses. The Young Turks pushed.

But JOT still hesitated. Not only did Minorco have no plan, it had no leadership. Who would actually run Gold Fields on its behalf? Here was an ominous crack at Minorco. A view now formed among the Young Turks that if Minorco was to pull off anything, Anglo American must be made to let go: that was the inner tension now building up in the relation between Minorco and its parent; the inner takeover battle hidden by the outer one.

At Minorco's secret terraced house headquarters in Ely Place, the Turks agonized over what to do. Lea and Phillimore were being brought increasingly into the discussions. They became members of the exco in all but name. And they had a good relationship with Hank – when they could see him. Hank had become Minorco's man on the flying trapeze – constantly in flight between New York, Johannesburg and Luxemburg. Like the Amazing, Incredible Zamo of some Spanish circus, he was never here and never there but flying in between. When other men had indigestion, Hank had turbulence. Recalls Lea: 'We looked at all the options. Gold Fields was almost obsessive. It was fast running out of money, and we could bring cash to the party. If we crossed that Rubicon it would achieve so much for Minorco. In one fell swoop we would get the public ownership of the shares immensely increased; the Anglo–De Beers stake would go down and we would get operational control. It was a colossal task. We looked at other alternatives. Uppermost in our minds was that we had to get the company moving.'

Minorco was contemplating a £3 billion bid for one of the biggest and best-known companies in the world. But Minorco employed less than 30 people, the bulk of whose time was spent in Luxemburg clipping dividend vouchers. Gold Fields had a payroll of more than 14,000. The new operational responsibilities would be massive. But who would undertake them?

Gold Fields' debt was now over £600 million – and rising. It was in a box. Who would open that box? It took the enchantment of a French château in May to help focus minds. The Château de Remaisnil, near Amiens, belonged to Adrian Doull, a former personal assistant to Oppenheimer who had worked at Inspiration Resources in Canada. Here, during a weekend in May, Minorco gathered. How could the discount be closed? How could Minorco acquire operational assets?

It took a cathartic session at the château to psyche up JOT and the Old Guard for crossing the Rubicon. There were plans to be drawn up, figures and budgets to be worked on, the structure and pitch of the offer to be decided, Newmont and the American front to be prepared. But time was running out: a head of steam was building up for the Dellums Bill in Congress designed to widen economic sanctions against South Africa. Any bid should be timed to coincide with the Presidential election in November, which would help minimize the political exposure – and the risk of being an early showcase victim of a possible Dukakis administration.

Above all, the tightest security had to be maintained. The last thing Minorco needed now was the Gold Fields price moving up against it.

Yet from this period, Gold Fields knew that a bid was almost certainly on the way. It was handed the information – the presenter was JOT. He and Neil Clarke were still on the Gold Fields board and were still receiving boardroom papers.

If JOT carried on getting them, and Minorco subsequently made a hostile bid, Gold Fields' lawyers would hit him for six, arguing that he had access to privileged inside information. On the other hand, if JOT asked to stop getting the papers, Gold Fields would rumble what was up. It was an almost impossible dilemma, and was resolved with operatic rigmarole: JOT still 'received' his papers – but they were delivered in ceremoniously-sealed Jiffy bags to his lawyers. As for Clarke, he could attend the Gold Fields meetings, but he could speak to no one and contribute nothing: all he lacked in this bizarre role was a wraparound plastic bag and ear muffs.

All this was an obvious signal to Agnew that the bid plans at Minorco were flashing amber. Short of Oppenheimer marching down Charles 11 Street with the Dagenham Girl Pipers singing, 'We're on the way, Rudolph', no message could have been clearer. Indeed, from that moment, Gold Fields was on bid alert.

Minorco was getting strategic advice from Lazard Freres, in particular Bill Loomis and Robert Agostinelli – head of its office in London and, at 36, one of the firm's youngest partners. A Wall Street Italian American with button-down shirt collars and a propensity to verbal hypertension, he was one of the firm's rising stars.

Morgan Grenfell handled the financial and regulatory detail. The two key men were Tony Richmond-Watson and Peter Cadbury. One of the City's oldest merchant banks, Morgan Grenfell had handled 97 merger and acquisition deals worth £7.3 billion during the previous year. But it was struggling in the wake of the Guinness scandal two years before, which had triggered the departure of three top corporate finance executives, and was already being pushed from its Number One perch in the Acquisitions Monthly league tables by rival Schroders – advisers to Gold Fields. Here would be a battle of the merchant bank leviathans.

Richmond-Watson, a quiet, stolid accountant who had been with Morgan Grenfell for 20 years, was a senior figure in the corporate finance division. Cadbury, a solicitor, had risen to become the corporate finance director responsible for 'long-term strategic financial advice' on mergers and acquisitions – City-babble for winning. At 46, he came to Minorco with knowledge of the South African scene and formidable experience in some of Britain's most fiercely contested battles.

The advice both sets of bankers gave to Minorco was as urgent as it was unanimous: on no account should it present itself as a South African company. The more distance it could put between itself and Anglo American in the public eye, the better. A company perceived to be controlled from South Africa would be a direct target for regulatory bodies and anti-Apartheid activists across the world. Any bid seen to involve an affiliate of Anglo American, Bill Loomis counselled, would be headed straight for anti-trust problems in the US courts.

Minorco needed to concentrate on getting the Anglo–De Beers shareholding down below 50 per cent. It needed Anglo American off the stage. Deny your parents; deny and deny again, was the advice.

Meanwhile, who was to 'open the box' at Gold Fields and break up the company? The job would need a recognized British corporate figure, someone tough enough, with vision enough, and proven skills in breaking down opposition. Once Gold Fields had been captured, this person would be the hammer of Charles 11 Street, and all its colonies and dependencies. JOT and the Young Turks had a firm choice in mind, and the man was at hand.

Meanwhile, there were repeated rows on underwriting – offering institutional investors a discount to take up shares issued in a bid. For Minorco, which was planning to issue 80 million of its thinly-traded shares, the case was compelling. It would put a floor under the price: Cadbury and Richmond-Watson argued that an under-written offer would stand a far greater chance of acceptance.

But the underwriting need ran slap into the security need. Minorco would have to brief institutional investors while still keeping the bid a secret. Lea was now torn. He needed that underwriting raft, other-wise Gold Fields would make Minorco shares, not Gold Fields' value, the issue. But 'pre-heating' might spring a leak. 'It's not just meeting one man from a bank,' Lea would tell his colleagues. 'The one man says: "I've got to talk to my fund managers", and suddenly there's six people in the room. Then someone says, "Hey, I've got to speak to my salespeople, or the regional boys", and now there's 12 in the room. And that's just one institution. It's too much of a risk.'

For Thompson, Lea was pressing on an open door. Thompson was opposed to underwriting almost on principle. 'Our shares are already standing at a discount to their underlying assets,' he pointed out. 'These assets in turn are standing at a discount to *their* underlying assets. Minorco shares are probably trading at something like a 60 per cent discount, all told. To offer Minorco paper at yet more of a discount to underwriters is pandering to greed on their part and succumbing to folly on ours.'

Some analysts feared that was arrogant and naïve. The row rumbled on through the summer. Morgan Grenfell reluctantly caved in and the offer was prepared without an underwriting floor. It would prove a near fatal error.

More, much more, would be heard about Minorco paper. Mean-while, precious little would be heard about Minorco. The same security priority ruled out any prospect of Minorco doing the rounds of analyst and press presentations. With no briefings and no press cultivation, Minorco was deep in problems long before its bid was fired. The men from Minorco, it seemed, were doomed to come from nowhere.

As the château meeting broke up, a final problem now preoccupied JOT. Minorco would be the anvil of the attack on Gold Fields. Now it needed the hammer.

As the directors climbed aboard the bus that would take them to Le Touquet airport, JOT slipped his briefcase on to the luggage rack, moved down the central aisle, and took a seat beside someone with whom he wanted to have a very serious chat. He waited till the coach had cruised out of the château grounds on to the motorway before broaching the subject. The man sitting beside him and now listening intently was a man who had begun his business life delivering timber round Port Elizabeth in a dilapidated lorry called 'Lucy'. He had risen from being the son of a Cape garage proprietor to boss of Britain's largest-volume car manufacturer. His name was Sir Michael Edwardes.

11

A Necessary Myth

■

Why did Minorco choose Sir Michael Edwardes to lead its bid? Many of Minorco's own directors still do not know. It was a boardroom coup to beat them all.

On the coach to Le Touquet, JOT's discussion with Edwardes was less to do with leading Minorco than with taking on Gold Fields. Throughout the discussions of the Minorco cabinet on Gold Fields early in 1988, Edwardes was increasingly drawn in. He was a non-executive director of Minorco and beyond argument was the most experienced industrial leader on the board. Phillimore and Lea looked to him as a catalyst. Slack and JOT, because of their geographic distance, were increasingly dependent on Edwardes' advice and his assessment on the taking over of Gold Fields.

The leadership of the bid itself was a different matter. JOT was chairman of Minorco, and the natural choice to lead the battle. He knew Agnew and Gold Fields better than anyone and had been with Anglo American for more than 30 years. He had been a director of De Beers for 22 years and its chairman for four. He had been an executive director of Anglo American for 18 years, and was closest to the ear of Harry Oppenheimer. And in terms of ability, experience, standing and charm, no man was better qualified to lead Minorco.

The sorting out of Gold Fields was something else. It required a tough, hands-on, operational manager who would be based full time in Britain. Gold Fields was not just a huge investment holding house but the aggregates business of ARC was a colossal activity in its own right. JOT could not run diamonds, dig gold and crush stone all at once. Leading bids is one thing; running businesses another. In the complex politics of Minorco in the spring and summer of 1988, the two became hopelessly and fatefully confused, and this confusion was cultivated and spread by the best corporate advice money could buy in New York and London.

In the political cross-currents swirling round Ely Place, JOT was reluctant to mount a hostile bid against Agnew. But the Young Turks were increasingly keen to make a break and go for it. Edwardes, meanwhile, was warning that Minorco would 'miss a window' if it did not move before October. This was talk that the Turks were all too ready to hear, and their advisers Morgan Grenfell and Bill Loomis at Lazard Freres too ready to give. 21 September was the date fixed for the launch of the assault on Gold Fields, code-named 'Countryman'.

JOT was not an enthusiast. Both Agnew and Simon Garmoyle of Warburgs had warned him that they would 'throw the book' if Minorco tried a hostile bid; they would call on every authority to have it stopped. That is why JOT hesitated, while the Turks pushed.

As for communication with 44 Main, the less of it from the Young Turks' view, the better. Edwardes' was the lead they wanted to follow, and the ponderous Anglo American machine would be a frustrating brake. But what of the powerful regulatory and political lobby in the United States? Despite meetings with Newmont's Gordon Parker in August, Slack could get no assurance that Newmont would play along. The only advice the Turks now listened to was the advice they wanted to hear.

There was no doubt that Edwardes had the will to tackle Gold Fields. His defeat of the British Leyland unions was legendary; in the late 1970s he was Britain's best known businessman. At BL, the workers in the TR7 plant called him 'Head and Shoulders' because, they said, they only ever saw him on television.

Edwardes own book on the saga, *Back from the Brink*,[1] revealed a courageous leader, but also a ruthless one. It also revealed him as an astute thinker and inspired pragmatist with a firm, if highly unorthodox, grip on the levers of corporate power. One of his first moves at BL had been to halve the board from 20 to ten. In terms of executive directors, the company was to have one of the smallest boards of any major industrial company: an executive team of just three. In his five years at BL, Edwardes became notorious for a

[1]   *Back from the Brink: An Apocalyptic Experience*, Collins, 1983.

savage de-manning. He was likened to Cromwell: 'A bloody-minded man called in to deal with bloody-minded opposition'.

Not only could Gold Fields expect a radical thinning out of board-room numbers (it had 18), but one that would be carried out within a very short time of the bid succeeding.

Another hallmark of Edwardes' style is his fondness for psychological analysis and testing of people. He put the entire senior executive strata at BL through psychology tests. The testing was intensive and reached right across BL's management – literally thousands of executives were subjected to them. He persuaded top psychologist Eric Jones to fly to England from Johannesburg. He also brought in the former New York Police Department consultant, Dr Charles Bahn, Professor of Psychology at the John Jay College of Criminal Justice. Hundreds of executives were asked to resign. Recalls Edwardes: 'Some had lost credibility, often through no fault of their own. Others had been over-promoted and needed to start again elsewhere.'

The grand total of jobs lost came to more than 90,000. The BL 'apocalypse' left everyone bruised, not least Edwardes himself. He had developed a cynicism towards politicians and a distrust of the media, particularly for the way it personalized events and issues. He was subsequently to turn down two high-profile jobs: the chairman-ship of Eurotunnel and the top slot at Westland. He returned to Chloride as chairman.

One particularly striking example of Edwardes' tenacity – some would say gall – stands out. Leaving a dinner party at Number 10 Downing Street, he was about to thank the Prime Minister for a pleasant evening when Lord Carrington remarked that BL was doing much better and added: 'Keep up the good work Michael.' The PM immediately pounced: 'So he should, he's paid more than I am.' Far from making light of the jibe, Edwardes, who had just been studying a paper on pension funding at BL, began seriously to argue the point, saying she was costing the taxpayer as much as he, if the cost to the state of funding her pension was included. If this was the man Oppenheimer thought had a winning way with the Prime Minister, clearly he had not had the benefit of Edwardes' advice on his pension arrangements.

Celebrity though he was, Edwardes did not enjoy a City following. News of his appointment to a board would not move the share price in the way that, for example, the name of Sir Owen Green or Nigel

Rudd might. And while Minorco may have seen him as its lamp-lighter through the Department of Trade and Industry, Britain had moved on from the early 1980s, and the issues which Edwardes had fought so successfully had been largely resolved. He was a Callaghan knight, not a Thatcher one.

There was a further fundamental misjudgment. And this, most of all, was to haunt Minorco. Edwardes was not, and never claimed to be, a mining man. He had no feeling for the world of natural resources; nothing of the golden enchantment had touched him. In the eyes of Consolidated Gold Fields, which had just celebrated its centenary year, this, more than anything, was an outrage. To Gold Fields, Edwardes was an industrial head-banger, cosher and slasher for the banking men, a crisis manager from another world and another age. Choosing him to take over Gold Fields implied that it was not just a bid target but a company in deepest trouble; a terminal case like BL or Dunlop.

When Agnew heard the name Edwardes, he reacted as a man not just attacked, but insulted. There was barely a day in which Agnew's face did not crease and darken at the thought of the former BL chief: was this not the ultimate corporate surgeon? The little doctor with the bag of knives? Edwardes for him was the ultimate slap from Anglo American; they could not, he felt, have more maligned his rank or threatened the company. Edwardes was a human dagger in his back, and JOT had plunged it there.

For JOT, too, there was barely a day when the lips would not purse and the brow furrow under the hail of one-liner venom coming from Charles 11 Street. Why, JOT was so often to ask his friends as Agnew daily jibed and taunted Edwardes through the Press, 'why is Rudolph so *hostile*? We were friends, I invited him to my home, we spent weekends on the game reserve, he stayed with us in Johannesburg. Why all this personal hostility and bitterness? Why is Rudolph so *angry*?'

Why did Minorco choose Edwardes to lead its bid? In truth, it had less to do with qualities of industrial leadership than with Minorco's own need to create a Necessary Myth. The Necessary Myth of Minorco was the political requirement to present itself as distant and separate from Anglo American – its own sovereign state, even though Anglo–De Beers had a 60 per cent shareholding. This Necessary Myth, reasoned the Minorco managers, would win the bid.

No less an exponent of the Myth were Minorco's advisers, in particular Bill Loomis of Lazard Freres and John Craven, chief executive of Morgan Grenfell. The urgent advice was that Minorco should be presented as a company separate from its controlling parents, Anglo American and De Beers – understandable advice, but in the City of London, it was fatefully naïve: investors and analysts were being asked to ignore the 60 per cent shareholding.

Within Minorco itself, Edwardes had been supported by the Young Turks, Phillimore in particular. JOT may have been the better man to lead the bid, but he would have destroyed the Myth.

Then there was Anglo American's own need for a Necessary Myth. By a complex osmosis, that discreet and elliptical path of hidden intent and faltering dissemblage, the choice of Edwardes gave an insight into the state of Anglo American. The empire had grown to be in need of an outsider and a free man who could somehow cut through all its compromises, stand-offs and entanglements and set it free.

It needed someone whose very separateness could break the bonds that tied it to its past, and to its flawed South Africa. It was hopelessly compromised with the world; it faced the exhaustion of its mines, the attrition of its power and the relentless pressure of costs on a base that was not commensurately expanding. It also faced a crisis of relationships, and that crisis reached across the world, to America where Oppenheimer had been banned, to Britain where Apartheid rendered Anglo American a pariah, and to Australia, which wanted to nourish its own.

Oppenheimer was trapped by the past. And here was Edwardes, the free, uncompromised catalyst who alone could break the curse of gold and help set Anglo American free. But here was the core of the dilemma: Anglo American could not intervene lest its past compromise the future; yet by that instinctive drive that had shaped its past and brought it here, it could not let go. It was a true crisis of power and impotence. To the extent it intervened, it would break the Edwardes Myth; to the extent it didn't, it would deny its own.

The choice of Edwardes exactly captured this dilemma: Edwardes, the free hero, was not quite free. 'He', Anglo American had to be able to say, 'is not one of us. He is not Anglo, he is British, unconnected. He is our *uitlander*'. Here, however, was another contradiction: Edwardes was a born and bred South African. He had been capped at Rhodes University by Sir Ernest Oppenheimer. He sat on South African company boards.

It was another symptom of that reluctance to trust or to let go. In Johannesburg, troubled by an inner insecurity and defensiveness, Anglo American was incapable of choosing a true *uitlander*: its idea of a non-South African was a South African; its idea of a non-Anglo American man was one who had sat for three years as a supportive director of Minorco; and its idea of a hero mistook familiarity for influence and profile for power.

Thus it was that the Minorco board assembled for critical meetings at the Boulevard de la Petrusse on 19 and 20 September, just a day before the launch of the bid, with two quite different perceptions of the leadership: the Young Turks (for Edwardes) and the old hands (for Thompson). The full board was not told of the choice of Edwardes as chief executive until a presentation on the afternoon of the 19th. It was a *fait accompli*, and that was disquieting.

There was no open dissent. Coming, as the announcement did, as part of a massive package of detail on the biggest corporate takeover ever, and one to be launched in 48 hours, with many pressing points to be assessed, the moment to debate the leadership issue had long gone. In any event, the whole package had come with the unanimous recommendation of the executive board, and of advisers Lazard Freres and Morgan Grenfell.

Older hands did wonder at the appropriateness of Edwardes. Where was his constituency? What support could he bring? From what they could see, Edwardes had no knowledge of mining and natural resources, nor a track record in winning contested bids. He was among them less through *appropriateness* than through *reputation*, and that reputation had a brusque and abrasive edge. The idea that this would set the tone of the bid appalled them. This was not Harry Oppenheimer's style: Anglo American had never before launched a hostile takeover bid.

Above all, there was consternation among the old guard that Minorco was set on denying its Anglo American heritage and connection: Anglo American was everything that gave Minorco substance; the school to which they had all gone. What was there to be downplayed or ashamed of? What sort of people deny their parents? But the doubts were too late: Edwardes had been smuggled in, like a rugby ball, by the Luxemburg front row.

The meeting in September was the culmination of months of work by Lea. Central to the launch of what was then the world's biggest bid was the question of finance. The doors of the British banks were shut to Minorco: either (like Barclays) they had business connections with Gold Fields, or (like National Westminster) joint directors, or they were reluctant to take on the South African political heat.

Lea faced a daunting task. But by September he had arranged a $1.4 billion loan from a consortium of four banks led by Swiss Bank Corporation. Also in the syndicate were Chemical, Bank of Nova Scotia and Dresdner Bank. It was a formidable achievement. Chemical, America's seventh largest bank, was to come under political fire, which it returned with interest. The Brits, Minorco suspected, would have caved in at the first shot.

Minorco's own firepower was considerable. Results for the year to June showed record earnings up 58 per cent at $104 million, net assets of just over $3 billion and cash holdings of almost $900 million.

Months of preparation came to a critical head on the eve of the bid, at the two-day full board summit in Luxemburg on 19–20 September. Details of the bid, with the code-names 'Achilles' for Minorco and 'Hector' for Gold Fields, were put by Morgan Grenfell to the executive committee in the Boulevard de la Petrusse on the morning of 19 September, and to the full board in the afternoon.

Lea's team had been working on the terms of Minorco's offer throughout the summer. There had been intense argument. Two issues were paramount: first, the overall value of the offer, and second, the element of Minorco paper. That in turn required agreement on how far the Anglo American group was prepared to dilute its 60 per cent holding. It was reluctant to go much below 40 per cent; and the market would have a problem absorbing the Minorco paper involved in further dilution. A holding of around 40 per cent in the enlarged group was the aim.

The bid would have to be pitched appreciably above the Gold Fields price. But that price, now highly volatile, was already inflated by takeover speculation. At the same time, there was the Gold Fields debt mountain. Something also had to be kept back for a final sweetener if necessary.

The terms were not finally agreed until the full board meeting on the afternoon of the 20th. As to the presentation of the bid, it was agreed that Anglo American would stay as much out of sight as possible. New executive appointments confirmed the arrangements that had emerged through the summer: Edwardes was to be deputy chairman and chief executive; Phillimore, the office workhorse at Ely Place, became strategic director; Lea formally gained the title of finance director but sacrificed his position as a director of Anglo American; Hank Slack was appointed head of Minorco's North American operations.

On a personal level, Minorco's confidence in victory was in no doubt. Hank was now moving his family from Johannesburg to a new home in New Jersey, while Tony Lea was moving his family from Johannesburg to London. Victory was the working assumption. Minorco, with the might of Anglo American discreetly behind it, would, it was believed, smash Gold Fields within 60 days. It was now all go for Achilles. The bid would be launched the next day.

As Minorco's private Hawker Siddeley jet took off from Luxemburg late in the afternoon of 20 September, much still had to be done. Minorco's public relations now had to warm up the audience – and from a deep freeze start. Piers Pottinger of PR consultant Lowe Bell had only been put on alert the previous Friday: preparation and distribution of press releases, background details on Minorco and the executives and briefings for journalists and analysts all had to be arranged.

Lowe Bell knew little of its client. It had no experience of handling a South African company or indeed, any natural resources business. To make matters worse, it was having to deal with Edwardes through an intermediary, John Mackay, a trusty press minder Edwardes brought from his BL days. Mellow Gold Blend it wasn't.

The background biographies on the Young Turks were scant. It was hard to discern whether Lea and Phillimore had any experience at all in mining finance. As JOT ruefully admitted months later: 'We tore up their CVs because they mentioned Anglo.' Here again, men from nowhere. Lea had even given up his directorship of Anglo American.

There was to be no break for Lea. On Wednesday evening, he was still negotiating with the banks on the fine print of the loan agreement. The discussions dragged on until final signature at 4am. Four hours later, Ely Place was like backstage at the Royal Opera House with the curtain due to rise.

Last minute briefings were held, with every stress on the loosening of that Anglo American tie. Robert Agostinelli tried to lighten the mood: 'All we need now', he quipped, 'is Nelson Mandela on the board.' No one laughed.

In a side room, Hank Slack could contain his boyish enthusiasm no longer. He dialled Gordon Parker, head of Newmont Mining at his home in New York. Slack had been keen to fly over to New York the previous evening and break the news over dinner. But Cadbury warned against. It was important, Slack recalled, that he speak to Parker before Agnew did. 'With hindsight, it was a mistake.' For the hypercharged Hank, the phone seemed to ring an inconsolably long time. Finally, he got through and gushed out the exciting as-it-was happening news. There was a sluggish acknowledgment. Then the phone went dead. Parker growled angrily and climbed back into bed, cursing at Slack and Harry goddam Oppenheimer. In New York it was three in the morning.

But the time of the men from Minorco had come. And they now started out on their journey, assured of success, across that huge rainbow of ambition that arced across the world, from Johannesburg to Luxemburg, the rainbow's end moving as they moved, from Luxemburg to London and from London to New York, the rainbow's arch to a golden future, out of Rheingold to Valhallah.

12

Charge of the Wildebeest

■

By 9am on 21 September 1988, the sun was well up over Anglo American's headquarters in Johannesburg, filling the first floor board-room and the sails of the Thomas Baines ships in the paintings of Table Bay. But the deputy chairman was missing.

JOT was in London, under a weak and struggling sun, a world away and an hour behind, but about to telephone Rudolph Agnew.

Agnew didn't even need to check his watch. He knew just by the timing of that call exactly what it was that JOT was about to tell him. And JOT duly told him little that he and the Gold Fields intelligence had not already divined: the bid, the terms, the advisers, the timing. Almost as an apology, he announced that the new chief executive of Minorco, Sir Michael Edwardes, was standing right beside him at the phone. That was the closest Michael Edwardes and Rudolph Agnew ever got.

Over the past two months, the tell-tale signs of a bid had been mounting for Agnew. First, there had been the John le Carré rigma-role of JOT's boardroom papers going in sealed bags to lawyers. Then there had been the warning from Gordon Parker in New York in August that Lazard Freres was up to something. But the clearest evidence of all, the phenomenon impossible to ignore, was the surge in Gold Fields shares. In Johannesburg, in the three days before Thompson's call, turnover in Gold Fields shares had soared to 15 *times* its normal level. However soft and reasonable JOT had tried to sound on the phone, Agnew's ears were already ringing with the drumming hooves of wildebeest charging his way. Minorco's bid for Gold Fields may go down as the worst kept secret in British company takeovers.

On 29 August, Gold Fields' shares stood at £9.75. They then began a steady and relentless climb: they broke through £10 on the following Friday, reaching £10.39. The next week they rallied from an early shake out to £10.43 on Thursday and £10.55 on Friday. On 18 September, they hit £10.75. On the following day, the eve of the bid, they went to £10.78.

Thus, in the three weeks prior to the bid, on turnover in London three and a half times the level of August, and in the teeth of a falling gold price, Gold Fields shares had risen by £1.03, or ten per cent. The equity value of the company, in that bewitching and anticipatory foreplay, had risen by $219 million.

But by far the most acute pointer to a confident foreknowledge of a bid was a surge in option dealings. At one point in the previous week eight million shares, representing four per cent of the company, were under option in the market. But who had been buying the shares, and building up the option positions? Might they have been friends of Minorco, buying through nominee companies? They would lie low until the bid was sprung – and then accept in Minorco's favour, reaping a profit in the process. Warning bells from the 1980 dawn raid reverberated deeply through Consolidated Gold Fields. Agnew could hear them pealing down through the years, a permanent reminder of Oppenheimer's clandestine rapacity, his readiness to strike by stealth.

Gold Fields had mounted a formidable guard on its share register in the form of Gisela Gledhill. A barrister by training and former head of personnel at Gold Fields, Gledhill was now company secretary and was to play a vital role in tracking the movements in the Gold Fields register. After the curious Liberian-registered names that had preceded the 1980 dawn raid, her job was to monitor and, where possible, identify the hundreds of nominee names.

The method was to send out 'Section 212s': forms which, under Section 212 of the Companies Act, oblige companies to disclose the identities of the beneficial holders. But in nearly every case, the returned form simply gave the name of another nominee company. 'When we got a straight answer,' Agnew quipped, 'we'd throw a party.'

During the summer, Gledhill came to know the register almost by heart. On 12 September, Gold Fields had sent a Section 212 to Savory Milln, the London stockbroker owned by Swiss Bank Corporation which had handled one large block of options in particular.

The response was unhelpful: a second 212 unearthed only another Liechtenstein name.

But such was the impact of the option dealing that a bid was suspected on the morning of the 21st. *The Times'* experienced mining sector watcher, Colin Campbell, had written of consternation among Gold Fields analysts fearful of leaving their desks for lunch because of rampant speculation that a bid was at hand. 'The danger with Gold Fields', he wrote, 'is that one can cry "wolf" once too often, but the heavy option trading is telling you something.'

The dealing volume was certainly telling something where it mattered – within the Stock Exchange itself. At 7.45am, 20 minutes before JOT picked up the phone to Agnew, its surveillance department launched an inquiry into dealings in Gold Fields shares.

When JOT rang off, Agnew stood by the phone and savoured a moment alone. For all that this at last was the real bid, the gun that really fired, it struck him with the spent surprise of a *déjà vu*. He thought briefly of Oppenheimer and those conversations of the past eight years: beseeching conversations, cajoling and insistent and beguiling and then, more recently, darker and menacing. In that call, Agnew had moved, without JOT admitting of the changed relation, from family outsider to utter expulsion from the empire.

And then he thought of Michael Edwardes. Harry's new thing! Harry's little drummer boy! What could Edwardes *know* of gold, or mining or natural resources? This was all of Agnew's life, all of his family's life, as it had been all of his grandfather's life, and of *his* family. And in one phone call JOT had waved all that aside, as if none of it had mattered and with not a hint of contrition or apology.

Agnew's life had been scythed in that moment. What else could he do now but fight? What option had Anglo American left him? Both Agnew and Simon Garmoyle had warned them that Gold Fields would pull out every stop if there was a hostile bid, but both in public and in private they had refused to listen. Thompson's call had been the throwing down of a gauntlet: now Agnew would pick it up. He would unleash not just a takeover defence but a total war against the empire.

Of the long list of calls Agnew now had to make – to Gordon Parker in New York; Robin Plumbridge in Johannesburg; and Campbell Anderson in Australia – there was one name on top of the list whose number he started to dial: the Cheapside office of Schroders.

Gold Fields' four managing directors – Antony Hichens, Humphrey Wood, Allen Sykes and Michael Beckett – were already on alert. Within minutes, the first inner-defence committee meeting was underway. By midday, the mezzanine floor of Charles 11 Street was in a state of upheaval. That morning, and for the rest of that week, phone lines, fax machines, tables, chairs, typewriters, files, wall boards, secretarial back-up, television sets and filing cabinets were on the move. The entire building prepared for a great siege – how great none of them could then know. The mezzanine floor was now Gold Fields' wartime headquarters, the boilerhouse of besieged Versailles.

Similarly intense activity was underway at Ely Place, a cramped warren of rooms by comparison to the ocean-liner elegance of Charles 11 Street. The cramped space and air of intensity at times reminded visitors of *Das Boot*, that interminable German film of life in a wartime U-boat. *Das Boot* was now at action stations.

After months of bid preparation, Minorco's press conference, the first it had ever given, was being hastily prepared. The Young Turks would now become public property. Few knew their faces, their backgrounds, their qualifications or their roles: an astonishing state of ignorance prevailed on Britain's most ambitious bidders, the men from nowhere.

The conference was held in the basement of Lowe Bell's offices in Red Lion Court off Fleet Street. Before the inelegant scramble of journalists, cameramen and sound engineers, Edwardes never felt more confident, even if the Young Turks shook a little. After the crisis days at BL, Edwardes had developed an assured and command-ing way at conferences, and this morning's was no exception.

The Young Turks smiled nervously as the cameras flashed. But it was the offer that was centre-stage. That morning, Gold Fields' shares had opened at £10.75. Minorco now offered a reasonable looking £13.06. The terms were: one new Minorco share (standing at £7.13) and £19 cash for every two Gold Fields shares. The package valued the whole company at £2.9 billion – then an all time record for a UK takeover bid.

The terms offered a 20 per cent premium on a Gold Fields price already inflated by takeover speculation. And while there was an element of Minorco paper, shareholders were being offered £9.50 in cash – just 50p short of the price at which Gold Fields had stood at the start of the month. As for Minorco shares, they were standing at a 35 per cent discount to assets, with every prospect of that closing once the takeover succeeded.

Minorco would immediately sell Gold Fields' 38 per cent stake in GFSA in line with the agreements between Gold Fields and Rembrandt which had first right of refusal over the bulk.

After Slack's stymied talks with Parker on Newmont, a skilfully worded paragraph discreetly hid the failure to reach agreement while keeping all the doors open: it would 'review' the Newmont holding. Minorco pointed out that Gold Fields was constrained 'by a long-term standstill agreement from exercising any reasonable degree of control over it for many years. The current dividend yield on Newmont shares is less than two per cent per annum'. No mention was made of Renison in the statement.

The combined Anglo–De Beers holding would come down from 60 per cent to 40.9 per cent. As for board representation, that, too, would be reduced. 'In today's climate, Minorco can best grow and prosper as an international company if it is properly independent. Anglo American and De Beers will not therefore seek to play any role in the day-to-day affairs of Minorco. As substantial, albeit minority, shareholders, they will participate through their board representatives in Minorco board decisions.'

Edwardes denied that Minorco was a front for Oppenheimer: indeed, it was on the assurance that Anglo American would play no part in day-to-day affairs that he had agreed to take on the role. 'Minorco is poised for a quantum leap. If the bid succeeds, we will unlock not only the true value of Minorco's assets, but of Consolidated Gold Fields' as well,' said Edwardes. Stress was laid on Minorco not being a South African company. 'We have no assets in South Africa,' he declared. Then, as if to fill the silence, he added that Luxemburg-based Minorco should be seen as a 'pan-European' company: 'We're almost living in 1992 already'. It went down like a Wobbly Rivet, clattering to the floor.

There was a second one. It was the manner and immediacy of Minorco's appointments which struck a disconcerting note: Edwardes appointed chief executive *yesterday*; Phillimore, strategic director *yesterday*; Lea, finance man *yesterday*; Slack, head of North America *yesterday*. What, the conference audience began to wonder, did Minorco do the day before yesterday? And why were all the Anglo American people still on the board? Why, if Anglo American was to take no part in day-to-day management, was it to have representation on the *executive* committee? The look of the board and the timing of these appointments, far from creating the necessary impression of distance from 44 Main, hinted instead at a contrivance, and in a manner that suggested rush and make-do.

There was a third Wobbly Rivet. The financial case for Minorco's offer rested on an assumption that the 80 million new Minorco shares to be issued would not only hold, but rise in value. It had the compelling logic of a precise interconnected mechanism of wheels and balls: Minorco would take over Gold Fields; down would drop the Anglo–De Beers holding; up would go Minorco's earnings; down would fall the borrowings on asset sales; and on the higher multiples accorded to operating companies as opposed to passive investment groups, up would rise Minorco's shares.

But there was another way of looking at this: 80 million new shares of a Luxemburg-based company would flood the market; many investors would want to sell, and those who didn't would be left with stock in a company certain to suffer the political discount problem of the controlling parent. From this angle, Minorco's logical mechanism looked like the perpetual motion of the Martin Escher Waterfall: precise, exact and correct, only the water was flowing *uphill*.

Above the buzz in the Lowe Bell conference basement could be heard a crack of thunder: the first splintering earful from Rudolph Agnew. The bid, he declared, was being made 'by a Luxemburg shell which was a front for South Africa', and was 'a simple and naked asset stripping operation. They are basic asset-strippers'. Explaining what he saw as the critical difference between Gold Fields owning assets in South Africa and having, like Minorco, South African owners, Agnew thundered, 'You can deny your bastard sons, you can't deny your parents.'

Agnew knew the full force of that remark; and he knew the speed at which it would travel by telex to Johannesburg, to the first floor of 44 Main, and then on, up Claim Street, past Joubert Park, through Hillbrow, to Houghton and on to Brenthurst, straight to the library and the private study of Harry Oppenheimer. It was a piercing shot.

It would also be the first of many one-liners Agnew would ricochet off the Press to cause exasperation in Ely Place. Of South Africa he said: 'They know that they are the pariahs of the Western world.' Of Minorco: 'These people speak with forked tongues, unconsciously at any rate.' 'Who *controls* Minorco?' he thundered in an interview later that week, 'ask yourself: who will appoint its *next* chief executive? That's the test.'

A collective view soon formed among the City's mining analysts. Jack Jones of Phillips & Drew led the pack: 'Minorco will have to raise its bid to £16 or £17 because Gold Fields will have a well-planned defence.' Peter Rolfe-Johnson of the broker, Williams de Broe, hinted that Gold Fields could come up with an asset value nearer £18 a share. By the close, the market was in no doubt that Minorco had a fight on its hands: shares in Gold Fields closed at £14 in late trading, up £3.22 on the day and 94p above the value of Minorco's offer.

The *Financial Times* made a telling point: 'Gold Fields is worth far more to Minorco than anyone else, and the market knows it.' Despite Minorco's strenuous efforts to the contrary, the financial Press almost unanimously saw Minorco as an Anglo American vehicle. 'In its modern manifestation,' declared *The Independent*, 'it has never been regarded as anything more than the external investment vehicle of the Anglo American–De Beers group and, to all intents and purposes, the Oppenheimer family's insurance against political disaster in South Africa.' The paper's City Editor opined: 'The record is undistinguished, residing in tax havens, widely viewed as the Oppenheimer family's offshore piggy bank, trading at a 35 per cent discount to net asset value and yielding two per cent.'

Edwardes and the Turks could scarcely believe the way in which their presentation of Minorco as a separately-motivated vehicle had been brushed aside. But it was only the beginning of a baptism by media fire: by the end of that week, Minorco's financial arguments were swept away in a gathering storm of alleged insider dealing and suspicions of concert party operations. Edwardes protested that Minorco had the least to gain by any leak or destabilization of Gold Field shares: every £1 on the price, he pointed out, cost Minorco £160 million.

It was even mooted that the Anglo American empire had deliberately depressed the world price of gold to smooth the way for the bid. It was certainly not a good week for gold: quietly, amid all the storm, oil giant BP dropped its plans for a £600 million-plus stock market float of its gold interests. Amid the din created by Minorco's bid for Gold Fields, few noticed the rustle in the undergrowth that would lead to a hugh shift in the natural resources world. Another massive deal was secretly underway.

Meanwhile, the Labour Party's City spokesman, Tony Blair, had called for an inquiry into insider dealing allegations, and Agnew wrote to the Secretary of State for Trade and Industry, Lord Young, demanding a probe. By now Gledhill had discovered that almost a quarter of the 8.2 million options traded in the three days before the bid had gone to Liechtenstein-based Verwaltungs-und Privat-Bank. The outcry was echoed in Johannesburg where, on 27 September, the Stock Exchange announced an official inquiry. By the 29th, the DTI had received a dossier from Gold Fields, and immediately summoned Agnew for talks.

Meanwhile, Swiss Bank Corporation began to feel deep heat. It was the lead banker in the syndicate behind Minorco's bid. It was also the owner of the London stockbroker, Savory Milln, where there had been massive option dealings in Gold Fields shares. Were the Swiss bank's Chinese walls truly intact? The bank denied any implication of insider dealing.

By the end of the second week, two companies based in Vaduz had been flushed out as holders of the mysterious option stake. Even if Gold Fields could not prove beneficial ownership it had evidence of *concealment*, and that was powerful ammunition in Gold Fields' battle for its first objective: a DTI inquiry.

But the row over alleged insider dealing was only one of a number of fronts on which the guns of the defence were opening fire. A strategy was now unfolding, first to encourage regulatory intervention, not only in Britain through a Monopolies and Mergers Commission inquiry, but also in Europe and the United States. Even if an MMC probe found no case to answer, there was a great tactical advantage to the defending company: it bought time.

The strategy was drawn up by Schroders and the Gold Fields inner cabinet, with Humphrey Wood in charge of day-to-day defence tactics. Recalls Gerry Grimstone of Schroders: 'One of the most important things in a bid defence is to stall. It might not succeed in defeating the bid, but one of the important things we had to do was to seize the offeror's timetable and make it ours. We launched a huge international campaign and the insider dealing scandal was all designed to put the pressure on for a DTI inquiry and a referral to the MMC. If we could pull that off, it would give us four to five months to prepare a financial defence. The whiff of insider dealing affected people's perception of the bid. It was very helpful for us to create a climate of opinion that this whole battle was good versus evil. The scandal helped us gain the moral high ground and the support of the Press.'

Good and evil! In the space of a few weeks, Gold Fields turned a modern day corportate takeover into a morality play: a great British company against 'a moral pariah'. It saw its task as alerting every regulatory authority against what it saw as no ordinary bounty hunter.

What legend must have echoed in Agnew's mind? He, too, had sat in the first floor boardroom of 44 Main. And he, too, had seen the paintings of Thomas Baines of the great Dutch ships at rest in Table Bay. Table Bay . . . and the ship of the Flying Dutchman. According to legend, it was a cursed and haunted galleon, blasted from Table Bay and doomed to roam the seas forever. Against its entry every little harbour manned the cannon and closed itself tight.

The cursed galleon from Table Bay! What a mission now for Agnew: Warn every coastline and every port! Beacons and great fires, one after another must now be lit. A chain of great fires! No harbour in Europe, Britain, Australia or America must open for the Dutchman from Table Bay!

Phillimore could scarcely believe Grimstone's remarks: 'We are businessmen. We launched a financial takeover bid. From the start our relationship with Gold Fields was a business one. But the bid was not being judged by business or financial criteria at all. That was the elephant in the room. And everyone was missing it.'

In the United States, Agnew hired Bruce Wasserstein and Joseph Perella as financial advisers, two of the brightest stars on Wall Street. Also brought in to man the cannon was the law firm of Paul Weiss, Rifkind, Wharton and Garrison. These were among the most expensive advisers in America. But expense was the last thing on Agnew's mind. After all, wasn't it sweet justice that Minorco, as Gold Fields' major shareholder, would be picking up 29 per cent of the bill?

Agnew now launched the most expensive corporate defence in British takeover history. From day one, Gold Fields was to spend approximately £170,000 a day on the battle. At the end of the first 100 days, the total amount spent or committed came to £16.9 million.

Agnew wrote to the chairmen of Britain's top 100 companies asking them to intervene in determining whether their company pension funds should back the bid. 'Investment decisions in a bid of this importance', he wrote, 'should not be left wholly to the discretion of professional fund managers.'

Next, Bill Brown, president of GFMC, pulled on that leper's bell of South Africa, warning that a Minorco takeover would put the group's American operations in jeopardy. 'You can take Minorco out of South Africa,' wrote Brown, 'but you cannot take South Africa out of Minorco.'

On 5 October, Gold Fields, together with Newmont Mining, appealed to President Reagan to block the bid on national security grounds, petitioning under legislation designed to protect US access to strategic and precious metals. Minorco's South African connections, they argued, would put control of key minerals used in defence work, such as zircon and titanium, under foreign control.

At Ely Place, there was consternation. It had been blasted back by the reaction to its bid and morale was badly shaken. Meanwhile, where was the offer document? The formal clock on a takeover bid only starts once the offer document has been despatched, and 12 days had now elapsed, during which Agnew had created mayhem.

Morgan Grenfell had been caught up in the painstaking process of drafting and redrafting in sessions with the lawyers Linklaters and Paines. There were times when it seemed not to be an offer document at all, but some baroque ecclesiastical text with every apostrophe scrutinized by Vatican scholars and carved by stone masons. Sessions at the printers lasted until midnight and beyond.

At Charles 11 Street, Gerry Grimstone could not believe his luck. He had used the delay and made every day of it *work* for Gold Fields. Recalled Graham Williams, the group's senior press officer: 'Anglo and De Beers seemed to totally underestimate the reaction both at home and internationally. Minorco's press relations were becoming so bad they were issuing releases that never got mentioned. Even on days when journalists went round to see Edwardes and we would brace ourselves for flak, they would go back to their offices and file pro-Gold Fields stories.' Says Beckett: 'We would have been dead in the water had their other document come out within five days. It was their huge mistake.'

Gold Fields was exploiting that vow of silence Anglo American had fatefully undertaken. When there came no answering fire, Gold Fields could pound again with soaring confidence at an enemy whose guns stood idle. Says Williams: 'They never played the Anglo card as we feared they would. They never said, "We are the non-South African arm of the greatest mining finance house in the world. This is our pedigree – and there's none better". They never made a virtue of Anglo, but tried to be non-South African. They could have made a virtue of their origin. But they didn't. And that was a terrible mistake.'

Meanwhile Agnew, in an exclusive interview in *The Times*, had given an account of the planned Wedding of the Romans deeply at variance with the recollection of Minorco – and of JOT in particular. 'As Julian Ogilvie Thompson outlined his plans, our mouths', declared Agnew, 'fell open.'

Minorco now decided to fire its Exocet: the full draft of the 1986 Gold Fields–Minorco merger plan. Lowe Bell had been hoping to save it for a weekend, when it would carry maximum impact. In the words of a Lowe Bell aide: 'Now it was being rushed out in an atmosphere of panic. The documents were hurriedly assembled and sent out late in the afternoon.' It was lucky to get the coverage it did: Lowe Bell's relations with Minorco cooled from this point. As one of the aides involved recalls: 'There was an appalling handling of journalists. Minorco wanted advice, they were given it, but they didn't take it up. Then they would turn round and say: "Get us out of this mess".'

Nothing could now halt the slide of Minorco's bid to the regulatory thresher. On 7 October, the Competition Board of South Africa launched an investigation into the consequences of Anglo American obtaining an effective controlling interest in rival Gold Fields of South Africa.

Meanwhile, Gold Fields hammered away at the damage Minorco's South African parentage might do to its business, and particularly to ARC when tendering for local authority work. It seemed to be drafting its case for a Monopolies and Mergers Commission reference line by line *in public*.

By now, Edwardes and Slack were fighting fires on other fronts. The move by Gordon Parker, head of Newmont, to join with Gold Fields in protesting to President Reagan over the bid was a glancing blow to the Minorco bid strategy. Recalls Lea: 'Newmont proved to be one of the biggest disappointments and misreadings of the entire campaign.' Slack had hoped to woo Parker to Minorco's side and overcome problems by some agreed, voluntary reduction in Gold Fields' 49.3 per cent holding, but failed completely.

When it was clear that there could be no deal with Newmont, Edwardes announced, on 10 October, that Minorco 'will regard the entire stake as being available for sale on the best possible terms'. This was seen as a major retreat. Whatever Newmont's debt problems, there was no doubt that acquiring a holding in it would have been a coup for Minorco, extending Anglo American's reach to the Carlin Trend – now not only the United States' biggest gold discovery, but the biggest outside South Africa. Agnew described Edwardes' announcement as 'a massive fit of bad temper. Parker wouldn't play. So Parker would be punished'.

On 11 October, Gold Fields and Newmont filed a suit in the New York federal court calling on it to prohibit 'the Oppenheimer syndicate' from acquiring any further stake in Gold Fields or its affiliates. The suit, filed against Anglo American and De Beers as well as Minorco, alleged violations of federal and anti-trust laws and claimed that they planned 'to achieve in the gold market what they have already achieved in diamonds, a monopoly'. The suit opened up a major new front in the war, one that was to contain a latent and deadly trap for Minorco.

In three weeks, it seemed the entire battle had swung 360 degrees: it was Gold Fields that was doing the attacking; Minorco was chasing six fires with one hose.

The mood at Ely Place was grim. Bad news was now rolling in from the most faraway places. From Papua New Guinea came news that the Government would force Renison to sell its extensive gold holdings in the country (the one-third stake in the Porgera project) if Minorco's bid succeeded. Declared Prime Minister Rabbie Namaliu: 'We cannot allow the Apartheid regime to benefit from our rich resources'.

That threat to Renison was another slash at the jugular of Anglo American's ambition. Australia had been marked out by Oppenheimer as a critical new area for Anglo American. It had just given up control of Anglo American Pacific, its 58.8 per cent-owned gold mining subsidiary to Poseidon. It retained an 11 per cent holding in the new company and clearly Oppenheimer was viewing this as a springboard to greater investment there.

Renison, with a major position in mineral sands, producing 30 per cent of the world's titanium and 45 per cent of zircon, would be a valuable prize for Minorco. But on 14 October came the news that Australia's Prime Minister, Bob Hawke, had added his voice to growing international opposition to Minorco's bid, writing to Mrs Thatcher and US Secretary of State George Schultz to point out the strategic importance of the two metals.

On 13 October came news that the European Commission was set to launch an inquiry. It was concerned that if the bid went through, 54 per cent of world production of titanium would be in South African hands. The EC's competition commissioner, Peter Sutherland, had already brushed with the British DTI and had made clear that whatever the British Government's attitude to cross-border takeovers, the EC would not be browbeaten.

Within a month, the charge of the Wildebeest had been stopped in its tracks. A pall of gloom hung not only over Ely Place but over Morgan Grenfell too. Recalls Cadbury: 'The greatest aggravation was the failure to obtain fair and objective press comment in the early stages and our inability to prevent inferences of destabilization and insider dealing from, at least, being believed by some of the media. Minorco was the victim of a well-orchestrated smear campaign which managed to discredit it for being South African, notwithstanding Anglo and the Oppenheimer family's links with the Progressive opposition party and its opposition to Apartheid.'

Lea was more blunt: 'We were ready for a hot political campaign. But no one expected it to reach the level of personal vitriol that it did.'

In just one month, from Australia, Britain, Europe and the United States, Agnew had let a storm break loose. And all the ships in the paintings of Table Bay began to rock.

13

Passing Go

∎

Das Boot was now under fire from bow to stern. Each day brought fresh shelling and public relations explosions that shook the crew. In the distance, the great protective battleship, the mother ship Anglo American, looked dolefully on. Its huge guns stayed silent and the lifeboats unmanned.

Anglo American now seemed in relation to Minorco as the United States to the Cuban exiles in the Bay of Pigs: for a Bay of Pigs Minorco's bid for Gold Fields was turning out to be. Having started a financial battle for Gold Fields, Minorco now found itself in the middle of a political one – against Anglo American. From the start, it had hoped to concentrate on the financial case for its Gold Fields bid and let the anti-South Africa campaign blow itself out. But it was blowing with hurricane force. As the Young Turks saw it, Agnew had embarked on a policy of scorched earth against South Africa and even Gold Fields' own interests there. But what would they make of Minorco's financial critique of Gold Fields? And what would Gold Fields come up with by way of financial defence? The constant digression into politics appalled them. They saw Agnew's crusade as a campaign that sought to substitute the political process for the financial market place.

In truth, until the bid had cleared the regulatory hurdles and Gold Fields had produced an asset valuation and earnings forecast, the financial argument could not be enjoined. If Gold Fields was fighting a phoney war, so too was Minorco; the time for financial argument was not yet.

On 19 October, the DTI appointed inspectors, under Section 442 of the Companies Act and Section 117 of the Financial Services Act, to investigate dealings in Gold Fields shares ahead of the bid, and also the allegations of concert party arrangements and insider dealing.

Pressure now grew on the Take Over Panel to freeze Minorco's bid until the DTI enquiry was completed – and that enquiry could take six months or more. The Panel met on 24 October, two days before the deadline for a decision by Lord Young on whether to refer the bid. Agnew now felt that if there were sufficient grounds for Young to order a DTI investigation, they must be sufficient, too, to compel the Panel to stop the clock on the bid. But he still had no hard evidence, either on concert party operations or insider dealing.

Minorco responded in an extraordinary move by presenting the Panel with affidavits, witnessed by the solicitors Linklaters and Paines, giving personal assurances that no person or entity in the Anglo–De Beers group held any shares or options in Gold Fields other than the 29.6 per cent declared. The affidavits covered Minorco's directors and their families. A separate affidavit, signed by Hank Slack, locked in Oppenheimer himself, the family and Anglo American chairman, Gavin Relly.

Breach of these affidavits would render the signatories liable to up to two years' imprisonment. And that weighed heavily with the Panel, which, in what it described as 'a deeply concerning case', was in the uncomfortable position of being asked by Gold Fields to decide on an issue with irreversible consequences, even before the DTI inspectors had embarked on their task. If it halted the bid it would be pre-judging the outcome of the enquiry. Equally, if it let the bid proceed, the evident leak of inside information would be effectively waived. While it could not take a view on the veracity of the affidavits, it noted the sanctions attaching to their breach and ruled that the bid should continue.

The relief for Minorco was short lived. Hardly had the news gone out from the Panel when Lord Young announced he was referring the bid to the Monopolies and Mergers Commission. If the decision itself was a surprise, the grounds were even more so: in addition to normal public interest, it was 'to assess the possible effects on competition in the markets for certain high value minerals and especially titanium and zircon'.

Titanium and zircon? In the City, hands reached uncertainly for dictionaries. Titanium and zircon accounted for just three per cent of Gold Fields' profits, and mining analysts observed that the raw material from which 'tit and zirc' were produced was in abundance.

The involvement of both Gold Fields and Minorco was tenuous. It was a reference made by a logic of sorts: Anglo American's mighty position in gold may have been the more obvious grounds, but Young could scarcely ignore the boundaries involved.

The MMC was in no position to make judgments on the state of competition in the international gold market beyond UK shores, and still less could Young hope to enforce any of the conclusions such a global investigation might reach. But it was hard to escape the conclusion that the Minorco bid was too hot politically to be ignored and, not wishing to be seen bowing to anti-South African prejudice, 'tit and zirc' were an expedient means of justifying a limited reference and getting Young off the hook.

The decision was a blow to Minorco. On almost every front it had underestimated the opposition to its bid, but this was the most devastating punch of all. It was equally a shock for Anglo American. 'Oppenheimer', nudged senior Gold Fields aides, 'would never submit to a MMC probe. It's curtains for Harry now.'

It was not the only blow that morning. Overnight had come news that a New York district court had granted a temporary injunction to Gold Fields and Newmont barring Minorco from acquiring any more shares in Gold Fields pending an anti-trust inquiry into the bid. Judge Michael Mukasey ruled that Gold Fields and Newmont 'and the public at large face imminent harm from the takeover's effect in decreasing competition in the world gold market'.

That further added to the atmosphere of crisis, both at 44 Main and Ely Place. Should they now see the inquiry through? Or pull out now, before further damage was done? The inquiry would take up to three months and all of Minorco's time and resources for an outcome that could be swayed as much by political considerations as any cool appraisal of the facts. But the terms of Young's reference clearly limited the enquiry to titanium and zircon – so they thought – and Edwardes was confident he could satisfy the MMC.

It was a week when Edwardes needed every ounce of his tenacity, and of that he had much. He had taken an extraordinary punishment over the past month, and whatever else his critics may have levelled at him, he had toughed it out with pluck. He had taken Anglo American and Minorco to a crossing of the Rubicon, and those who thought he would back down did not know the man. The week after the referral he lunched with Oppenheimer in London. He told him of all the problems, but of his determination, too. And that impressed Oppenheimer.

But seldom, if ever, in the history of the Monopolies and Mergers Commission, had two companies approached an investigation with such sharply divided perceptions on the grounds for inquiry. Minorco felt that concentration in high-value strategic minerals was the relevant issue at hand. But Gold Fields saw the reference as *carte blanche* for an inquiry into *all* competition considerations and *all* high value minerals.

That is why, over the next two months, an extraordinary situation now arose: Minorco would arrive with their papers in standard size wallets and briefcases. The Gold Fields material, covering every aspect of the world market in diamonds, gold, platinum, palladium, zircon, titanium and the UK aggregates market supplied by ARC thrown in for good measure, was delivered by the carload.

Grimstone and consultants Sallingbury Casey now trawled everywhere. For them, the MMC inquiry was open season on everything and anything that Anglo American mined or did. Minorco's case was more focused, but Edwardes could barely take the zircon issue seriously – Minorco used none in any form. He had been enjoying a Christmas break in Thailand and was shopping with his wife Sheila when she spotted sets of stunning 'diamonds' for sale – £7 the pair. The stones were made of zircon.

Edwardes immediately pounced. At the MMC hearing the following week, he produced the stones from his pocket with a dramatic flourish, rolling them across the table in front of the MMC chairman, David Richards. 'There, gentleman,' he declared, 'is the entire stock of zircon in Minorco's possession – and you're welcome to keep it!'

*   *

Through those winter months, there fell a menacing and uneasy quiet between the two camps. The battle would intermittently rumble in the distance like a faraway electric storm. An occasional flash of lightning, like the anti-Apartheid clamour at the Gold Fields annual meeting, would light up the sky. Then came an ominous flash over Luxemburg followed by a clap of thunder: Minorco had pitched a man overboard. At the annual meeting, there was an empty chair where Neil Clarke should have been.

It followed a sudden and quite unexpected palace coup at Charter Consolidated. According to a tersely worded announcement on 7 November, its chairman, Jocelyn Hambro, and its deputy chairman and chief excutive, Neil Clarke, had resigned. The new chairman was to be Sir Michael Edwardes. Joining him as non-executives were Tony Lea and Chips Keswick, chairman of Hambros merchant bank.

Shares in Charter sped to a new high as analysts divined that its dominant 36 per cent shareholder, Minorco, was now bent on a hands-on activation. And shares in Johnson Matthey joined in the rush. The move sent all the bid bells ringing and nowhere did they ring louder than in the Hatton Garden office of chief executive Eugene Anderson, a wry laconic Texan. Neil was his chairman. What, he wondered, was Minorco trying on?

Behind the sudden resignation of Clarke lay differences of personality and approach about Charter and a power struggle which tested Anglo American's commitment to Edwardes at a critical time. Charter, in Edwardes' view, was not getting to grips with its strategic problems quickly enough. Now that Minorco was being activated, the differences and the problems were more starkly highlighted.

Clarke immediately appealed to Johannesburg for back-up, but Edwardes was given the support. It left Clarke with no option but to resign. It also raised questions as to whether Minorco's hands-on approach needed to adjust kin relationships in so abrasive and confrontational a manner.

Anderson heard the gunfire half-a-mile away at 40 Holborn and feared that other bodies might now slump bloodily to the floor – his included. The two had been rival contenders for the top post at Chloride and had strongly contrasting personalities.

Minorco's annual meeting in Luxemburg's Royal Hotel on 10 November thus opened with Clarke's nameplate swept from the table into a plastic bag by a fretful PR aide. In the politbureau line-up of Luxemburg he had ceased to be.

JOT used the meeting to attack the 'world-wide orchestrated programme of vilification and abuse against Minorco, Anglo American, De Beers, Harry Oppenheimer . . . anything that was South African'. And he also moved to scotch an intriguing report that Lonrho's Tiny Rowland had secretly met with Oppenheimer the previous week and had sought to buy Minorco's Gold Fields stake.

Yes, JOT confirmed, there had been meetings, including one at Rowland's home attended by Edwardes and Tony Lea. But no deal was discussed as the stake was not for sale. Oppenheimer and Tiny Rowland had also met – socially. As for secrecy, the two, said JOT, had met 'in the rather public forum' of the dining room of Claridges Hotel. What a flash of insight that provided into what, in the top Anglo American universe, is a 'public forum'.

Throughout the annual meeting, Oppenheimer's brow seemed locked in permanent furrow. But if he was entertaining doubts that Edwardes may have been a mistake at Minorco, he said nothing. He sat with a hand partly covering his face and stared at the table. He caught no one's eye. He took no notes. Outside, the middle-aged ladies of Luxemburg were doing what pleased him most: lingering at shop windows full of gold rings and diamonds in platinum settings. He had just turned 80, and had marked his birthday two weeks previously by a gathering of some 200 friends and associates in the Brenthurst library. It was not a year to have a cherry missing from the cake.

*　　*

Meanwhile, at the Monopolies and Mergers Commission, a six-man panel chaired by David Richards was looking at Anglo American and the implications of Minorco's bid right across the spectrum: gold, platinum, zircon and titanium, together with the effects that South African control might have on ARC.

Its concern was to assess the competitive implications of the merger *in the UK*. Gold Fields' objective was quite different: to expose Anglo American's grip *on global markets*. It sought to compile a catalogue of every cartelistic misdemeanour, actual or latent, real or potential, and put Anglo American on trial.

The report began with titanium dioxide, used mainly as a pigment in the manufacture of white paint, and in producing titanium metal, used in the nuclear and aerospace industries. Renison in Australia is the biggest producer, accounting for 24 per cent of world supply. Other major producers are Gencor with 11 per cent and Richards Bay Minerals in South Africa with 18 per cent.

Gold Fields argued that if the bid succeeded, South African interests would control 54 per cent of Western production of high-grade titanium and enable the formation of a price cartel. The MMC dismissed this argument. Renison is itself a naturalized Australian company, a requirement for which is that majority ownership and control should be by Australian nationals; the largest shareholding in Richards Bay Minerals is held by a British company rather than Gencor; the bulk of new reserves available for exploitation lay outside South Africa; and in any event, Minorco now said it would sell the Renison stake – yet more luggage dropped en route.

Zircon is used in cladding fuel for nuclear reactors. Renison is again the Western world's largest producer, accounting for 41 per cent of total production. As with titanium, the Commission found the threat of collusion 'difficult to accept'.

Platinum is concentrated principally in South Africa, the Soviet Union and Canada. South Africa is the world's largest platinum producer. It supplies 93 per cent of the total Western world mine production. Rustenburg, part of Anglo American, is the world's largest producer, accounting for 49.6 per cent. Impala Platinum, controlled by Gencor, produces 37.4 per cent. Gold Fields argued that Anglo American and Gencor between them controlled 88 per cent of the Western world production and there was evidence of collusion in pricing between these two and the Russians.

What of the prospects for the new Northam platinum mine in which Gold Fields had a direct 13 per cent shareholding and GFSA 70 per cent? Northam had signed an exclusive refining contract with the German concern, Heraeus. This would provide a source of platinum outside of the Anglo American cartel. Not only would competition be lost in the event of Minorco taking over Gold Fields, but it was also in Anglo American's interests to prevent the Northam development.

But, concluded the MMC, 'we find it difficult to be confident that the development of Northam will significantly increase competition in the refining of platinum for users in the United Kingdom'. It again noted that Minorco, in any event, intended to sell its holding in GFSA.

Gold Fields' most serious contention was that the merger of the world's largest and second largest gold producers was anti-competitive. If the takeover succeeded, the share of world production controlled by the Anglo American group would rise from 20 per cent to 32 per cent, enabling it to manipulate the world gold market.

Anglo American would also have acquired control of production outside South Africa which would enhance its ability to manipulate the price. Anglo American could be expected to extend its cartelistic practices to Gold Fields' gold mining interests in the United States through production restraint – shutting down the mines.

However, adding together Anglo American's and Gold Fields' interests in world gold production exaggerated the effects of the merger and the Anglo American group's enhanced ability to manipulate production and price. Even accepting the broad Gold Fields definition of 'interest', the Anglo American group's total share of world production would rise by a very small amount, from 20.2 per cent to 20.7 per cent once the disposals of Newmont, Renison and GFSA were taken into account.

As for the Anglo American group's enhanced ability to manipulate the gold price, the bulk of the two groups' production is in South Africa where all gold production is sold to, and marketed by, the Reserve Bank of South Africa. The merged group's influence on the supply of this gold to world markets would be negligible.

The MMC concluded that it did not believe Anglo American would be able to abuse its position: first, it was obliged to market all gold produced in South Africa to the Reserve Bank; and second, there were extensive stocks of gold, equivalent to over 70 years of current world production, together with unmined gold both within and outside South Africa. 'We do not believe that any attempt at manipulation by Anglo American would seriously increase the instability of the gold price, nor do we see that such instability would be in the interests of Anglo American as a producer. The Bank of England has expressed no concern to us.'

Finally, there was Gold Fields' attack on 'the nature of the beast' – the character of Anglo American itself: 'secretive, authoritarian and centralized' were the hammer words. Indeed, the nature of Anglo American and its patriarchal style seemed the central charge.

It told the MMC that it saw the bid as a move designed to entrench the Oppenheimer family more strongly outside South Africa, almost regardless of the ongoing profitability of the assets acquired. Minorco was merely a front. It claimed that the group had always operated through complex interlocking shareholding and management systems designed to optimize the benefits to the Oppenheimer family. The boards of all the companies where Anglo American was a major shareholder were not independent bodies acting in the interests of shareholders, 'but in sum beholden to the Oppenheimer family'.

To pass judgment on the nature of the beast was not what the MMC was asked to do: its brief was to assess the competition implications of the proposed merger as they affected the UK public interest.

But it made a general point about the 'exodus' motive of some force: 'The merger is not in itself being financed by any further funds from South Africa, but even if the overall aim of the Anglo American group is to diversify outside South Africa, we see no reason why it should have any less regard for the profitability of its investments than any other multinational organization.'

Doubts were then raised about Anglo American's competence: its capacity to manage businesses acquired and its overseas record. Here was something of an Open Day for Anglo American's critics. John Du Cane, former chairman and chief executive of Selection Trust and an employee of Anglo American, took a ferocious swipe. The idea put forward by Edwardes that his hands-on management could run Gold Fields better than the present board 'would be laughable were it not for the very real danger of being put to the test'. Outside of South Africa, the group's record in exploration had been abysmal. But it was not related to competition policy, and doubts on an acquiring company's track record were, the MMC considered, matters best left to shareholders.

Overall, the MMC concluded: 'We do not believe, as it was suggested to us, that the proposed merger would operate against the public interest on account of the characteristics of the Anglo American group, or Minorco's South African associations in general.'

The MMC's verdict was released on Thursday, 2 February. Phillimore took a telephone call at his home the previous evening tipping him off on the verdict. It is a prescient sign in any battle when moles change sides. This was Minorco's first victory since the bid started. Phillimore sent every one of the advisers a case of champagne.

Four months later, a tiny packet arrived for Edwardes at Ely Place from the MMC. He was baffled as he opened it gingerly. Out rolled, sparkling like fiery diamonds, the small zircon stones. Edwardes later had them made up as earrings for Sheila.

At Charles 11 Street there was stunned disbelief. 'The message', Agnew declared bitterly, 'is do not, for God's sake, be British and look to the authorities for protection.' The MMC had taken a parochial view and if the London Stock Exchange followed its example 'it will end up as a market for British pubs and Scottish funeral parlours. . . Absurd,' he railed, ' . . . like the Mad Hatter's Tea Party'.

In the operations room, Gerry Grimstone stared blankly at copies of the piles of evidence Gold Fields fed to the MMC. 'I don't think', he recalled, 'those part-time commissioners could handle the complex papers about the world gold market. Maybe we suffocated them with *too much* information.'

But in that long winter trench warfare of statistics, Grimstone's flair for the surprise attack and guerilla raid had not deserted him. While all eyes were on the MMC investigation, Gold Fields had rolled a grenade into another part of the Oppenheimer empire. And the noise of its explosion now sent a consoling thrill through Charles 11 Street: an Office of Fair Trading probe was announced into the De Beers diamond cartel.

While Minorco's bid had hogged the stock market's attention, one of the biggest transfers of natural resources had taken place without a finger raised. Midway through the MMC's inquisition of Minorco, mining giant RTZ announced it was buying one of the biggest parcels of gold, copper and precious metals in the world: the minerals division of British Petroleum, in a deal worth £3 billion.

The entire package would increase RTZ's gold production from 400,000 ounces to one million ounces immediately, with good prospects of that climbing to 1.7 million in the 1990s, making RTZ one of the largest gold producers outside South Africa. BP Minerals alone would add some £260 million to RTZ's profits. Not a single regulatory body in the world batted an eyelid.

The new RTZ poses a tremendous challenge to the Anglo–De Beers empire which now has a rival set to overtake it in size and topple it from the world's number one position. That such a deal could have been pulled off from under the noses of Anglo American and Minorco, further added to the crisis enveloping the empire.

Meanwhile, in the United States, Minorco had to contend with Agnew's foxes loose among the chickens. First, there was pressure on the two principal banks in the Minorco syndicate – Bank of Nova Scotia and Chemical Bank. The Canadian bank's involvement was the subject of discussions at the Commonwealth Committee of Foreign Ministers on Southern Africa. Political pressure was also stepped up on Chemical Bank by the New York city authorities to force it to withdraw its £300 million loan agreement with Minorco because of its South African ties.

The anti-South African campaign even reached into the Governor's office of the state of Michigan. A particularly vocal campaign was mounted against State Governor James Blanchard over a holding by the state pension fund of a 5.4 per cent stake in Minorco. Keith Orrell-Jones, chief executive of ARC, wrote claiming that it fell foul of the state's policy not to invest in companies with South African ties. The Governor fired back a strongly worded riposte: 'The transparency of your efforts is matched only by your profligate waste of corporate money in this self-servicing advertising campaign.' Nothing more was heard from Gold Fields on the subject of Michigan.

Slowly the tide was beginning to turn for Minorco, but time was now the problem. Under UK takeover law, companies have 21 days from clearance by the Monopolies and Mergers Commission to relaunch a bid. Now time was speeding on. Minorco was now poised to relaunch its bid. Lea, with his advisers, had put the finishing touches to a renewed offer. But Minorco was worried by a belief in the market that Minorco would pay any price to get Gold Fields. What it planned was an offer that would pull back expectations.

But Minorco was loathe to fire until two further hurdles had been cleared: the European Commission inquiry and the US court action.

It did not have long to wait. On 17 February, the Commission announced the rejection of Gold Fields' complaint of a platinum production monopoly. Minorco was over a crucial hurdle.

A favourable outcome in the US court battle looked less certain. Slack flew back from New York on Thursday, 16 February to report to a meeting of Minorco's board in Luxemburg, called in conditions of tightest secrecy for the following Sunday. Oppenheimer and Relly had already slipped into London the previous week.

Minorco's lawyers, Shearman & Sterling, now gambled on an appeal rather than risk a court case which might take too long. Now they tried to speed up a ruling from the three American appeal judges ahead of the deadline for relaunching the bid, now just four days away. Unless the judges overturned the temporary banning order granted to Gold Fields and Newmont pending a full antitrust hearing, Minorco could not buy another Gold Fields share.

But there was a second problem: any offer Minorco made, no matter how generous, could not be declared unconditional or closed until the appeal was resolved. And that firmly wedged Minorco like a ham between two different clockwork slicers: it had to fire a renewed bid in four days under the Take Over Panel clock.

But it did not want to fire a bid until the appeal was out of the way: because in launching a new bid it would start another takeover clock which would tick for 28 days precisely. And on that day time was up. All this, of course, assumed that the court decision, when it came, would be to throw out the Newmont/Gold Fields injunction. If it was upheld, and the case went for full trial, Minorco would face a year in the courts. Maybe more. Tick tock went the clocks at the Boulevard de la Petrusse.

Morgan Grenfell had sounded out the Take Over Panel on the dilemma to see what its view would be of a request for an extension of the 28-day deadline if a New York court ruling was still outstanding. The response was sympathetic. But the uncertainties of the New York legal outcome nagged at them. No one round the table needed reminding of the litigation-happy American corporate attorneys and the devastation they could wreak.

In addition, Gordon Parker had been round this track before with the T Boone Pickens raid. The problem for Minorco was that any renewed offer would have to be made conditional on the New York appeal being successful.

But what if the appeal was rejected? Another submission to the New York district court. And how long would that take? And could Newmont come back and challenge that? Everyday's delay further widened the gap between the Gold Fields price and the new Minorco terms. Further hesitation and delay could ruin the impact of the new offer. Tick tock went the clocks in the Boulevard de la Petrusse.

Slack and Thompson were confident they could win. Morgan Grenfell were confident the Panel would back them if Newmont's fight in the courts was seen to be frustrating action designed to filibuster the bid out of time.

Minorco had come so far. It had cleared the Monopolies and Mergers Commission. It had cleared the European Commission. Its bankers and investors had seen off political pressure. The uncertainty over the outcome of the New York legal hearing was a nagging worry. But the Turks were not to be held back now.

Tick tock went the clocks in the Boulevard de la Petrusse. Amber! Amber! flashed the lights as Minorco hit Green for Go.

14

Tweakers and Slammers

■

Across the departure lounge of Luxemburg airport, late in the after-noon of Sunday, 19 February 1989, there came a startled cry from among a group of men, followed by a gust of laughter.

Minorco's board meeting in Luxemburg had been convened in great secrecy following a tip-off that Gold Fields had brought in the American security and private detective firm of Kroll Associates – Wall Street's 'Private Eye'. However much the firm insists that its work comprises counter intelligence, anti-fraud and routine company research, Kroll's name conjured up images of furtive gumshoes in alleyways, strange clicks during telephone calls – and bugs in the boardroom.

Kroll had been used by Newmont during the T Boone Pickens raid and the firm was now retained by Gold Fields through its New York lawyers, Paul Weiss, to supply information on Oppenheimer companies, Minorco and the movements of its directors. A total of 45 legmen were now reputed to be involved digging into every aspect of the Anglo American empire. One of Kroll's claims was that the Tie Rack chain – a small 'niche' retail operation set up by South African expatriate Roy Bishko – was part of the Oppenheimer empire. The claim astounded Bishko as much as 44 Main. It was based on a coincidental use of a bank nominee facility. There is no Oppenheimer shareholding in Tie Rack. Or an Anglo American one. Jules Kroll was later to boast in a magazine article of the 'intellectual challenge' provided by the Gold Fields brief. The same might be said of the constructions placed upon Kroll's research.

Forty-six Kroll detectives! News of Kroll's involvement had been greeted with stunned amusement by Minorco's directors, followed by an unpleasant sensation that their every move – personal and professional – was now being watched. For the families involved it was no laughing matter. Every privacy was at risk of being invaded and everyone was now on guard. A major problem was that board meetings had to be held in Luxemburg, and for critical meetings which might give a vital clue to the timing of any bid relaunch, it was assumed Kroll would have airport surveillance cover during weekdays at Luxemburg. Minorco hoped to catch Kroll napping by meeting on a Sunday.

Now, as the directors waited in the late afternoon darkness to board the private Hawker jet back to London, Sidney Spiro felt a tap on his shoulder. 'Psst! Look over there,' came an urgent whisper from a colleague. 'There's a Kroll detective staring right at you!' Spiro spun round and gasped as he suddenly caught sight of a dark figure about to leap out of the duty-free shop. It was a cardboard promotion for Sandeman Port.

In London, the market had been on tenterhooks waiting for the renewed Minorco assault. Shares in Gold Fields had raced to £14.35. Minorco, surely, had to top this.

At 9am on Monday, 20 February, the Minorco guns blazed into life – but with dummy bullets. Edwardes had fired a cash and shares package valuing each Gold Fields share at £14.06. The groan was almost audible: the terms were seen as little more than foreplay designed to draw out the crucial Gold Fields asset valuation and profits forecast. Shares in Gold Fields climbed even further out of reach, to £14.43.

The bid was made conditional on a satisfactory outcome of the legal action in the US courts. But most commentators still regarded this as a vexatious irritant that would be overcome. Wrote Neil Collins, City Editor of the *Daily Telegraph*: 'It is hard to imagine that even the averagely arrogant American court will stand in Minorco's way now that its assault on Gold Fields has been blessed by the Monopolies Commission and the European Commission.'

The battle now entered a central phase that was to reveal much about the characters of the two companies. It also brought home several deep-seated problems for Minorco: its corporate style, its public relations problems, its underestimation of events in the United States and its own internal division: between tweakers and slammers.

Five months into the bid, Minorco still had to establish itself as a credible company, capable of taking on the operational management of Gold Fields. It had additional public relations problems. Edwardes had promised to keep Minorco's shareholders informed, 'as if it were a UK company'.

But it wasn't and had chosen not to be. The remark had been prompted by a press question on directors' salaries, declarable under UK disclosure requirements, but hidden from view under Luxemburg accounting. Edwardes was reckoned to be on a £1 million success fee and the Young Turks on secret salaries from Oppenheimer Swiss accounts.

The reality was different. But the question touched on a wider problem about the acceptability of Minorco and its paper. Here was a dollar-denominated stock registered in Luxemburg with a dominant shareholder based in one of the world's most politically unacceptable countries. Corporate image buffers Lowe Bell had worked hard to polish the brassplate and improve the accessibility. But it was proving a struggle. Minorco bore the traits of a South African affiliate registered in Luxemburg. And behind that anonymity some detected an arrogance, bred of Anglo American's easy dominance of economic life in South Africa.

The Young Turks had hoped that with the fall in the Anglo American group's holding, the South African issue would just 'go away' provided Minorco did nothing to draw attention to it. It was never tackled head on as it should have been. Minorco desperately needed a more informed view of its parent. That it was consistently counselled against such an effort effectively doomed it to fall into a ditch when the bridging of it was an essential prerequisite of success.

Minorco was not a British company, and it showed. Visitors to Ely Place in those early days could not but be struck by the furtive atmosphere it seemed to exude. Entry to 35 Ely Place was effected by a bell on a weather-beaten entryphone. Callers were asked to give their name and company. When the front door finally clicked open, callers made their way up a steep flight of stairs, monitored by a remote-controlled close-circuit camera. At the top of the stairs, another door, with steel bars and more locks.

Even a phone call to Minorco created a sinister impression: the response was never a bright, silver-tongued 'Minorco, good morning!' but the number whispered in furtive tones. It was like trying to penetrate some dubious and exclusive club.

And inside, what picture did the global arm of Anglo American present? The effect was that of pleasant town flat, furnished with an eye to the Georgian period, which had been commandeered by a family firm of solicitors. It was less Minorco than Edwardes, Slack, Lea and Phillimore, Commissioners for Oaths. As for the Anglo American influence, the only clues to Minorco's parentage were small framed watercolours of hippopotami and wildebeest.

At the far end of the corridor was an inner sanctum where Lea and Phillimore sat. Edwardes had banned Phillimore from smoking his cigars in front of the Press. Here he could puff in safety.

But the pace was often hectic. Edwardes had brought a hyperactive style of command and a habit – irritating to his colleagues – of bustling in and out of simultaneous meetings in a sort of frenetic rotation. This made it difficult for meetings to proceed in an orderly way through their agendas. Often, they would have to restart 'from the top' on Edwardes' arrival.

Minorco's day began at 7.30am with a meeting of the Turks attended by the sharply dressed Italian American Agostinelli from Lazard Freres, Cadbury or Richmond-Watson from Morgan Grenfell, Richard North from accountants Coopers and Lybrand, representatives from Minorco's stockbrokers James Capel and aides from Lowe Bell. The meetings would often be held across the road in the cavernous seventh floor boardroom of Charter Consolidated. Each time Minorco used the boardroom the new innervated Charter under Edwardes charged £200 a session.

Phillimore would often take the chair; Agostinelli, when in town, would sit next to him on his right, exuding the air of the seminal strategic thinker; while Cadbury and Richmond-Watson were pushed a little down the table to take their notes. By contrast, Agostinelli never brought a notebook or documentation to the table: notes were for wimps. He would sit, his head back, with the smoke from a huge cigar drifting down the table to the Morgan Grenfell end. But for his sense of humour, they would have murdered him. A parallel committee, steered by Bill Loomis, would meet in New York.

Lunch was an economy affair, with press interviews conducted over soft drinks and rolls served in paper bags from the local delicatessen. Occasionally Lea and Phillimore would slip down to the Diamond Trading Company a few doors down in Charterhouse Street. The headquarters of the world's diamond trade would frequently double up as the Minorco bistro.

With the Press, Edwardes was always on guard, and to the end, tape-recorded every major interview. It was, he insisted, because of

Take Over Panel rules banning him from saying anything which would require a formal circular to shareholders. But journalists found it intimidating. And Agnew never used one.

Indeed, the contrasts with the Gold Fields headquarters could scarcely be more marked. Number 31 Charles 11 Street had once been the London home of Prime Minister Lord Derby, situated close to St James' Square and with the great clubs of London – Brooks, the Reform and the Carlton – just a stroll away.

On the second floor was Agnew's eyrie, a spacious, high-ceilinged green and yellow drawing room, free of any taint of 'executive' furniture. It was a room made for high politics and good cigars. Here was where Agnew would greet his institutional investors, hold heart-to-hearts with Grimstone – and tell all to Augusta, his labrador. Augusta was to become a very wise dog in the course of Britain's biggest takeover. 'I tell Augusta everything,' Agnew confessed. 'We have long discussions. The Take Over Panel would not at all approve.'

The operations floor on the mezzanine level was regularly electronically 'swept' for phone bugs and listening devices. The main operations room, manned twelve hours a day, was dominated by a group of desks clustered in the centre. Here was the nerve centre of Versailles, where advisers and the home defence team congregated, sustained by a constant flow of beverages and snacks.

To the rear of 'ops' was the inner sanctum: the strategy room with a horseshoe-shaped table littered with ashtrays. The day would start with a communications meeting at 8am chaired by Agnew's chief of staff, Grimstone, or by joint managing director, Humphrey Wood. It was one of the most powerful defence teams ever mustered in a takeover battle. Among the dozen or so present would be finance chief Antony Hichens, company secretary Gisela Gledhill, Michael Casey (from Sallingbury Casey), Sir Gordon Reece, John Reynolds and Roy Blackman (from public relations consultant, Shandwick), Stephen Carden (from Cazenove) and Gold Fields' own experienced press team – Hugh Impey, Graham Williams and Neil Chapman. Grimstone would go round the table for latest reports. Tactics would be drawn up for the day – even deciding which journalists and analysts Agnew would meet for lunch.

And lunch with Agnew was a different experience to the austerity sandwiches of Ely Place. It would be served in an elegant first floor room with a meticulously prepared table. Despite erratic timekeeping by Agnew and his guests, the chef, Jean-Pierre Rochet, never disappointed. While guests enjoyed the wine, Agnew, an unabashed intercourse smoker, demolished Diet Coke and Gitanes.

His day would typically start with a few moments working on a giant jigsaw puzzle at his home at The Clock House, in Chelsea's Cheyne Walk (ironically one floor above Nicky Oppenheimer) and he would arrive at Charles 11 Street just before 9am. 'Vespers' – the top level evening meeting – would be held at 6pm, consisting of Agnew's inner cabinet of advisers and chaired by him.

On both sides, drafting sessions and proof reading of documents at the printers would last long into the evenings. The travelling, particularly on the Minorco side, was punishing. Weekends and bank holidays went by the board. So, too, did family life for many. Takeover bids, with their hectic meetings, briefings, late drafting sessions, weekends in the office and business being conducted up against one deadline after another, day after day, week after week, take their toll. Wives soon began asking: 'What did he *do* before Minorco?'

As each week passed, the battle became a test of endurance. Grimstone likened it to an epic medieval siege, with constantly renewed assaults with battering rams and hails of arrows and cannon slings. Lines of supply were crucial to both sides. 'The gravest threat all along for us', Grimstone recalled, 'was that Anglo had unlimited financial resources. If Minorco could keep up the pressure and maintain its lines of supply then it would win. So we had to maintain ours. The people being besieged always end up having the worst of it.'

Behind the scenes, Agnew's manner would sometimes give rise to friction. He had no eye for detail and exasperated colleagues would wonder whether he had read any of the constantly discussed defence material. But he possessed great qualities of leadership and an ability to rally and inspire people. The bid was the proving of Rudolph Agnew. Never before had he exercised such leadership over Consolidated Gold Fields and never was a company more fiercely defended.

Over at Minorco, the prickly atmosphere began to change. The telephone was now brightly answered by: 'Minorco UK, Good Morning!' and the air of menace softened. That change was helped with the arrival of Keith Irons, a tough corporate public relations warhorse who had worked for Blue Circle and latterly for Charter. He brought an intuitive insight into Minorco's predicament and a much more proactive response by Minorco to the daily twists and turns of the battle. He also saved Minorco from a PR disaster that teetered on farce.

To counter the Gold Fields portrayal of Minorco as a group of stony-faced accountants who knew nothing about mining, it had been agreed – against Irons' stern advice – to photograph Edwardes, Lea and Phillimore grouped together, as if at a pithead, wearing miners' helmets.

The photograph, with accompanying blurb, would appear as a full page advertisement in the *Financial Times* and space was booked. A photo session was organized in a West End studio and the three, jackets and ties now removed, were suitably bedecked with hard hats and miners' lamps. Then they were given pick axes and shovels to hold in their hands. To add authenticity, shoe polish was liberally applied to the brows and cheeks. Edwardes removed his half-moon spectacles and Phillimore his watch.

As the camera clicked away on this bizarre scene, the mighty roar of London's traffic could be heard through the curtains, buses chugging past and taxi horns hooting. When the pictures of the glistening three were developed, pioneers of the Witwatersrand they were clearly not. Irons took one look at the photographs and made two decisions very quickly: destroy the negatives, and cancel the ad.

But if Agnew's anti-South African 'scorched earth' phase was over, the phase of 'scorched Edwardes' was stepped up. He launched a ferocious assault at a press conference at Charles 11 Street on 23 February. Few who attended would forget the experience.

Agnew, Gitane in hand, came to the rostrum, centre stage of two large velvet curtains. From this moment the event took on the atmosphere of opera. He introduced the Gold Fields swingometer. The bizarre gadget was used to illustrate the life cycle of a mine, from initial exploration through to development: 'We thought it might be useful in case Edwardes slipped in.' Then came a well primed assault on Edwardes and Minorco.

'They held a smoking cheque book to my head. [Their bid] could be described as a form of financial terrorism . . . Minorco is a thinly traded Gamma share. They are parasites. They feed on their own parent in South Africa and make it clear they would feed equally on the brilliance of Gold Fields' management.' Up on the screen popped a plunging graph of the Chloride share price where Edwardes had been at various times chairman and chief executive – a graph damningly contrasted with Gold Fields' own.

Grimstone, 'my Gauleiter', as Agnew now referred to him, sat at a side table with his head in his hands as the Gitane machine plunged on. Phillimore, Oppenheimer's godson, was brushed aside as an 'office manager'. Agnew then referred to Edwardes as 'a pipsqueak, making the pips squeak' and he likened him to a mixture of Napoleon, Wellington and Ghenghis Khan. Grimstone looked as if he was already mentally composing a reply to a wigging from the City Take Over Panel to whom Minorco duly thundered in a complaint.

At Ely Place, Irons tore off the first rushes from the Exchange Telegraph printer and showed them to Edwardes. 'If I was a Gold Fields director,' he said, 'I would wonder whether he is losing his self-confidence.' As for the £18 million defence costs, these, Edwardes vowed, 'will be submitted to the closest scrutiny'. Warning letters were fired to Charles 11 Street.

In the City, arguments now raged about how much Minorco would have to pay to win Gold Fields. Mark Wood, analyst at Kleinwort Benson Securities, worked out a figure of £15.30 a share. That was arguably the least Minorco could fire by way of final shot and it proved a prescient piece of research. But it left little room for doubt about Minorco's paper which now loomed large.

Meanwhile there was speculation that Agnew, as an ultimate act of 'scorched earth', would sell or partially demerge the aggregates giant, ARC. In the City, anticipation rose to fever pitch on Agnew's next move.

It came on Thursday, 9 March. So great by now was the media crush at Agnew performances that the Charles 11 Street opera house was no longer big enough. The presentation was held at the Bakers Hall in the heart of the City. It was capable of holding 300. Agnew now produced a defence document extending to a numbing 28 pages, setting an all time record for corporate defence statements. It bore the stamp of Antony Hichens: the keeper of statistical munitions, the great Krupp of facts. Broken down under such headings as 'Your stone in Britain and the United States', it was a Teutonic effort, packed with statistics and diagrams and charts. It told of ARC's 1.8 billion tonnes of stone reserves in Britain, ARC America's 1.3 billion tonnes and production of 26 tonnes of crushed stone a year; profits from both forecast to soar 55 per cent to £158 million that year.

But instead of an overall asset value, Agnew kept everyone guessing with a document which stopped short of putting on an actual number. Investors were left with a 'join-the-dots' puzzle – with the key dots missing. The nearest clue it gave was a pricing of Gold Fields' North American gold interests (including Newmont) at between $3.25 billion and $4 billion – equivalent to between £8.44 and £10.39 a share.

Yet slowly the tide was turning in Minorco's favour. In January, the Turks went on a hectic European roadshow and a lightning tour round fund managers in Johannesburg. Minorco was now throwing everything into a Continental European and overseas campaign designed to encourage support for the stock that was not so forth-coming in London. Out of earshot of the Gold Fields rhetoric, that campaign was starting to pay. A European refresher tour in the first week of the renewed bid saw the Minorco price climb 26p to £8.09, raising the value of its offer to £14.29. Could the Minorco bandwagon be rolling at last? On 6 March came more heartening news: Minorco's bid had been cleared by the South African Competition Board – the third regulatory clearance in six weeks.

Piece by piece, section by section, that great Agnew Orchestra of the Apocalypse was being closed down. Now it was Minorco's turn to go on the attack. What lifted morale was the reception for Lea and Edwardes in Johannesburg in the first week of March – the first stop in the Minorco roadshow.

Agnew had angered the Johannesburg business community with the 'moral pariah' attack on South Africa. Donny Gordon, chairman of Liberty Life Association of South Africa, had been aghast at the Agnew campaign. 'It was all quite ludicrous. It seemed to be based on the assertion that being born in South Africa is a mark of Cain.' Not only did it further heighten the sense of isolation in Johannes-burg, but by attacking the country's most liberal and politically pro-gressive employer he had weakened his own credibility. Johannes-burg now found itself cynically branded in a political campaign by a company which held the largest single block of shares in one of the Republic's biggest and most right-wing gold mining companies – Gold Fields of South Africa.

Agnew's remark, 'You can deny your bastard sons, but you can't deny your parents', had a cutting double edge: GFSA was also, by implication, Gold Fields' 'bastard son'. How, Johannesburg asked, could Agnew deny GFSA, deriving as he did £34 million of Gold Fields' profits from the company?

GFSA's 7.5 per cent shareholding in Gold Fields had been pledged to the Gold Fields cause, although chief executive Robin Plumbridge insisted he took no part in the debate. That stake could prove the decider. Agnew was thus caught between his campaign to separate Gold Fields from GFSA in the public mind while relying on GFSA to back him up.

The audacity of this alliance infuriated Thompson and Relly because Anglo American itself, with its 20 per cent shareholding in GFSA, had been allowed no say in how GFSA's Gold Fields stake should be voted. GFSA's other major shareholder, Rembrandt, was also under pressure to intervene. But the difficulty was that, while Gold Fields had 38 per cent of the GFSA equity, it retained 48 per cent of the votes. Plumbridge looked impregnable.

Minorco now turned on the heat by investigating the legal validity of GFSA's support. It had not, Anglo American argued, been considered by an independent committee of the board. And that put a question mark on whether it could deliver the votes.

The GFSA board had other reasons to reconsider. The block of Gold Fields shares was now worth over £220 million at Minorco's bid price. And there was now mounting financial pressure on GFSA, whose Northam platinum mine was now eating money. It was strapped for cash, and secretly planning a rights issue.

Meanwhile, the main concern amongst an audience of some 50 analysts at a Minorco presentation at the Rand Club was a refreshing contrast to their London counterparts: they were worried Minorco might *overpay* for Gold Fields.

In the evening of 6 March, Lea and Edwardes flew out of Johannesburg for a whistlestop tour round Europe. Since Edwardes had now formally ruled out a full cash alternative, Minorco paper had to take the strain. And with no underwriting safety net, Agnew struck and struck again at what he saw as Minorco's weak link: the lack of support for Minorco paper and the prospect of a price collapse if the bid went through. 'Gamma stock!' was the taunt of Charles 11 Street.

Lea and Morgan Grenfell worked flat out to maximize support in Europe where the South African issue was viewed more coolly: fund managers in Zurich, Frankfurt, Paris – and interestingly, Edinburgh and Glasgow, too – were more predisposed to listen to the financial argument.

By 9 March, Minorco shares had risen further, to £8.13. And at this level, its offer now valued each Gold Fields share at £14.31 compared with a price in the market of £14.23. For the first time in six months, Gold Fields seemed to be within its grasp. But by the first closing date of the offer, on 18 March, Minorco received acceptances from Gold Fields shareholders representing just 0.2 per cent of the equity. They included, Tony Lea later confessed, his mother.

At Ely Place, there was now a sharpening division of the group into two camps: 'tweakers' – those, like Edwardes, who argued that only a small increase, if any, on the terms was necessary to win; and 'slammers' – those, like Morgan Grenfell, who urged a knock-out £16 a share final shot that would put the battle beyond doubt. Almost all of Minorco's advisers were in the slammer camp. An offer which triggered an avalanche of acceptances would put enormous pressure on Gold Fields' advisers and non-executive directors to urge acceptance. Against the slammers the tweakers were outnumbered. But why, the tweakers argued, with the current offer now worth more than Gold Fields shares, should the terms be increased *at all*?

Edwardes wanted to win on his terms: for him, the true machismo of victory lay not in triggering an avalanche of acceptances, but securing just the handful needed to take Minorco over 50 per cent. Minimal victory was his counter to Agnew's total war.

A lengthy meeting of Minorco's board in Luxemburg, on 16 March, broke up with the deadlock between tweakers and slammers unresolved and, more ominously, with a numbing report on the legal deadlock in New York. On Saturday, JOT flew back to Johannesburg a preoccupied man. First, he had to explain to colleagues in 44 Main how a company Minorco nearly won on agreed terms two years ago at £8.66 a share could cost up to £16 now. Second, why did a bid by a Luxemburg group for a British company now wait upon a New York legal ruling? Louder even than Agnew was the sound of the takeover clock ticking to midnight.

On 22 March, the US Court of Appeal upheld the injunction preventing Minorco buying more Gold Fields shares. Anglo American, through Minorco, would be likely to dominate the world gold market. It instructed the New York district court to deal with the anti-trust and the securities laws issues. With the takeover deadline fixed at 26 April, the ruling put a gun to Minorco's head. Shares in Gold Fields tumbled £1.75 to £12.44. The ruling also widened the front by allowing a case that could force further disclosure from Minorco under US securities laws.

The ruling dumbfounded JOT and 44 Main. It appeared to take no account of Minorco's stated intention to sell GFSA, Renison and, above all, Newmont; or of clearance the previous winter through the US Justice Department and the Federal Trade Commission who had found no anti-trust problem. As for further information, that to Thompson seemed beyond the court's jurisdiction to order: how could American judges intervene in a bid where the two companies were registered outside the United States and where less than five per cent of the equity of the complaining company, Gold Fields, was in American hands?

Criticism now rained on Edwardes and on Morgan Grenfell for making the offer conditional on a favourable legal outcome, thus endorsing what was seen as the questionable authority of the court over a non-American takeover. Others argued that it had lost the initiative through an inadequate offer which brought no support.

The blow was softened by news of regulatory clearance in Washington. The Committee on Foreign Investment ruled that the bid did not justify a review under US trade legislation. That was a milestone for Minorco: it had now cleared *every* regulatory barrier to its bid. But its legal problems were compounded by being up against the Take Over Panel clock – and it was ticking remorselessly towards the 26 April deadline. Morgan Grenfell contacted the Panel to find out whether it would still be sympathetic towards a request for an extension.

Meanwhile, Jeremy Epstein, lead attorney for Minorco's New York lawyers, Shearman and Sterling, frantically scrambled for an expedited hearing to offer undertakings to sell Gold Fields' stake in Newmont and to find out what additional information was required to meet the securities issue.

But now Minorco faced a new nightmare. Michael Mukasey, the judge in charge of the case in the New York southern district court, announced he was taking a two week break – to attend an economics seminar. He would not be back before 17 April – just nine days before the bid would run out of time in London. The signals from the Panel suggested that unless Gold Fields also agreed to an extension, the bid deadline must stay in place. Not only had Gold Fields no intention of agreeing, but it was intent on causing Minorco maximum embarrassment on the disclosure issue.

At Charles 11 Street, Agnew could barely conceal his glee. He remembered Thompson telling him of how Oppenheimer had looked after his senior people, the payments through Switzerland, the discreet arrangements through a private company, Central Holdings, and how Rudolph would be 'looked after'.

All that, he gloated, would now be forced out in court by his ferrets: Lewis Kaplan of Paul Weiss was already filing for details on the size and source of payments to Edwardes and the Minorco directors and whether they were paid through Central Holdings. Agnew sensed a kill at hand: 'We will strain every sinew to find out. Shareholders should know what they are getting into. They keep repeating that assurance that Minorco is independent. Well, who pays the executives is relevant to Minorco's independence.'

Agnew railed against JOT, the appointment of Edwardes, the 'bully boy' tactics against Gordon Parker at Newmont and what he saw as JOT's vacillation and helplessness, a man now being battered as the Edwardes hammer banged on the anvil of Anglo American. Tweakers and slammers! How Agnew revelled at the split. 'Tweakers and slammers!' A great jet of Gitane blew across the room. 'Knowing JOT, he's probably both!'

Minorco now looked trapped in the pit of the New York district court and with the pendulum of the takeover deadline inching nearer with every hour. Epstein now went back to the court offering to post a $100 million bond as evidence of Minorco's intent to sell Gold Fields' interest in Newmont, GFSA and Renison and abide by a 'hold separate' order until the sales were effected.

Gold Fields' eagerly awaited final defence was now played. On 4 April, at the offices of the City's most powerful and exclusive stockbrokers, Cazenove, Agnew and Hichens ran through the presentation rehearsal with Stephen Carden of Cazenove and the ubiquitous Grimstone.

'What should I say', Agnew asked him, 'if I'm asked about some of the low analysts' valuations on our assets?' Grimstone's face tightened. He had steered Agnew through six months of conferences and presentations and here was the final and most important. On high pressure occasions like this, Agnew's personality could take on the properties of sweating gelignite. One chance remark now would set the Press leaping at his throat and the Take Over Panel elegantly reaching for the trapdoor button.

Sometimes, Grimstone felt as if his every waking moment was spent waiting for the Agnew one liner that would murderously backfire. 'Say nothing, chairman,' he urged. 'Nothing. And don't move. Not even a turn of the body. It might be seen as body language.'

Agnew now unveiled Project Adam: the code-name for a top secret defence ploy drafted by John Grieves, corporate finance partner of Gold Fields' legal advisers, Freshfields. It set a target of 20 per cent compound earnings per share growth over the next three years, failure to achieve which would oblige Gold Fields to swallow what appeared ominously like a poison pill: if the target was not met, shareholders would get a special preferred share entitling them to a pay-out of £6 a share. It would cost £1.3 billion.

For the press conference, the curtains were drawn and the lights dimmed. On the screen was a seemingly endless procession of Hichens' slides: marching soldiers of statistics on aggregates, crushed stone and gold reserves. Hichens was having a great war, guns of facts pointed ahead and blazed away: bullets into the brains of idiots.

Agnew came to the rostrum. Grimstone sat, head in his hands, his eyes and ears now alert, waiting for the maverick firework. 'As for some of the lower estimates of our asset value by brokers' – Grimstone pressed his hands hard to his head – 'I am not allowed to indicate my opinion, not even' – Agnew's knee rose slowly upwards – 'by body language.' The audience collapsed.

'This bid', he growled, 'is for the godson and son-in-law of Harry Oppenheimer. These absurd people at Minorco should be seen out of the City of London for good.' Grimstone's face puckered. Jesus, chairman. Get on with it. Agnew looked up for the final sally and paused at the name of Edwardes. He now pronounced it 'Edwar*dees*': 'Edwar*dees* has said there is nothing new in our document . . . Well, we love the Edwar*dees* publicity. We think Gerry Grimstone is writing it for him.'

In the market, Gold Fields shares rose 25p to £13.48. Minorco fell 11p to £7.43. So this was the final Gold Fields answer to Minorco: it would willingly set the torch to a final bonfire of itself if necessary, a corporate *Götterdämmerung*. Gold Fields would do anything, anything but surrender to Minorco.

Three days later, on Friday, 7 April, Minorco's board met in Luxemburg to fix the terms of a third and final offer. It was urged to put the bid beyond doubt with a £16 a share offer. This was a battle on the world stage, too important now for Anglo American or Minorco to lose. Edwardes, stung by the latest Agnew attack, dug in.

The terms were fixed at £15.50 a share. The tweakers had triumphed.

15

Where Do We Send the Sheriff?

■

From the wall of a cluttered office behind the court-room of the New York District Court in Lower Manhattan, a large portrait of George Orwell looks down on a desk cluttered with papers.

It is the desk of Judge Michael Mukasey. Orwell is a hero of his. Mukasey, born in the Bronx, and with a face younger looking than his 47 years, had earned a reputation for busting corrupt politicians and civil servants. Among the papers are legal submissions on product liability, affidavits in disputes on late delivery, tax frauds and money laundering. The most pressing case, near the top of the pile, and marked urgent, is a dispute involving a boat-load of bananas that had rotted *en route* from Ecuador to Marseilles.

Nestling in this pile was a submission from Jeremy Epstein, attorney for Shearman & Sterling, acting for defendants Anglo American and Minorco *Société Anonyme*. Here is where the fate of Minorco's bid now rested, wedged between the banana boat and the tax frauds in a Mukasey case docket packed with a few hundred civil cases and some 15 to 20 criminal cases at a time. George Orwell looked impassively on.

The scene could not be more removed from the tumult of London. When Minorco's new £15.50 a share terms hit the London stock market, shares in Gold Fields tumbled £1.40 to £13.35, a damning verdict on the prospects of the final, long awaited, knock-out offer. It seemed to lack the compelling force that would have gathered institutional support behind it to force Agnew and his directors to drop the US action.

But it was a fair offer, one that would have swept the board in a conventional bid battle. It priced Gold Fields at over 14 times earnings and the cash element now stood at £11.75 per share. This represented 75 per cent of the offer. Further, were no bid in place, and Gold Fields rated on the same basis at RTZ, its shares would be standing at around £10. Investors were thus being offered a premium of more than 50 per cent on what Gold Fields would otherwise be worth. Meanwhile, interest rates were going up – and the gold price down. Second thoughts duly crept in. Gold Fields shares began a fitful but telling rise.

Over the next week, Edwardes and the Turks launched themselves on a whirlwind tour round institutional shareholders in Britain and Europe, a campaign more intense and punishing than anything so far. In all, Minorco made 83 institutional visits during the bid. But a split now opened up within the institutions: the traditional long-term funds (such as the Prudential and Legal & General) supporting Gold Fields, while the shorter-term or performance funds were proving more responsive to the high element of cash now in Minorco's offer.

Earlier that week, Agnew had gone on a similar lightning tour of Europe, striking deep into Minorco's heartland. If the sessions with British institutions were heavy going, those with Swiss investors quite sapped his spirit. The Swiss would sit with barely a twitch of the facial muscle to indicate whether life was still flowing through. For Agnew, it was like kneading granite. 'My greatest achievement', he was later to gleefully boast, 'was to get Swiss investors to laugh. We showed them a graph of the Charter Consolidated share price.'

Back home, Gold Fields produced a defence video which attracted 5,000 requests – a record for any corporate video in Britain. A telephone hotline was also installed which would handle more than 20,000 enquiries. On the first day, the line was inadvertently crossed with an anti-AIDS jingle warning against 'sleeping around'. Callers pondered. Was this Agnew's latest toot to Minorco?

Gold Fields also released a circular on the 'secret payments' to Minorco directors made through the Central Holdings Swiss account, details of which Epstein had filed in the American court. Two directors were paid through Central: JOT, on the grounds that he worked for three Anglo American companies (and did not qualify for pension rights from any) and Slack, who was now stationed in New York. It also hammered at 'Oppenheimer's son-in-law and godson on the board' and that Minorco was just a 'gamma stock' with no investor market for the 80 million shares that would be issued. 'Minorco', the release was headed, 'is an unsafe investment.'

Lea felt it would cut no ice with fund managers. An informal poll conducted by the *Sunday Telegraph* showed the battle swinging Minorco's way. Its survey of Gold Fields' top 20 institutional investors found that Minorco 'should scrape through with sufficient acceptances to take it over the 50 per cent level'.

But doubts persisted on Minorco's paper. And a number of fund managers expressed concern over Minorco's management ability and absence of track record. What could it possibly know about aggregates, the core business it was planning to retain? But there were also reservations about the Gold Fields special preferred share: it was far from being the popular device Grimstone had hoped.

But Minorco was soon to face its greatest crisis. Late on 17 April came Judge Mukasey's ruling on whether the injunction barring Minorco from acquiring more shares in Gold Fields should stay in place.

As Mukasey himself was vividly to comment, Gold Fields' lawyers, Paul Weiss, had 'carpet bombed the landscape with affidavits and other material from day one of this litigation'. Mukasey filed a 45-page judgment on the Monday, with the deadline for shareholders to accept Minorco's bid just nine days away.

To meet the anti-trust objections, Minorco had proposed a 'hold separate' order under which Gold Fields' shareholdings in Renison, Gold Fields of South Africa and, most crucially, Newmont would be held in a suspense account pending disposal within a year. It had further agreed not to sell its Newmont holding to any company affiliated to itself, its parent shareholders, Anglo American and De Beers, or any company linked to the Oppenheimer family. It had offered to post a $100 million bond to the court as evidence of good intent. Finally, it had further offered to submit the whole arrangement to inspection and policing by an auditor appointed by the court.

It was a comprehensive package. Surely, faced with this, Mukasey would lift the injunction and let the bid proceed?

Here was a critical ruling. If Mukasey rejected the hold separate proposal and kept the injunction in place, Europe's record breaking takeover would be dead in the water – and with it Anglo American's credibility. The MMC, the European Commission, the United States regulatory authorities, and now, the gruelling meetings with the institutions stood to be wiped out as irrelevant.

Most far reaching of all, a continuing block on Minorco would raise complex questions on corporate and sovereign jurisdiction. Where lay the fulcrum of regulatory approval now in transatlantic takeovers? Newmont stood to be put 'in play' if the Minorco bid succeeded. But what right had a New York judge in a civil action to block a takeover involving two companies not incorporated in the United States and where the total number of American shareholders in the target company totalled under five per cent?

Moreover, how relevant now to the bid were the findings of the US Government authorities which had cleared the bid on anti-trust grounds? What implications did this battle hold for the way the MMC went about its work? And where, in all this, were the rights of *shareholders* who owned the company? If shareholders voted to accept a bid, where would that leave the directors and the civil suit they were pursuing? If shareholders' interests were to lie secondary to a civil action unendorsed by them in the US courts, it opened the prospect of a torrent of frustrating suits by managements fearful of takeover. The precedent-setting implications of the resort to American civil action was already deeply troubling London institutional investors.

Those who thought Judge Mukasey's economics crash course betrayed a lightweight lawyer out of his depth in a corporate lawsuit were in for a surprise. Mukasey was little known and badly underestimated both by the Press and by analysts. He had previously served as the assistant attorney for criminal cases in the New York southern district and became head of its anti-corruption unit. He developed an expertise in complex commercial cases, and it was already clear, from some sharply observed and keenly put interventions in the court proceedings, he was well up to speed with this complicated case.

In the battle for Mukasey's mind, Lewis Kaplan for Gold Fields had led a ten-strong team of attorneys from Paul Weiss. For Minorco, Epstein led a team of eight from Shearman & Sterling. For Newmont Mining, the company at the heart of the battle, there was just one attorney: Richard J Holwell of White & Case.

From page one of the ruling it was clear Mukasey had done considerable research. And he approached the issue with deference.

Agencies of four governments, he noted, had examined the anti-trust aspects of the bid and found that competition would not be impaired.

The United States Government had looked at it under the Hart-Scott-Rudino Anti-Trust Act and found nothing to warrant further investigation. The Committee on Foreign Investment, whose members include the heads of five cabinet departments, had considered the bid for five months and had also taken no steps to block it.

What, then, could Michael B Mukasey, of the Southern District Court of New York usefully add? He first proceeded to kick away some vital props to the Kaplan case against the hold separate order. Gold Fields' case on serious anti-competitive harm was not strong enough that it could not be adequately addressed by a hold separate order: under the definition of the gold market most favourable to Gold Fields – current non-communist mine production – the degree of concentration was insufficient to be challenged by the Justice Department. 'Plaintiffs' showing on the merits of this case is hardly overwhelming'.

Indeed, Mukasey added, 'when one considers the takeover has not been challenged by the US Justice Department, the Committee on Foreign Investment in the United States or by the British or Europeans . . . the public interest weights slightly in favour of Minorco'.

Gold Fields had contended that breaking up the company itself would be anti-competitive, felling as it would Anglo American's largest competitor; that Minorco's retention of GFMC violated anti-trust; and that Minorco could retain influence at GFSA through Anglo American's 21 per cent holding. On top of this, Gold Fields insisted, Newmont itself would be debilitated: management would leave and it would be tarred by the South African brush. Finally, Newmont was going flat out to triple its production by 1990 and Minorco would have an incentive, because its holdings are in higher-cost South African mines, to thwart Newmont's plans and, ultimately, shut down the mines.

Mukasey held that breaking up the second largest gold company would leave the largest (Anglo American) free to dominate the market. 'The gold market is not so concentrated nor so fractured that such a result could occur'. The anti-trust laws, he pointed out, were enacted 'for the protection of *competition*, not *competitors* . . . Breaking up Gold Fields and selling off Newmont, GFSA and Renison would serve that interest'.

179

Nor did he find Gold Fields more convincing on the anti-trust argument about GFMC. The company accounts for just 0.8 per cent of the non-communist world gold market. The concern over Anglo American's continued holding of 21 per cent of GFSA was also without merit: the only way Anglo American could become the largest owner would be if Gold Fields' 38 per cent interest were to be parcelled out to many owners, rather than sold to one company. But that was not the plan at all. As Kaplan would have known, Gold Fields' interest was most likely to be sold as a block to Rembrandt, a buyer chosen by Gold Fields itself and to which it had granted the right of first refusal.

But Mukasey was only now about to bring a blush to Gold Fields' cheek. It came over the Gold Fields contention of damage to Newmont through the South African 'tarred brush'. For it was this aspect, more than any other, that had stood to incite lay opinion against the Minorco bid.

Here, surely, was Kaplan's strongest suit, an easy blow on behalf of Caring Corporate Attorneys against South Africa: the approved progressive punch-bag. *Good versus Evil*: back to the paint box with just two colours!

Mukasey was having none of it: 'Gold Fields itself has significant ties to South Africa, ties which are at least as damning as Minorco's. Indeed, Gold Fields' connections are, if anything, more perceptibly tied to the injustices of Apartheid.

'GFSA has one of the largest private armies in South Africa, complete with dogs, armoured vehicles and its own patented rubber bullets which it uses in labour strikes. It has also allegedly discouraged unionization by black workers and has exploited the excess of unskilled black workers to keep their wages low, while skilled white workers receive far more. As a result, only seven per cent of its black work force belongs to the South African National Union of Mineworkers . . . GFSA's record on race relations and unionization is so bad that any responsible American company should be ashamed to be associated with them.'

If Kaplan was tempted at this point to ask what all this had to do with Newmont Mining Corporation, he wisely bit his tongue. The chairman of GFSA, Robin Plumbridge, sat on Newmont's board as a representative of its largest shareholder – Consolidated Gold Fields. But Mukasey's purpose here was not so much to expose Newmont's South African links than to cut through the hypocrisy he had detected in the anti-Anglo American depositions, and he did so incisively. The remembrance of Orwellian truth may have helped a little.

By this stage it appeared as if Mukasey was ruling for Minorco on all material counts: public interest; the validity of a hold separate order; and anti-trust. On all of these he had looked into the eyes of Minorco and found in its favour.

But Mukasey's gaze did not stop there. It reached over Minorco's shoulder to Anglo American, and Anglo American had declined to put itself before the court. From this point on, Mukasey's judgment slid steadily, remorselessly, against Minorco.

What, he asked, might Anglo American do? Anglo American had an incentive to hold Newmont's head under water because it would own a lower percentage of low-cost Newmont than of its high-cost South African mines.

But what of Minorco's assurances that it would divest itself of the Newmont stake within a year? The existence of Anglo American affiliates outside the court's jurisdiction made it impossibe for a hold separate order to guarantee no anti-competitive harm.

Said Mukasey: 'The Anglo group could easily set up corporations in countries which protect the identity of the owners, and through these corporations purchase shares in GFSA, Renison and Newmont. The Anglo group has every incentive to stifle the competitive energy of these direct competitors . . . I find that the proposed hold separate order would not effectively check interim anti-competitive harm, largely because of the possibility that an Anglo group affiliate not subject to this court's jurisdiction could purchase shares in the companies and suppress their competitive conduct.'

Even if Minorco secured from the purchasers of these stakes undertakings that they would not be sold on to any member of the Anglo American group, nothing could legally stop Anglo American from buying them.

And how could a court-appointed special master trace the identity of a buyer bent on secrecy? Where could he send the sheriff? 'The world abounds with jurisdictions where incorporations need not be disclosed, where ownership is evidenced by bearer shares . . . Indeed, plaintiffs note that South African laws, such as the Protection of Business Act, enable South African companies to conceal the source of their overseas investments in order to avoid the effects of anti-Apartheid laws. The Anglo group could easily use these laws to help create new entities to recapture the three companies.

'Neither the proposed special master, nor any of the three companies, nor this court, can be certain to prevent such anti-competitive
results . . . I have every reason to be concerned that the order might
be undermined by an Anglo group affiliate over which this court has
no control.'

Buy why was Mukasey driven to make assumptions about the
intentions of a company from which he had heard no direct evidence?
Here he came to the core of his rejection: Anglo American could
not be trusted: 'The Anglo group's record in circumventing legal
restrictions and engaging in anti-competitive behaviour is not
reassuring.'

And what led him to this view? The moment when Anglo American
affiliates purchased 16.4 million Gold Fields shares in 40 minutes;
the event which, as Mukasey put it, 'Gold Fields refers to melodra-
matically as the "Dawn Raid"'. Back to that! Nine years after the
event, that furtive gulp at the Gold Fields Grail returned to haunt
Oppenheimer. It had come to warn people of his coming, like a
leper's bell.

This, coupled with the past cartel behaviour of De Beers, 'compel
the conclusion that this court's lack of jurisdiction over the other
entities in the Anglo group could frustrate a hold separate order and
divestiture remedy'. Mukasey ruled against Minorco and upheld the
Gold Fields injunction.

It looked to be a breathtaking slapdown of one of the world's
largest companies. But there was more to it. Mukasey had reached
deep into the folk memory of corporate America and had touched
on a long-rooted distrust of Anglo American. Here was a sign that
nothing had been forgotten, or forgiven. For Anglo American, it was
the return of the curse.

Little wonder in London Rudolph Agnew had Mukasey's quotes
typed out on a sheet of A4 paper which he kept in his breast pocket
and whisked out for repetition. For the Young Turks at Minorco, it
must have seemed that the demon in Anglo American's past was out.
Not by Gold Fields' scorched earth had the ground now darkened
before them, but the shadow thrown by their parent.

It was a moment Edwardes in particular had dreaded: all the
assurances he had been given on autonomy, all the plans he had
spelt out for an independent and credibly self-determining Minorco
were suddenly shrinking back before the ancestral ghosts. In the
Oppenheimer house are many mansions, and no matter how far flung

they are or how wide or deep the moats between them, the ghosts of yesteryear walk through them all.

What was Mukasey getting at here? The distrust and unease about Anglo American reached back much further than the 'Dawn Raid', to the early 1940s when the United States was desperate to secure a stockpile of industrial diamonds for the defence industry. As the United States saw it, Sir Ernest Oppenheimer had taken advantage of that need to force the Justice Department to overturn the ban on the De Beers diamond cartel opening up in New York.

Why had neither Anglo American nor De Beers agreed to appear before Judge Mukasey in the District Court? On the record stood a 1974 grand jury indictment of De Beers and two American companies for conspiracy to rig prices and share markets.

De Beers had refused then to appear before an American court. And it was certainly reluctant now. Under the American legal process of 'discovery', the court can compel companies to produce corporate documents for scrutiny and examination. Not only had Anglo American every reason to fear an examination driven by present-day American standards and attitudes into a cartelization process that had deep historical roots and which arose out of a unique set of historical and economic circumstances; the process once started, would be lengthy, complex, a gravy train for the vexatious and, in the end, irrelevant to the merits of Minorco's bid.

Lewis Kaplan had also brought six complaints alleging securities violations, ranging from irreparable harm to failure to disclose relevant information. Arguably the most serious of these was the allegation that Minorco had failed to warn Gold Fields investors that Minorco shares would fall sharply if the offer went through. All these claims were brushed aside by Mukasey: 'Plaintiffs' securities claims are trifling . . . their claims look feeble and contrived'.

But few had stayed to the end of the ruling. When news that the injunction would stay in place hit the London stock market early on the morning of Tuesday, 18 April, shares in Gold Fields plunged 58p to £12.90. Judge Mukasey's ruling in favour of Consolidated Gold Fields had set back its shareholders more than £100 million.

This whole dimension had been severely underestimated by Minorco: barely a week previously it had brushed the litigation aside as 'simply frivolous'. It proved to be one of the most serious misreadings of the entire battle. The briefest reading of the recent history of Newmont would have acquainted Minorco with its readiness to resort to litigation, very little of which was 'frivolous'. Minorco had again betrayed a sense of arrogance with which it had approached this battle.

The mood at the prayer meeting on the morning of the 18th was one of irritation and impatience. Around the table – Edwardes, Lea, Phillimore, Irons, Cadbury and Agostinelli – there was no doubting the sense of frustration and setback. But two immediate tasks lay ahead. The first was to seek a rehearing of the case in New York.

A London war council was immediately convened. Throughout the battle Anglo American and De Beers had taken pains to remain outside the reach of American law, from a fear that once Anglo American put a foot inside the Southern District Court all the attorneys in town would be out for the kill. The absence of Anglo American and De Beers had been quickly spotted by Mukasey. He had ruled that it was not sufficient for Minorco alone to be a guarantor of good behaviour: Anglo American and De Beers must come forward too.

Oppenheimer now flew in from Johannesburg. Anglo American and De Beers offered to submit themselves to the American court and pledge that they would not buy any shares in any of the companies that would be sold by a Minorco-owned Gold Fields for at least ten years. They also offered bonds of $100 million each as a guarantee of good behaviour.

The second task was to minimize the impact on the financial battle in London. While it was clear Minorco was legally blocked, momentum – that vital effect that had constantly eluded it from the start of this battle – was desperately needed now. The setback had to be down-played if the entire campaign was not to grind to a sodden halt in the mud of Mukasey's court.

In one perverse way, reaction to the Mukasey ruling worked to Minorco's advantage: the further the price of Gold Fields fell, the more attractive the offer looked. But the slump was signalling a collective belief in the market that Minorco's bid was going to fail. And the perception of failure would work powerfully against the bandwagon effect Minorco needed.

Minorco's press release picked out Mukasey's dismissal of Gold Fields' securities claims as 'feeble and contrived'. 'Minorco presses on' ran the scribbled headline underlined at the top of Irons' notepad. It gave notice of Minorco's intent to battle on for Gold Fields through the court.

But how to break the legal impasse? The earliest an appeal could be held was on Monday afternoon – with less than 48 hours to go before the bid closed in London. Richmond-Watson was now convinced Minorco would sail through 50 per cent. The only question was the margin of victory. He immediately began to check with the Take Over Panel to find out what would happen if Agnew still pressed on with the case. That, he felt, would be frustrating action under Rule 7 of the Take Over Code. But would Gold Fields play by the rules? And could such a ruling be binding on Newmont, co-party to the legal action?

Not only was the battle now widening in legal and territorial scope; it was also rising to an unprecedented level of intensity – both in London and New York. Legal teams on both sides rushed to prepare fresh statements for Mukasey. In London, Gold Fields' operations room was now canvassing every major institution and large private investor. Everything was being thrown in to halt the Minorco advance. For all sides, it was yet another crisis weekend of late meetings, phone calls from New York, briefings for journalists, cancelled dinners and fraught relations at home. Jeepers, was there ever life before Minorco?

Agnew and the entire Gold Fields board, including the non-executives, had taken legal advice on their positions in the event of a Minorco victory. Could they still persist with the legal action? The advice they received from Freshfields was that they had a duty to the company as a whole, not just to one group of shareholders, even though it might form a majority.

What a drama now opened up. With only days to go, the outcome was on a knife edge; Agnew and his directors were ready to barricade themselves in behind the boardroom table if necessary. Minorco would have to capture not just the company but the building, floor by floor, room by room, down to the last bullet in the last revolver. Total war, Agnew had vowed. Total war it had proved to be.

Edwardes and the Young Turks had barely a moment to spare. Virtually the whole of the week had been booked for meetings and presentations with institutions and fund managers. And in this final week fell the crucial ones: M&G (holding some two per cent of Gold Fields), the Prudential (2.75 per cent), Legal & General (just over one per cent), Royal Insurance and the Pearl. These long-term funds tended to stay loyal to companies fighting off bids. But elsewhere the Turks were making progress. By Wednesday, they were confident a bandwagon effect was starting to take hold. There was no doubt that they would get 50 per cent.

But news from GFSA in Johannesburg was soon to bring fresh consternation to *Das Boot*. Minorco had been tipped off that the company which had pledged its 7.5 per cent holding in Gold Fields against the bid was planning to launch a rights issue. But by accepting the bid terms, GFSA would have received more than £160 million for its shares, a sum which would have largely met its financial needs. Agnew, a director of GFSA, had not mentioned anything about the rights issue though details had been circulated in a secret memorandum of 13 April. The memo was leaked via Peter Gush, Anglo American's man on the GFSA board, to the Minorco camp.

Morgan Grenfell pounced immediately. A rights call was a material fact that should have been disclosed in the final defence documents. Agnew said the plan had 'not been formally considered' by the Gold Fields board. But a behind-the-scenes scramble erupted to find the mole.

Meanwhile, in a cramped office in New York under the benign gaze of George Orwell, Judge Michael Mukasey and his four-strong staff had never been busier. The Gold Fields–Anglo American–De Beers–Minorco–Newmont saga was now taking up an inordinate amount of time in a bulging case docket. And there was still that boat-load of rotting bananas.

Rotting bananas! Agnew would have had no lack of ideas on where to send those. According to some accounts he had already, some weeks earlier, sought to wreak havoc by mischievously ordering a ton of aggregate slag to be delivered to Ely Place.

Late on Monday, 24 April, Mukasey again ruled against lifting the injunction. And once again he founded his ruling on doubts about Anglo American. 'Minorco's motion', Mukasey ruled, 'must lie denied as an attempt to relitigate an issue already considered.' Minorco's new submission, he argued, was 'inadequate . . . It still does not ensure full enforceability because members of the Anglo American group, other than Anglo, De Beers and Minorco[1] remain free to purchase shares in the three companies. Furthermore, given that the Anglo group and the three companies (Renison, GFSA and Newmont)

---

[1] The company cited in the ruling at this point was Renison, although clearly Minorco was meant.

are direct competitors in the non-communist world gold market, the Anglo group will have every incentive to purchase shares'.

Mukasey was still faced with the original problem: where do we send the sheriff? 'There was no assurance that the auditors' report to the special master overseeing the court order would be able to find out whether Anglo and De Beers, or other members of the Anglo group, are purchasing shares or whether shares have been purchased by an entity not formally affiliated with the Anglo group, but none the less acting in its interest.

'Anglo and De Beers could not voluntarily provide information to the auditor without violating South African law, except with the consent of the South African Minister of Economic Affairs.'

Orwell gazed approvingly down on Judge Michael Mukasey. There were now just 36 hours to the bid deadline.

16

A *Judge Too Far*

■

Gerry Grimstone, still trying to work out what had happened to seven months of his life, gazed out of his window at Schroders across Cheapside to the clock on the little Church of Mary le Bow. It kept the time for all between Saint Paul's and the Bank of England. He waited for the clock to strike. But then, he had been waiting since the previous September, and now it was well into spring for the clock to strike an end to this gruelling, epic battle against Minorco.

Of all the talents Minorco had run up against, his was the most understated but outstanding. He had slowed down Minorco, stolen its timetable, outmanoeuvred Lazard Freres and Morgan Grenfell, kept the guns blazing and guarded the mouth of the company chairman. He had come far in seven months. This bid had been the proving of him.

First he had compared it to being in a shooting gallery, having to fire at all the figures that popped up, not knowing for sure which one carried the loaded gun. Then he had likened it to a long medieval siege. Now he saw it as a scene from the First World War: a blasted landscape of shell holes, abandoned trenches, burnt-out tanks and bodies as far as the eye could see.

Agnew and Edwardes now emerged for the final showdown – and few dared bet on the outcome. This had been Britain's biggest, longest, loudest, fiercest and costliest takeover battle. And Agnew was in no mood to give up now. Resistance against Anglo American and Minorco would go on to the last minute of the last hour of any clock Grimstone could find in the City.

Deadline Minorco – 1pm Wednesday, 26 April – was now at hand.

Its offer was worth £15.41 for each Gold Fields share at the close. Gold Fields shares stood at just £12.45.

The count, at the New Issues Department of National Westminster Bank in the heart of the City, lasted four hours and 17 minutes. Acceptances had been arriving, too, at other centres: Johannesburg, Brussels, Frankfurt, Paris and Zurich. In London, inspectors from the Department of Trade and Industry scrutinized the count to check for insider trading and concert party activity – further witness to the suspicion and bitterness roused in the battle.

Still more drama was to come. Royal Insurance, one of Britain's biggest institutions, which held 1.9 million Gold Fields shares, was caught out in a bungled *volte face* at the last minute. Its directors found out that morning the investment manager had accepted the offer and tried to withdraw. For the Royal's board, there was a sensitivity to criticism that it was succumbing to 'short termism' – and in any event, one of its number, Sir Derek Alun-Jones, was himself a director of Consolidated Gold Fields. But it was told acceptances could not be withdrawn by phone – or by fax. And it was too late to send someone round now.

Afterwards, Edwardes was to enjoy some fun at the Royal's expense. He and his wife had been invited to a reception given by the Royal's chairman, Lord Cuckney. He wrote back saying he was delighted to accept – and would not, at the last minute, be withdrawing. As the letter lay in the Ely Place out-tray, Phillimore could not resist doodling on the envelope: 'By Royal Mail'.

Minorco emerged as the victors with 54.8 per cent of Gold Fields' equity. By the close, it held directly 29.9 per cent and won acceptances for its bid covering a further 53.2 million shares, or 24.9 per cent. Minorco had passed the winning post. Or had it?

An extraordinary debate now erupted. Agnew saw no victory for Minorco at all. Not only did he not concede – a convention normally observed when the bidder crosses 50 per cent – but he now redoubled his efforts to repulse Minorco. 'We will look carefully at the votes. They have only got 35 per cent of the "free vote", so 64.6 per cent are staying with us. We know our duty. We will fight for victory.' For Agnew, Minorco's failure to capture a majority of the independent votes robbed its numerical majority of any force.

It was an argument that seemed predicated on a view that some votes are more important than others, and in this case the 29 per cent already held by Minorco did not count. This smacked of treating certain votes as 'not counting' just because they did not go Gold Fields' way – not an altogether healthy position from which to enter a debate about 'shareholder democracy' – or any other democracy, for that matter.

Minorco claimed a majority of institutional shareholders – 17 out of 30 – voted to accept the bid in respect of at least part of their holdings. But Grimstone and Agnew counted off all the major institutions – the Prudential, Sun Alliance, M&G, Pearl, Legal & General – and the vast majority of the 'long-term' funds had turned down the offer. The 54 Per Cent Club, they seemed to say, was not a one to which gentlemen belonged.

Top institutions had split their vote, the long-term funds staying with Gold Fields and the short-term, performance-orientated funds going for Minorco.

But what did votes matter? Agnew's refusal to accept the wishes of the majority of his shareholders was unprecedented in a takeover battle and, in Minorco's view, a clear breach of the rules. Cadbury and Richmond-Watson immediately protested to the Panel and urged an extension beyond 17 May, the final date by which the offer must go unconditional. For Minorco could not go unconditional – and thus take control of Gold Fields – until the New York injunction was lifted.

Agnew was boiling at the prospect that the Panel should change the rules for Minorco now. Edwardes was in a trap – and he was determined that he should not be allowed to wriggle out of it. 'Minorco', Agnew thundered, 'made a satisfactory outcome of the US action a condition of its bid. They cannot close the bid while the matter is unresolved. Our board has a duty, confirmed by Counsel, to continue to pursue the legal action.'

Now came a dramatic twist in New York. Unmoved by the majority vote of Gold Fields' shareholders in London, Gordon Parker ordered Newmont's lawyers to reaffirm that Newmont would pursue the legal action to keep the injunction in place. As Parker saw it, the shareholder vote changed nothing. Nothing at all.

Not only did Agnew not sound like a beaten man, he did not look like one, either. Despite numerous low points in the battle, the vote only seemed to inspire him to fight harder: it had quite recharged his spirit.

And so, too, that of Antony Hichens. The fight, as he saw it, was not a last ditch resistance, but a continuing moral crusade against

Anglo American and De Beers. Declared Hichens: 'Anglo and De Beers are fearful of the American process of "discovery" – the production of papers and documents about all aspects of their business. Newmont knows this. That is why it is going on with the trial. Why should it swap a standstill agreement with us for a leap into the unknown?

'It all comes down to the fact that Anglo American is not trusted. The second nature of these people is the avoidance of the open ground and the avoidance of regulation. Why else do they operate through Swiss, Luxemburg and Liechtenstein companies and not in open court? It's all part of a pattern, a way of thinking for them. How can Minorco stand surety for its own parents? To get someone to go into court for you? It's a most damning thing.'

There was no way that Gold Fields was going to roll over and die just because Minorco had a majority of the votes. 'How can the Panel argue that it is not correct for a company to appeal to a legal court? This is not a vexatious suit. The Panel set the rules. It can't play about with them now.'

Declared Agnew: 'The injunction is just the first step. If Anglo and De Beers are not prepared to put their case the judge won't be pleased. JOT and Anglo were joint signatories to the standstill agreement. Removing the injunction would be the best invitation I've heard for suit lawyers to hit the Newmont board.'

Agnew quickly ran through the Newmont position. Parker was worried that American Barrick was preparing a bid. Its Goldstrike mine was next to Newmont's Deep Post on the Carlin Trend. Barrick had to mine deep down to get at the sulphides. But it couldn't get access other than through Newmont property. 'Shrewd men with balls are watching this,' was Agnew's crisp summation.

As for his own legal position, he sat as a director of the Newmont board, together with Hichens and Robin Plumbridge. While, he insisted, they could not vote on the question of whether Newmont should pursue the legal action, they were bound, as they were at Gold Fields, to act in the interests of the company. A Panel ruling forcing them to drop the Gold Fields legal action did not oblige the Gold Fields directors to urge a similar course on Newmont. 'We have to dig deep into our integrity.'

But not, as Minorco saw it, 54 per cent deep. Even if Minorco forced him to drop the Gold Fields action, he would be bound to continue support for the Newmont action: an extraordinary position.

What a merciful thing JOT could not see his old shooting partner now. Agnew was so charged up and energized that he almost had sparks flying out of him. Not a defeat, but a new phase of battle! Not a setback, but a pause for breath! Even Hichens' charged account of the past now seemed mild in comparison to Agnew's salivation at the coming showdown. 'It's taken us right back to September. And I've got masses of energy. Masses. I'm not so sure the audience has. The fact that shareholders voted for the bid does not change anything in law. The directors still have to carry responsibility for the company and act in its interests . . . The judge isn't going to change his mind. Newmont isn't going to change its mind. Minorco won't go away. We've all got problems now.'

He stood up and walked quickly back to his office. He had a plane to catch. He was going on a journey to the Second Front: a diplomatic visit planned months ago, but which now had much greater significance – and could not be more opportune. Newmont Mining and Gordon Parker were keenly awaiting Agnew's arrival in Denver.

At *Das Boot*, Edwardes and the Young Turks now faced huge problems. They had fired the torpedo, watched as it hit Versailles amidships and waited for the Mayday and the SS Rudolph Agnew to lurch gurgling into the sea. But nothing happened. Far from capitulation and a scramble for the lifeboats, Gold Fields looked as buoyant as ever. Its guns were now winched into new positions as it changed course, steaming for the United States and the protection of covering fire from its sister ship, Newmont. So much for the shareholder vote: the Exocet that bounced.

Edwardes now launched counter-attacks on four fronts. The first was to get the Take Over Panel to agree an extension of the bid deadline. The second was to call immediately for a rehearing in New York on the basis that a majority of Gold Fields' shareholders now backed the bid. The third was to mobilize Gold Fields' institutional investors. And the fourth, final resort, was to dynamite Newmont out of the legal water. A full-scale tender offer would have to be made for the company. Newmont shareholders could then appeal to the court that the injunction was frustrating an offer being made for Newmont itself. In one strike Minorco could thus turn the legal tables and put Gordon Parker and his directors under intense pressure. 'The only way out of the legal morass', Edwardes now decided, 'is not a court solution, but a market one.'

On Minorco's behalf, Felix Rohatyn of Lazard Freres had told the

New York court that five approaches had been made to Minorco from parties interested in buying the Newmont stake in the event of the bid succeeding; two American, two Canadian and one Australian. The two clear front runners in the market's perception were American Barrick and Placer Dome. Minorco now needed one of these approaches to crystallize into a full-scale bid.

But here it had to tread carefully: who picked up the telephone to whom was more than a point of diplomatic nicety. Minorco could not of its own solicit a bid – that would fall foul of the injunction. But it could signal that its lines were open. The clock ticked relentlessly away: Minorco desperately needed a further approach soon if the whole machinery of a tender offer was to be in place in time.

Meanwhile, a full meeting of the Take Over Panel was called for Friday, 5 May. It would hear an application by Minorco that Gold Fields was in breach of General Principle 7, which obliged companies to seek the approval of shareholders in general meeting for action which might frustrate a bona fide offer. The battle was now more deadlocked than ever.

Agnew and his board, backed by top legal opinion, felt bound to continue with the legal action; Minorco, determined to consummate the bid, saw Agnew's defiance as frustrating action designed to deny the wishes of the majority of shareholders. It was a civil action which could be withdrawn by Gold Fields immediately. A Take Over Panel ruling forcing Gold Fields to put the issue before shareholders would see to it.

But what of Newmont's position? Newmont had now reaffirmed its determination to continue with the action in New York. And so long as the injunction persisted the takeover could not be consummated. Throughout the period, Agnew robustly maintained that, although Gold Fields held 49 per cent of Newmont, the company was independent of Gold Fields and that none of the Gold Fields directors had any operational control of the company.

But here lay a logical flaw. The whole basis of Gold Fields' and Newmont's civil action was that Minorco, by acquiring control of Gold Fields, would have operational control of Newmont and its gold reserves and the power to shut down its mines. That was the premise at the heart of the anti-trust case. If, by its own admission, Gold Fields controlled Newmont then, Minorco argued, it could prevail upon Newmont to lift the action.

Agnew could not, in logic, argue on the one hand, that by taking over Gold Fields Minorco would have 'control' of Newmont and, on the other, maintain that no such power of control existed. It was one or the other. This was the contradiction into which Agnew had stumbled: control, not control. Which was it? Agnew's position *vis-à-vis* Newmont was now the pivotal hinge on which everything swung. If he could not influence Gordon Parker to drop the legal action then Minorco could not influence Newmont to vary its gold production. One or the other. But which?

Edwardes could make little headway in persuading any of the major institutions to make a public stand on the principle of shareholder democracy. Some said privately that they were concerned at the precedent-setting implications of what Gold Fields was doing. Others said they had no wish to be drawn into public controversy, preferring to leave it to the Panel to rule on the rights and wrongs. Not one spoke out.

From Gold Fields' seven distinguished independent non-executive directors – ranging from Foreign Office diplomat Lord Bridges to the intense, chain-smoking ex-Hill Samuel merchant bank chief Christopher Castleman – there was silence. Some 54 per cent of shareholders had voted to accept a bid. But no director could be found who would speak for them.

Never before had a meeting of the British Take Over Panel been preceded with so much expectation and controversy. Argument raged as to whether it should change the rules of British takeover practice; others pleaded that for any justice to be done, the will of the majority of shareholders must be respected and an extension allowed.

There were more disturbing questions. How had a situation arisen where the rulings of a New York judge were effectively forcing British takeover rules to be changed? Here, surely, was a judge too far. An incisive comment in the *Wall Street Journal* hit on the question of territoriality Mukasey had posed: 'What is this case doing in a US court-room in the first place? Everyone agrees that Britain is the location of the takeover fight. . . Entrenched managers the world over will be encouraged to come running to the US courts to stop unwanted takeovers, regardless of takeover regulations in their own countries or whether there is any real US interest in the case. . . The only true loser so far is the costly and erratic US court system, which has proven once again why its reach does not deserve to extend the world over.'

On the 23rd floor of the London Stock Exchange, at 9.30am on 5

May, the ten members of the full Take Over Panel, together with their chairman, Lord Alexander QC, took their places. In front of them, to one side, was grouped Consolidated Gold Fields, with Rudolph Agnew, his senior directors and the ubiquitous Grimstone. On the other side was Minorco: Thompson and Edwardes, flanked by Lea and Phillimore and Richmond-Watson and Cadbury from Morgan Grenfell. Specially summoned from the United States was Dick Leather, vice-president of Newmont, accompanied by his adviser Robin Broadley of Barings. The entire session was held in camera.

The hearing lasted all day, with a short break for lunch. Neither Agnew nor Edwardes spoke throughout the hearing. Grimstone opened by stating that an extension of the bid was unwarranted as it would be unprecedented: Minorco itself had made clearance of the American legal action a condition of the bid going unconditional. Further, it had since last October to put all the necessary arguments to the New York court: it was Minorco, not Mukasey, that was responsible for this last minute, breakneck, race against time. Allowing an extension would create a dangerous precedent and companies looked to the Panel to uphold the rules that it itself had set out for the conduct of takeovers. They cannot suddenly be revised and amended in the course of bids for the convenience of one party.

Further, far from the New York court case being frustrating action, the anti-trust issue was central to Gold Fields' whole defence against the Minorco bid; its directors had taken advice of leading Counsel and were advised of their duty to continue to defend the company's interests. Finally, Gold Fields had no control over Newmont, which had every intention of continuing with the action.

Richmond-Watson came forward. In a dry, unemotional submission, he reminded the Panel of all the regulatory hurdles that had been cleared by Minorco; the acceptance of Minorco's offer by a majority of Gold Fields shareholders; the continued action of Agnew and the directors with neither the consent nor support of the owners of the business. Rule 7 clearly stated that Gold Fields needed the authority of its shareholders in general meeting to continue with its legal action, and this it had not sought. It was not Minorco that was seeking to rewrite the rules, but Agnew and the directors of Gold Fields. They should now abide by the rule, and that rule was written to ensure shareholder democracy would prevail. As for Newmont, Gold Fields had argued throughout on the premise that a Minorco

victory would give it control of Newmont and its gold mining operations. That was the case before the New York court. It could not
now argue the reverse before the Take Over Panel by saying it had
no control over Newmont's involvement in the action.

Broadley for Newmont pointed out that, with the best will in the
world, a United States company headquarters in Denver could not
be ordered by a quasi-legal British body to desist from actions it
clearly felt to be in stockholders' best interests. Gold Fields and
Newmont were signatories to a standstill agreement under which no
disposal of more than 15 per cent of the company by Gold Fields
could be undertaken without prior knowledge and consultation with
its board.

Finally, there were clear concerns of anti-trust that had led to a
reaffirming of the injunction four times by the American courts. This
was no vexatious, frustrating suit, but a matter of central importance
to the world's gold market, in which Newmont was the largest American producer.

At 5.30pm, chairman Alexander brought the proceedings to a close.
The Panel would consider the matter over the weekend, judgment
would be finally composed on Monday and most likely released some
time on Tuesday morning. It was as English and laid back as a request
for a decanter of sherry, Madeira cake and an Anthony Trollope
novel. Alexander was not a man to be rushed.

That Sunday, Edwardes could scarcely believe the battle had been
raging since September and was now in its eighth month. Not just
in length but in intensity, too, this had been an Everest of a bid. He
had taken Minorco over such a distance, through every regulatory
board and hurdle, a distance far greater than any travelled in any
other bid by any other company. He had won the majority of shareholders. But still there was no victory. How much longer could they
deny Minorco!

Agnew escaped London that weekend with a set of emotions quite
different, but in every way as potent as those of Edwardes. To the
end, he would carry with him two dark secrets. Against all the odds,
he had held out against the financial onslaught of a bid backed by
the world's largest mining company, one that lacked for nothing in
power and resource. He had fought for the survival of Consolidated
Gold Fields and he had defended it without any help from the British
financial or political Establishment. On the contrary. As he saw it,
the MMC had caved in with a supine verdict that was the laughing

stock of every analyst in town. And though the financial pillars had stayed loyal, those pillars were of crumbling mortar.

And as Agnew, too, looked back on those seven months, and the eight years before those seven months, and as he considered the new era of global takeovers, it struck him with a sense of helplessness that British companies, no matter how deep their history, could no longer count on a protective establishment. There was no guardian now. Against the new breed of nomadic global marauder, Britain could offer only little men and little rules. Nothing now seemed to be valued at any more than the realizable break-up value of its parts. Nothing was allowed in that valuation in the way of history or heritage or merit. Britain was now an industrial Sothebys, and every day was a sale.

And here Agnew now could not help but dwell on one of those secrets. For Gold Fields, he knew that its days were finished. Even if he fought off Oppenheimer, there would be someone else. And the saddest aspect of all was an evident indifference to this dismemberment, from the highest levels in the country down. Who *cared* any more?

The Panel's ruling was released just before the market opened on Tuesday, 9 May. It could scarcely have looked worse for Agnew. After much handwringing and admonition that this in no way set a precedent, the Panel duly set one: it came down seemingly in favour of Minorco, ordering Gold Fields to have the legal action sanctioned at a shareholder general meeting, and extending the final deadline for acceptances to 7 June.

'The continuance of the US proceedings without shareholder approval', declared the Panel, 'clearly has the effect of frustrating the offer . . . The majority view of the shareholders as to the future of the company should be respected.' 7 June! At *Das Boot*, a triumphant euphoria broke loose.

But like so many of Minorco's incipient celebrations, all it needed was for Edwardes to reach for the champagne for the bubbles to vanish. Gold Fields immediately announced it would comply with the Panel ruling and would withdraw from the legal action *forthwith*.

At one stroke Agnew had nullified the grounds for the Panel's extension. He thus sidestepped a foredoomed battle for shareholder votes and drop-locked the original 17 May deadline back into place.

It knocked any advantage of the Panel's ruling clean out of Edwardes' hands. And it left Minorco just eight days to blow

Newmont out of the water. What a poisoned chalice: Minorco was back in the pit of Judge Mukasey's court. . . with the pendulum now swinging closer than ever.

17

Shootout in the Last Chance Saloon

∎

It was a passage Edwardes had cause to know well. A few moments into Act III of Puccini's *Turandot*, the great tenor aria begins its climb, an ascent of Puccini genius: *Nessun Dorma (No one shall sleep)*.

On this evening in the first week of May, it held the audience of the Royal Opera House in its palm – and several members of that audience specially: in the front stalls, Edwardes and his wife; and, unknown to him a few rows away, senior officials of Consolidated Gold Fields. *Nessun Dorma!* Over the next two weeks, no one would sleep at Gold Fields or Minorco.

The Take Over Panel's ruling could not, of course, apply to Newmont: it was free to pursue its injunction – and Gold Fields was under no pressure to seek to change Newmont's mind. As the Panel saw it, Gold Fields did not control Newmont: it had little alternative but to note both Gold Fields' and Newmont's own submissions on this point.

Since the request was made for the Panel ruling, 12 precious days had ticked by; and though it upheld Minorco in the unique circumstances of this case, the reward for Minorco was to be a setback, not an advantage. It had until 17 May to declare its offer unconditional or the offer would lapse.

In New York, Hank Slack scrambled to put a final appeal in before Judge Mukasey. But the only real hope now hinged on getting a bidder to come forward for Newmont – and fast. Minorco was now deep in talks with Placer and American Barrick. Every minute now counted. In the market, Gold Fields shares went up 10p to £13.28. Newmont went up $3 to $40 – and on abnormally high turnover: over a million Newmont shares changed hands. Something was definitely underway. In New York, and London, and Luxemburg, and Johannesburg, the tick of the clock grew louder.

Barely had the implications sunk in then Newmont went on the attack, slapping in a motion to the New York court that Minorco had now violated the injuction by the very act of appealing to the Take Over Panel. It further sought a ruling on the grounds that Minorco had been attempting to find a buyer for Newmont.

Epstein now worked furiously on a reply and on a last ditch submission for a rehearing. Minorco, he argued, had every right to put its case before regulatory bodies in the UK. As for Minorco's attempts to find a buyer, Epstein pointed out that a month previously Newmont had faulted Minorco for not having lined up one. It could hardly claim now that efforts to remedy that now constituted contempt.

The plea for rehearing was to be Epstein's most trenchant and (for Newmont) damningly researched submission yet to get the injunction lifted. Its opening words set the tone: 'This injunction has been fraudulently obtained and should be dissolved.'

Epstein seized on the opposing positions Agnew had adopted on the Newmont control issue and hammered away at the contradiction. As for the standstill agreement, that, he argued, 'has been used for whatever purposes seemed most expedient to ward off the gremlins of the moment. When it was initially put in place at Newmont, the company had strenuously and successfully argued at the Delaware courts that Gold Fields would not control Newmont. When it became expedient in this litigation to argue the reverse, that was done'.

Epstein quoted extensively from the statements Dick Leather had made the previous week to the Take Over Panel, that 'Gold Fields is plainly not in a position through its board position or its shareholding to impose decisions about Newmont's management or board'. This and other statements made clear Newmont's perception that Gold Fields could not influence or control Newmont against its wishes. He then contrasted this with Newmont's statement to the court the previous October, that 'Minorco's contention that Gold Fields does not "control" Newmont and that Minorco therefore would not acquire "control" via a successful bid for Gold Fields, is absurd'.

Newmont, as well as Gold Fields, now looked caught out. Epstein closed in: 'Because it became expedient, Newmont and Gold Fields have successfully argued that Gold Fields' 49 per cent stake does not permit Gold Fields (and, by necessary implication, any future owner of this block) to control Newmont or significantly influence it to do anything contrary to the best interests of Newmont and all of its shareholders. By so doing, they have pulled the lynch pin from this court's anti-trust injury analysis.' The injunction should now be thrown out – both because the premise for the injury finding had been removed, but also because the court had been 'improperly led down the primrose path into error'.

Epstein cited 'another about face' – this time on Newmont's view of the gold market. Leather, he claimed, had tried to back-pedal on a statement he had made to Congress in 1987, explaining why it was impossible to establish a cartel in the gold market. Parker, Epstein pointed out, had also gone on record with the view that investors, not gold producers, determined the price of gold.

Whatever may have been Newmont's true position on these matters was a secret it seemed determined to take to the grave.

Throughout that week, the phone in the Denver office of Jim Hill, Newmont's self-proclaimed 'vice-president in charge of talking to people', rang with journalists seeking a briefing on Newmont's position. His phone seemed clamped by a Denver boot. Earlier that week, Newmont shareholder Blake Thomas, attacking the board's position, pointed out that when the Minorco bid looked like winning, Newmont's shares had risen. The board was now holding out against stockholder interests. It was not an argument the directors were evidently keen to enter at that point.

At the New York offices of Lazard Freres and at Ely Place in London, Minorco now desperately awaited to hear from potential buyers. Placer Dome was believed in the market to be the prime contender. But discussions kept foundering on the injunction and the practical impossibility of getting a tender offer in place almost immediately.

Meanwhile, Mukasey had ordered that Felix Rohatyn and Bill Loomis of Lazard Freres, together with Slack and Edwardes attend the offices of Newmont's lawyers, White & Case in New York's Avenue of Americas, to submit to questions in camera and under oath on all documents and information that may have been disclosed to potential buyers.

For Edwardes, that involved a 10am flight from Heathrow on Concorde to New York on Saturday morning. Seven hours earlier, at three in the morning, the bedside phone at his Surrey cottage burred into life. Edwardes struggled awake. It was a call from Canada – a potential buyer for the Newmont stake.

Nessun Dorma! This could be the last minute key to the door. Edwardes scribbled feverishly on small yellow sheets torn from a *Stick-It* pad. The numbers from Canada were way below Minorco's minimum. The enquiry came to nothing. But every piece of paper scattered over Edwardes' pillow that morning had to be solemnly submitted for scrutiny to Newmont's lawyers in New York. The deposition took three and a half hours.

As the minutes ticked by, Minorco's chances of securing an offer for Newmont grew more remote. In the market, Gold Fields shares were £12.73 at the Friday close, £2.70 below the value of the offer. The market didn't rate Minorco now. Its last hope now lay with Mukasey, who said he would rule on final submissions the following Tuesday.

Just 24 hours would be left on the clock. Denver, London, New York, Johannesburg, Luxemburg: all now waited for the shootout in the Last Chance Saloon.

The ruling, on Tuesday, 16 May, came a little after high-noon New York time. Lunch arrangements were instantly abandoned. Small groups gathered nervously in front of the Reuters screens. The outcome of an eight-month battle that had ranged across three continents was now pending at last.

At 12.33pm the headline flashed on the screens: 'US judge refuses to lift injunction barring Minorco from Gold Fields takeover'. Waiting in the offices of White & Case was the *Observer's* George Pitcher: 'Clenched fists were raised, chairs knocked backwards. Even lawyers allowed themselves to smile – though perhaps not Minorco's Jeremy Epstein.'

The ruling was the end of Minorco. The Young Turks in London and the older hands in Johannesburg were united in exasperation. In truth, Mukasey's ruling could hardly have come as a surprise. On three previous occasions he had ruled for an injunction: to reverse these now, with less than 48 hours to go to the final deadline, would not only involve a public abandonment of all his previous reasoning, but would expose him to the charge of knuckling under pressure. And of all the principal parties involved in this extraordinary case on this side of the Atlantic, it was Mukasey who was by the end the most *individually* exposed.

In addition, the civic culture in which Mukasey operated and the peer group of corporate attorneys before which he played, looked for an anti-South African verdict: that was the one most appropriate to Mukasey's own record and that of the powerful New York lobbies that had already publicly roasted Chemical Bank for its participation in the banking syndicate behind Minorco. Mukasey was being asked to go against the grain. And finally, he could afford the decision: this, after all, was only a ruling on whether there were reasonable grounds for an anti-trust trial, not a ruling on anti-trust itself.

What, then, of the Fourth Protocol of Judge Mukasey? His rebuttal of Epstein rested on an assessment of both the qualitative and quantitative extent of Gold Fields' control over Newmont.

Even though Gold Fields may not have been a dominant influence in the launch or continuance of Newmont's legal action, it still enjoyed considerable influence over the general direction of Newmont's affairs. 'Newmont's representations to the Panel that it was not legally controlled by Gold Fields do not undercut its earlier position that Gold Fields, or any entity controlling Gold Fields' shares, could inflict significant anti-trust injury on Newmont's operations such that Newmont has anti-trust standing.' It was a breathtaking distinction: if Newmont was not legally controlled in one regard, how was it now legally so in another?

Minorco, Mukasey went on, 'confuses absolute control with substantial influence. Even assuming Minorco could not exercise absolute control on Newmont, it would have great influence over Newmont's future'. But that influence could only be translated into control with the agreement of the representatives of the other 51 per cent, and with Newmont's executive directors.

And the objections to the hold separate proposal still persisted: 'Problems of enforcement and detection would remain. Unidentified members of the Anglo group remain free to acquire shares . . . Many of the Anglo group members are not subject to this court's jurisdiction and thus could easily evade this court's or the special master's detection'.

Epstein must have asked himself why he bothered. But Mukasey was not finished yet. He was not going to allow Minorco space to complain that it now had only 24 hours left to appeal. 'Minorco had ample time to appeal this court's 17 April and 24 April decisions. It should not now complain of unfair prejudice because it chose voluntarily a strategy which now leaves it little time to appeal.' *Ample* time? Judge Mukasey's definition of 'ample' seemed to many more Irish than judicial.

Not just a closing of the door, but a slamming shut: caught between the 12-day deliberations of the Take Over Panel and this latest ruling, any lingering hopes Minorco may have had of going back to Mukasey were blown away in this judicial blast.

In London, the news came through late in the afternoon. But even now Agnew could not uncork the champagne. There was speculation that Minorco was planning an immediate appeal. Then came a report that it was seeking a meeting with the Panel.

Another appeal! Another extension of the bid deadline! In his drawing room, Agnew lit a Gitane and flopped on to the sofa, drained at the prospect of going another round with Minorco. In the entire eight months, this was, according to his closest aides, his darkest hour, the lowest point.

Then, in a terse statement released in London that afternoon, Edwardes formally conceded: 'We tried our best. We felt our latest position was powerful, but he [Mukasey] threw it all out.' Lea added: 'We are looking at the deadline of tomorrow and have to face reality.'

In Phillimore's office, an inflated party balloon gorilla, to which he had stuck a label, 'Mukasey', sagged to the floor. The mood was one of defeat and bitter frustration: of being cheated of a victory. And victory had been so close. It would take some time before the full reality sank in: the Myth that was Minorco was over.

At Charles 11 Street, the collapse of the siege was celebrated in champagne. Said Agnew: 'We can hardly believe it. We have always believed this is a bad bid. And we have won on a technicality.' A technicality! Lewis Kaplan offered the kindest description of all: 'The result was a unique convergence of improbables.'

How would the market react? Every morning for months BZW's mining analyst, Alan Richards, had climbed on to the stand, nick-named 'the pulpit', to address the main dealing floor on the latest developments in the battle. It was a moment he had come to dread: each day a gutteral groan had risen up at the very mention of Minorco–Gold Fields. All the boys wanted was the bottom line: were the shares going up? Or down?

But now, as Richards announced Gold Fields' Houdini-like escape, a cheer began, and it swirled across the floor, gathering volume, a cloud of noise, fists banging on the desks and thrust into the air.

At Charles 11 Street, Agnew threw a final press conference. It was a subdued affair, as if he and Hichens and Grimstone could not quite grasp that the battle was over. The total costs of the defence, these were now estimated at £30 million.

As the conference broke up for champagne, Agnew slipped up to his private suite on the floor upstairs to take a phone call. As he finished, the quietness of the room and the absence of bustle for the first time in eight months now enveloped him. He sank slowly into his armchair and lit a cigar. On a sideboard table, the little statuette of Cecil Rhodes, that gift from Oppenheimer, looked stoically on. Rhodes and Orwell: a unique convergence of improbables!

What had this battle been all about? 'What we proved in New York was that South African control is just not acceptable in large areas of the world. The harm comes from direct political opposition right across the spectrum to subtle denial of business by local authorities and private industry, people who are members of the anti-South African industry.

'The second reason was the dead hand of Anglo American: the examples are a multitude of the failures of Anglo investments overseas. And when they came to make their biggest acquisition move overseas in what was the largest takeover ever, the dead hand appointed a godson and a son-in-law to lead the bid.

'You see, at Anglo there is a family agenda and a corporate agenda. And the two are mixed up.'

As for fraternization during the battle, there was none. The only personal communication Agnew received from Minorco was a letter from Edwardes threatening legal action. But then several people got those.

During the bid, Agnew had kept two dark secrets to himself and they had haunted him increasingly. But there was one on the other side he could not fathom. A hand came to the brow. '*Edwardes*,' he suddenly hissed, the face twisting and the head slowly shaking, 'why *Edwardes?*'

There was a long Agnew pause. He drew on the cigar and gazed out of the window. After eight gruelling months he could now let one secret out: Gold Fields had escaped without producing either a profits forecast or an asset valuation.

'This', he said, his face disappearing behind the billowing cigar smoke, 'was the most winnable bid in history.'

CHAPTER

18

Enter Lord Silken Gloves

■

Not an ending, but an interval; not a victory, but stalemate; not a solution, but a problem compounded. At Ely Place and 44 Main the mood of frustration gave way to a sulphurous, vengeful brooding. The crisis of defeat was beginning.

As for Gold Fields, there were few plaudits. 'Inglorious victory' ran the headline on the *Financial Times* Lex column. 'The fact', it declared, 'that Gold Fields' shareholders have been prevented from accepting this bid by the vagaries of the US legal system is clearly unjust.' A leading editorial in the *Financial Times* rumbled with disapproval: 'The circumstances surrounding the bid . . . reflect none too well on takeover practice in Britain . . . In failing to obtain share-holder approval for legal proceedings in the US which posed a threat to the Minorco offer, Gold Fields ran counter to one of the more important principles of the Take Over Code.'

If Gold Fields was downhearted by this criticism, it did not show. A great victory dinner and dance for around 200 staff and families was planned. It would be held on 4 July – American Independence Day. The venue was London Zoo.

There was no party mood at Minorco. As the blood urge for scapegoats mounted, it moved to keep up the pressure. It lodged a further appeal against the New York injunction. A priority was to lessen the damage done to the standing of Anglo American and Minorco in the United States and the barriers thrown up against future corporate advance.

As for Edwardes, he was in no mood for magnanimity in defeat. There would be no concessions: the appeal would go on, the pressure would be kept up, the 'preferred share' vigorously opposed. As for selling on the Gold Fields stake, 'all options', Edwardes firmly declared, 'are open'.

Edwardes looked across the oval table that filled the visitors room at Ely Place, took off his glasses and sucked thoughtfully at the stem. His face darkened. He had started the bid with five aces. Now there were none left to play. 'We'll let them stew.'

Gold Fields had a problem. Its shares had tumbled 45p to £12.28; institutional investors were restive. Matters could not settle back to where they were. Pressure was already mounting on Agnew to split the roles of chairman and chief executive. And the board's commitment to the Special Preferred Share now looked less certain. From its public affairs office came the new line that well, of course, a shareholders meeting would have to be called to vote on the plan, it would be quite wrong for the directors to tie themselves to unalterable courses so far in advance . . . surely, the new line went, it would be best to leave a final decision on a capital pay-out to investors to be made in the light of events at the time? It was hardly a ringing endorsement.

Minorco had a problem. A board meeting loomed in June, and with it a post-mortem. The knives were already flashing round Edwardes. The only doubts voiced in the City were not whether he would resign, but when. Minorco was no nearer its ambition to be a hands-on manager of assets. Further, under Take Over Panel rules, it would have to wait a year before bidding again. As far ahead as Edwardes could see, that 29 per cent stake would be the source of friction and combat, an obsession that would slide into neurosis.

Out of this depressing, frustrating stand-off there seemed no escape. Then came a glimmer.

On 17 May, the day after Minorco had thrown in the towel, Lea and Phillimore had picked up, through their City contacts, a report that Lord Hanson was 'sniffing round', enquiring about Minorco's stake in Gold Fields. They took the news to Edwardes.

Was there any substance to the rumours? If Hanson was really interested, why not phone him and see if something could be set up? The more Edwardes thought of a Hanson solution, the more intrigued he became. In the log-jam that the situation now presented, a Hanson move could create the space that everyone now needed. What was there to lose? Edwardes now dialled Hanson's headquarters in Grosvenor Place.

The conversation was brief, and as Edwardes played it back in his mind, it was all the more elegant for its brevity: 'I said, "James, about our shareholding in Gold Fields, now the bid is over why not have your people meet mine?"' And Hanson had replied, barely without waiting for Edwardes to finish: 'Done! Super!'

Edwardes left Hanson in no doubt about why he had called: 'What we said to the Press is the truth. We want to buy all of Gold Fields and if not, sell the stake. We're ready to hear any proposals you may have.' But something Hanson now said made Edwardes catch his breath. Hanson told Edwardes he had been asked in the course of the bid to intervene by Gold Fields as a white knight. But, he added, 'I didn't want to foul up other people's business.'

So there was the Agnew second secret!

Hanson had not intended to throw Edwardes off balance, but that was the effect. Amid all the Agnew diatribes about the break up of Gold Fields' business and the fulminations about asset stripping, Wyn Bishoff, head of his merchant bank advisers Schroders, had put in a call to the most accomplished corporate dissector of them all: breaking up other people's businesses was what had shot Hanson to prominence on the world stage.

There was no thrill more bitter sweet than the prospect that now presented itself to Edwardes. How could Agnew fight a bid against the man he had approached to be a white knight? If he started a defence, Edwardes now had the information to blow it out of the water. He would now move this knight to have Agnew not just in check, but checkmated.

*   *

In 20 years, Hanson had built a tiny north of England textile business into an international corporate legend. Ever larger acquisitions, embracing Britain's leading brickmaker, London Brick, tobacco and brewery combine, Imperial Group, and SCM and Kidde in the United States, had created an empire with sales of £8 billion and pre-tax profits headed for £1 billion, up from £123 million in just four years. Hanson now carried a stock market price tag of £8,360 million and a net cash balance of around £2,000 million.

Hanson had become not so much a company as a phenomenom, one which attracted a huge following among investors. It is one distinctive through both content and form: not just what Hanson does, but how he does it, has helped create one of the great stock market legends of all time.

Working with Sir Gordon White in the United States, he had developed an approach to company takeovers that was as elegant as it was formidable. Successfully bidding for companies and then breaking them up is a clinical and ruthless exercise. To this carnal voracity Hanson brought a peculiarly English coolness and style that not only helped legitimize the activity, but created around it a positive and approving light.

Hanson, at 67, had achieved this extraordinary charisma in three ways. First, his target companies would in almost every case comprise a business that was not performing at its best. Second, through acquisitions and disposals, he had created a formidable earnings per share and dividend growth performance that became a model for dozens of young copycat entrepreneurs of the 1980s. The Hanson group became an unarguable force in the market, not because of its bigness, but its performance: not once in 26 years has the Hanson earnings growth and dividend machine faltered. And third, he effected his executions with a clinical and brisk panache. The process of Hansonization involved the slashing of overheads, sale of surplus businesses and assets, and the enforcement of Hanson accounting methods. The sword would chop away – and with every downward swish of the blade the analysts and the Press would cheer. Journalists, rarely witness to the post-bid cannibalization process, made him out to be a shining Lohengrin. Hanson became a polished performer, the white knight of Thatcherism who talked of the entrepreneurial release and the more efficient allocation of assets: the executioner with the silken gloves.

Such was his standing by the late 1980s that there was barely a company, not even BAT Industries, that was not now considered to be within his grasp. It was a reflection of that standing that some of the biggest propositions were brought to his door. Such was the case with Gold Fields.

Recalls Hanson: 'When Wyn Bishoff of Schroders rang me during the Minorco bid asking if he could come round, he hinted at a white knight role for us. We didn't want to get into an auction. But the call emboldened me to take an interest once the bid had failed.

'Gold Fields was an attractive company to us, in particular the crushed stone business which is the basis for all building materials.

It had continuing growth, stability and extensive reserves. Gold Fields was a valuable, well run company which had been trying to change its spots in a way we thought was right, and ARC had an excellent record. And it was well capitalized. So you see, it was quite unlike other companies we have acquired.'

Hanson's interest in Gold Fields was also unique: because he had no previous involvement in gold and precious metals. But this was not a primary cause of Hanson's interest. 'For us, this was not a run at precious metals. We felt that Gold Fields had all the right qualifications in terms of asset value. Gold Fields was not a way for us into precious metals *per se*.

'Yes, we were strangers to the gold business, but so what?' A distinctive feature of the Hanson style is that it has rarely sprung a bid that was synergistic or indeed contiguous: 'Indeed,' says Hanson, 'we see in other company takeovers a premium having to be paid for synergy. That is why other companies come to pay over the odds'.

The fact that Gold Fields had an 100-year history had no bearing on how Hanson viewed the business. 'We looked at it in a purely financial way. We didn't look too hard at the gold price. As in all the acquisitions we've done, what we look for is positive earnings gain.'

This was the man Edwardes now set up for Rudolph Agnew: Minorco's cyanide kiss of goodbye.

On Monday, 19 June, Hanson phoned Ely Place with outline terms for the purchase of Minorco's 29 per cent stake. Edwardes had already drafted Minorco's proposals. Detailed negotiations then began between the two sides. Provisional agreement was reached on Tuesday.

Minorco now had to get board sanction – and fast. On Wednesday, Edwardes headed a press conference at noon on Charter's results at 40 Holborn. No hint was given about the pending deal as questions rained on Charter, 'but all my attention', Edwardes recalls, 'was on the negotiations with Hanson'. Immediately the Press conference broke up, he sped out across the road to the Central Selling Organisation in 17 Charterhouse Street and rushed to the roof where Nicky Oppenheimer and Thompson were waiting in a helicopter. By 2.30pm, a formal Minorco board meeting was underway in a hotel near Luxemburg airport.

Agnew, meanwhile, had been enjoying a day at Ascot, oblivious to the drama.

By 7pm, Edwardes was back in Ely Place. Phillimore and Lea had already set out for an expectant Hanson headquarters to sign the formal papers.

Done! Super!

Just before 8.30pm, two Bentleys drove up outside Gold Fields' headquarters. Out stepped Lord Hanson and Sir Gordon White. Waiting for them on the second floor was Agnew, flanked by Wyn Bishoff and Gerry Grimstone. Agnew smoked impassively as Hanson broke the news: he would be launching a formal bid the following morning having secured an irrevocable acceptance from Minorco of £14.30 a share in respect of its holding. The terms would now be put to all shareholders.

He knew Agnew would not like the terms and would seek to put up a fight. But did he have the will to resist? And did he have the strength? Hanson had made some shrewd assumptions here. He had seen press photographs of the Gold Fields chairman towards the end of the Minorco battle and the pictures had caught the strain of eight months of battle. The air of war weariness hung over Agnew's party. Moreover, Hanson was banking not just on his greater acceptability as a bidder, but also the response of Gold Fields' shareholders to an all-cash offer – especially against the background of a volatile share price.

Agnew watched intently as Hanson came quickly to the point with the terms. As he listened, Agnew caught sight of a curious feature about Hanson: around his right wrist, occasionally slipping out from under the sleeve of his jacket, was a gold chain bracelet. Agnew did not expect that. Was this Hanson's sole attachment to the world of gold? Something he slipped lightly on and off his wrist, as he would slip it on and off the wrist of his company? Agnew could never wear gold like that. No mining man could.

But more disturbing for Agnew was shareholder reaction to the price. He could scarcely ask them to accept £14.30. But neither could he totally reject it. The price was some £1.20 below the value of the cash and paper terms from Minorco he had roundly rejected two months ago. But why had Minorco accepted it? Hanson looked to have out-negotiated Edwardes. But the closer Agnew looked, the more deadly the Minorco–Hanson deal appeared. The fine print showed that Minorco was locked into accepting £14.30, even if Hanson increased the offer. Further, were there to be a rival higher offer, and Hanson withdrew, Minorco would have to pay to Hanson one-half of the excess price above £14 a share.

It was a cunningly constructed deal which not only assured Hanson of 29 per cent at no more than £14.30 a share, but removed from Minorco the incentive to play footsie with a rival bidder. 'We felt', said Hanson, 'that if we had to increase the offer, we didn't see that Minorco was entitled to any part of the increase.'

For Agnew, the implications were numbing: Hanson had him in a box. He could not go to war against Hanson having signalled to him an invitation to come to Gold Fields' rescue as a white knight, while at the same time the scope for leveraging a higher offer looked limited. In any event, after eight months of all-out war against Minorco, the Gold Fields leadership was exhausted: it was in no state to mount a similar war against Hanson, even if it morally could. And advisers pointed out that shareholders were not in a mood to go through a second defence, particularly against a cash offer. There would be a show of resistance by Agnew. But the independence of Gold Fields was over.

Outside, in the fading light, a car cruised slowly past. According to some witnesses it then drove round St James Square and came back to Charles 11 Street a second time, on this occasion passing even more slowly. In the car was Sir Michael Edwardes. For him, no moment was more gratifying, none more golden, than the moment of the Hanson blow on Agnew.

As for Agnew, right to the end he went blazing at Minorco. In a statement the following day, he could not resist another swipe. At least, he declared, this was a bid 'from a serious company, unlike Minorco'.

Less than three weeks later, on the day of the party at London Zoo, Agnew accepted an improved Hanson offer of £15.30 a share. But there was not immediate extra cash: 40p of the extra £1 comprised a special interim dividend paid from Gold Fields' own coffers. Also thrown in were warrants valued at 60p apiece to subscribe for new Hanson shares. 'We were surprised', said a Hanson aide shortly after, 'at how quickly Gold Fields caved in.'

Hanson was not the only one. In the City, fund managers were also taken aback, particularly after the vehemence with which Agnew had resisted the higher Minorco terms. David Prosser, head of investment at insurance giant Legal & General, Europe's largest pension office, confessed himself baffled: 'I can only assume that Agnew was exhausted after the long battle and had no stamina left. I was surprised at the lack of any real consultation over the Hanson offer.'

The sale brought $1.6 billion (almost £1 billion) to Minorco and a profit on the cost of its holding of $645 million (£400 million). Shares in Minorco jumped by 12 per cent to £10 a share on the news, a rise of almost 40 per cent since the bid started.

Edwardes: 'I said again and again at press conferences, and I wasn't believed, that we had no fixation about Gold Fields. People thought we had an obsession. We never had. If another bidder came along, we would have baled out immediately. We were happy to sell at £14 and cap it at £14.30 because of the elegance of the solution for us.'

Irony rather than elegance was the preoccupation of one of London's leading mining analysts, Mark Wood of Kleinwort Benson: 'It was ironic', he wrote to clients, 'that Rudolph Agnew should have announced the terms of an agreed bid for Gold Fields at London Zoo. There are some shareholders who would have liked to have put Mr Agnew behind bars for agreeing to a bid which offered them less than Minorco.'

And that, for many, was a pitiful irony: Gold Fields had spent some £30 million of shareholders' money in fighting off a bid from a company that assuredly wanted to invest in the business and take on many of its employees. Moreover, that bid had been accepted by a majority of Gold Fields shareholders.

Hanson, by contrast, was set to dismember the business, shut down the head office and sell off any part he thought fit. Did such an outcome still really call for a champagne party at the zoo?

The lawyers and financial advisers had cause to celebrate. Minorco's profit on Gold Fields was struck after $40 million (£25.47 million) in fees and costs relating to the bid. Adding this to the £30 million spent by Gold Fields, the bid battle all told cost £55.5 million. It worked out, over the eight months of the battle, at almost a quarter of a million pounds a day. Finally, the executive directors of Gold Fields would not be destitute: a judicious alteration to their remuneration package earlier in the year meant full pension entitlement on departure. For Agnew that meant, on his salary of £315,000, a pension at 55 of £208,000 for the rest of his days.

*　　　*

The Hanson capture of Gold Fields was as swift as the strike was opportune: the time between the announcement of the bid and gaining control was just seven weeks – a record for Hanson. By contrast, Hanson's conquest of Imperial had taken five months.

Seven weeks it need only have taken Minorco. But it was put through the hoop. And its higher bid failed to capture the prize. Why did it fail?

Mukasey was the immediate cause of Minorco's defeat: his judgments – 'rationally unsustainable' is how Relly described them to Anglo American shareholders – prevented Minorco from declaring the bid unconditional by the drop-dead date. The fact that the first of these judgments was made before the Federal Trade Commission ruled that there was no anti-trust case to answer left the Anglo American camp particularly bitter. But Mukasey is not the total answer, for he was ruling in a civil action which could have been avoided, or more successfully addressed by Anglo American earlier in the battle.

The leadership of Edwardes was blamed for Minorco's failure. In the immediate aftermath of defeat his was the back to which the knives predictably lunged, and if tongues were daggers, there would be little left of Edwardes to recognize him by. But a popular prejudice is seldom a reliable one, and for Anglo American, such culpability would have avoided the facing of deeper questions on the greater group's leadership and direction while neatly lifting responsibility from its own shoulders. Edwardes as convenient fall guy is just too glib.

Edwardes was not the best choice or the most appropriate one, but his conduct throughout the bid was honourable: he demonstrated pluck and determination; he stuck firmly to the financial arguments and never responded to personal attack in kind; and his institutional presentations won respect. Edwardes was not the ultimate cause of Minorco's defeat.

A predictable scapegoat was the Press: certainly the financial Press overall never warmed to the bid, but the reasons for that lay with the many errors and misjudgments of its prosecution. And tactical errors abounded. All these were a tap on Minorco's credibility. But neither individually nor in aggregate, were they more than secondary or contributory causes.

Minorco's bid ultimately failed to triumph because both the company and the arguments it presented lacked sufficient conviction to give the bid a necessary momentum. Its claim to be able to run ARC better than Gold Fields never seemed credible. Its rationale for acquiring ARC appeared even less so when one considers that, two years previously, Minorco had been entertaining the idea of a joint bid with RTZ under which it would retain the gold mining associates and leave ARC to RTZ. Now it had pledged to sell the gold mining associates and retain ARC: a complete 360 degree turn.

Minorco failed to gain active support because of deep-seated doubts both over the nature of the vehicle and of its ultimate purpose. Coming to this bid as a hitherto passive investment holding company in a tax haven, it never credibly painted a picture of how ARC would be better run or operationally expanded: it brought neither vision nor a sense of value added. Minorco's management came over as a young and inexperienced team of lightweights. Its most telling error was in denying its parent, the one element that would have brought provenance and weight to its case.

In asking the market to go along with this denial, it drew to itself all the negative perceptions of Anglo American (and the keen suspicion of a hidden agenda) while barring the many positive elements of Anglo American's operational experience, commitment to natural resources and its record as a progressive employer opposed to Apartheid. It drew all the brickbats while denying the bouquets. Admitted Slack: 'Denying Anglo was the biggest mistake we made.' Gold Fields' Michael Beckett was more scathing: 'In my view, the whole fiasco was created by the tradition of Anglo arrogance and parsimony and a belief that what the Establishment told them was correct – that there would be no trouble.'

Minorco was thus left with a financial argument alone and it assumed, with some arrogance, that this was sufficient. It was a substantial package. But it baulked at accepting the ultimate logic of a bid predicated on financial argument alone: the knock-out premium.

For all this the Young Turks must bear responsibility. They were the ones who pushed and champed and chivvied for a Gold Fields war. And the final responsibility for Minorco must lie – as it always must in public companies – with the chairman, Julian Ogilvie Thompson. JOT was a man caught between two magnetic poles: Oppenheimer and the Young Turks on the one hand, and the conservatives within 44 Main on the other. He wavered and vacillated between Ely Place and 44 Main, neither fish nor fowl, one or the other. He was chairman of Minorco and deputy chairman of Anglo American: the point where the denial and the affirmation met.

JOT was also pulled a third way: towards Agnew. The most fascinating aspect of the whole Gold Fields–Anglo American relationship was the remarkable friendship between Agnew and JOT. Seldom in the history of multinational corporations could there have been a personal relationship that was at one and the same time genuinely friendly and so disastrously misread and misunderstood.

It is interesting that the insiders in both sides start their accounts of the bid, not with September 1988, but with December 1986. The agreed draft merger plan, not the 54.9 per cent shareholder vote, was the nearest Minorco got to winning Gold Fields. Here was the real fulcrum of the relation. JOT approached the merger scheme with a conviction that the future of Gold Fields could be resolved as a private deal between friends.

JOT, so to speak in the family way of Anglo American, was not used to the culture of a boardroom. He misread the weakness of Agnew's position *vis-à-vis* his board, and was blind to a situation starkly obvious to others, that the heads of three Gold Fields associates on the board, together with the non-executives, were against the deal and four of Gold Fields leading executives who also had a vote stood to lose their rank as a result of the merger. The shooting weekends with Agnew blinded him to the gut realities of the Gold Fields board and all its underlying tensions and feuds: an orchestra with an embattled conductor and players with some highly individual notions of the score. Here the JOT shot misfired. And that miss cost Minorco.

Hanson now had control of £5.4 billion of gross assets for £3.2 billion. It could sell off the gold business and retain ARC for just £1.2 billion – a knockdown price.

Within a week of taking control, Hanson sold the bulk of its 38 per cent interest in Gold Fields of South Africa to Rembrandt for £36.8 million, or 22 per cent above the market price of the shares – a revealing pointer to the dismemberment profits in store.

Shortly after, GFSA duly announced a R1,000 million rights issue – the one Agnew had so hotly denied in the final days of the battle against Minorco's bid. A few minutes walk away from GFSA's headquarters in Fox Street, Johannesburg, Peter Gush, head of Anglo American's gold division and Anglo American's representative on the GFSA board, allowed himself a wearisome smile.

As for Newmont, Hanson was happy to keep his options open. He had met with Gordon Parker and told him that the 49 per cent stake was viewed on economic and not sentimental terms. On GFMC:

'We're learning a lot about the gold business in North America. We are in no rush to sell'. And little wonder. Within weeks the gold price began a dramatic rally that was to see a rise of more than 15 per cent to over $410 an ounce.

But he did not look set to build on the business, either. By the end of September, Gold Fields' headquarters in Charles 11 Street was locked in an elegiac stillness. All 85 head office staff had been made redundant. Almost all the directors, too, had gone. The building stood empty. After 102 years, the heart of Britain's gold empire had ceased to beat. Nor at 44 Main was there any comfort at the emptying of Gold Fields. JOT, depressed by a sense of needless, fratricidal tragedy, likened the outcome to the final scene of *Othello*: a pathetic, piteous waste.

Next to be sold was ARC America for £417 million and the remaining shares in GFSA. By December, Hanson had realized more than £1 billion in asset sales. Meanwhile, the Hanson scalpel plunged into ARC in Britain. Keith Orrell-Jones quit and tiers of management were removed. Few at ARC had expected that.

As for Agnew, the only person to be taken on by Hanson, he was undecided on whether to stay or move onto something new.

Meanwhile, the archives at Charles 11 Street had been crated up and sent off to GFSA in Johannesburg. After all the anti-South African clamour, it was a final irony for Gold Fields. But it was a coming home, all the same.

While the Hanson bid had been agreed deal, there was not a person connected with Charles 11 Street who did not feel profoundly saddened and angered at the outcome. One of the world's biggest concentrations of mining expertise had been abruptly broken up and let scatter to the winds as if nothing of Gold Fields' history or achievements had mattered. Agnew was defiant to the end: for him it was not humiliation but the necessary price of principle. 'History shows that companies that fall under the influence of Anglo American either conform or are rejected in a brutal way.' He knew that Gold Fields was doomed, not from 1988, or from 1986, but from 1980. It was a bitter end to one of the proudest names on the London Stock Exchange and arguably the worst outcome for everyone – other than Hanson. Knowledge, expertise and the greatest British name in precious metals mining: for how little did these now seem to count. Hanson's deputy chairman, Martin Taylor, was unapologetic: 'The expertise should be in the companies where the assets are. The expertise is better located at the operating centres than at the head office.' Nevertheless, many at Gold Fields could not help but regard it as the destructive and bludgeoning edge of Hansonization that the public never got to see: the breaking of careers and loyalties, the permanent loss to Britain of a bank of mining expertise, and in this case, the snapping of a link with history, too. But then, who cared any more?

All that was left in Agnew's elegant room was the little Oppenheimer statuette of Rhodes. Of the many Gold Fields assets of value to Minorco, this was the only one it asked Hanson if it could have. But much to JOT's chagrin, the founder stayed with Gold Fields to the end, looking out on an empire that had ceased to be.

19

The Crises of Anglo American

∎

A defeat abroad and a mounting drama of change at home: against this background Anglo American finds itself facing not one crisis, but three.

It faces an *investment* crisis, both at home where inflation and political uncertainty have put a question mark on long-term investment, and abroad where there are few natural resource areas which would not challenge the entry of Anglo American or its affiliates – a stigmatization heightened by the Gold Fields defeat.

It faces a crisis of *management succession*: to the already problematic passing of the Oppenheimer mantle is a top management weakened and compromised by the Minorco débâcle. Anglo American's High Command never looked more undecided or more unsure of itself.

Finally, it faces a *political crisis*: how it can assist the process of black empowerment within the group itself if it is to have a future in an internationally acceptable South Africa. Here Anglo American faces a central Catch-22: how, on the one hand, it can help speed up political change at home and, on the other, protect itself against the consequences of that change – one likely to result in a multi-racial state where the principal new actors are committed to socialist solutions and, at best, a limited role for the market economy.

Anglo American shows every sign of having woken up late to its political crisis in South Africa and to the realities of a changing order.

Nowhere more dramatic can the group's investment crisis be seen than at the headquarters of Minorco. Here, too, a crating-up had taken place. In late 1989 it moved out of Ely Place to new offices in Hammersmith – Elsinore House by name. The aim was to be nearer

Heathrow Airport. But the name suggested Minorco was no nearer to shaking off its ghosts. A year to the day it launched its ill-fated bid for Gold Fields, Minorco released from Luxemburg annual results that were as problematic as they were stunning. The company was awash with cash. After collecting $1.6 billion from Hanson for its Gold Fields shares, Minorco's cash balances stood at $2.5 billion. The interest on that cash mountain was running at $500,000 a day. Net asset value was $3.7 billion or $21.65 a share, of which $14.68 represented cash.

For all the opportunity the cash mountain afforded, it was a dramatic manifestation of the problems at the heart of Anglo American. Two years on from the switch to Luxemburg, Minorco was no nearer to achieving its original aim: operational control of assets. This central issue now looked more problematic than ever: after the anti-South African clamour raised by the bid, how would Minorco invest the money? Indeed, *could* it invest the money?

Because of the potential anti-trust problems on platinum, it could not move on 36 per cent-owned Charter, now looking ever more left out on a limb. Yet neither Charter nor Johnson Matthey could expand and grow as autonomous, independent companies. Eugene Anderson, JM's chief executive, felt increasingly frustrated by what he perceived as Minorco's stifling hand and quit truculently in December. His chairman, Neil Clarke, resigned the following day. Ironically, that same week, Edwardes also quit as chief executive at Minorco. The Minorco–Charter–Johnson Matthey *ménage à trois* looked never more fraught or irreconcilable. Hank Slack moved up to become *primus inter pares* in a management troika with Phillimore and Lea. The moving of Slack back to Europe indicated a surrender of ambitions to get hands-on in America. Post the bid, that looked fraught with difficulties. And Australia almost equally so.

Minorco's stockbrokers, James Capel, in a post-bid battle circular, sought to put a brave face on matters by citing as a plus point of the bid the achievement of 'a good understanding of the various regulatory bodies' – as if Edwardes had deliberately set out on an academic study course. It also betrayed a view that Minorco was destined for further journeys round the regulatory track. In truth, that was the last thing Minorco wanted. The working assumption from now on was that any acquisition Minorco sought would have to be agreed. Hostile assaults were out. That was another reason for Edwardes to go.

But the latent, and most problematic legacy of the failure of the Gold Fields bid was the additional premium that was now in danger of attaching to anything Minorco wanted to buy, regardless of size or corporate logic: to overcome the political and regulatory stigmatization, it runs the risk of having to pay more by way of entry cost which could wipe out the financial argument for the acquisition. As it was, Minorco faced an earnings dilution on any purchase it made because of the high interest income being enjoyed on the cash.

But at the same time, Minorco could not sit idly by. Across the natural resources industry there has been an unprecedented level of bid activity and scramble for assets. Morever, the gold price was beginning to move – and with it the price of precious metal-producing assets. Minorco could not afford to miss out.

What a daunting picture this presented to 44 Main. At the twice weekly meetings of the inner executive on the first floor, the Thomas Baines paintings now taunted Thompson and Relly: Minorco never looked more like the cursed Flying Dutchman, blasted from Table Bay and doomed to roam the seas forever. Here was a galleon full of cash – but one to which all the harbours shut themselves tight. But Anglo American was now desperate for results: it needed to have the sting of defeat eased away by news of agreed acquisitions or new natural resource ventures. But with high interest rates, the bank was the place to be.

Just as Minorco was dependent on an improvement of perceptions about its parent and South Africa, Minorco was also the gateway to the deeper problems within Anglo American. The interplay between external events and Anglo American's domestic crisis was never more evident than in the importance Anglo American was now to attach to exploration and acquisition success abroad.

While a successful bid for Gold Fields could never have masked the problems the Corporation faced at home, it would have provided a dramatic new lease of life for Anglo American overseas: a second coming of the empire. In 1988, South African gold production had fallen to 619 tonnes, 38 per cent less than in the peak year of 1970. At the same time, working costs per ounce of gold produced had increased at an annual rate of 23 per cent. By mid-1989, the cost price squeeze in the South African mining industry had intensified to the point that an estimated 20 per cent of the country's gold mines were losing money. The need for new and lower-cost gold was now more pressing on Anglo American than ever. As Rob Davies, mining analyst at stockbrokers Shearson Lehman Hutton, chillingly observed in the aftermath of the Gold Fields bid: 'Slowly, the new mines of Nevada and Papua New Guinea are squeezing the South Africans out of business'.

Anglo American, through Minorco, vitally needed access to the lower-cost mines of Gold Fields Mining Corporation in the United States. But the acquisition was strategically important also for the foothold in the United States it would bring, together with an international structure on to which all sorts of other acquisitions could have been bolted.

But there was another compelling reason why Anglo American needed success abroad: the acquisition of Gold Fields would not have involved the export of capital from South Africa; but it would have had a profound impact on the balance of Anglo American's equity accounted earnings, investor assessment of the quality of these earnings and the Corporation's perceived entrapment within South Africa.

But if the capture of Gold Fields would have provided a new lease of life for Anglo American and a talisman of endorsement for its leadership, the losing of it was more than a setback. Thompson in particular had cause to rue the blind and manic overruns of secondary issues upon primary ones that had so ruinously blighted Minorco's effort.

Defeat was the conduit which brought home to many the growing paralysis of leadership at 44 Main. While the gold price surge in late-1989 has brought immediate relief, some challenging questions now confront it. Not least of these is whether the structure of control is still appropriate. Equally problematic is the nature of the leadership itself.

Anglo American's leadership felt that a political silence throughout the bid would somehow belie the fact that with De Beers it still held 60 per cent control of Minorco. But Anglo American held the strings, and holds them even tighter now. The perception of Minorco as Anglo American's overseas arm can only be strengthened by the expectation that one man was lined up to become chairman of Anglo American in addition to the chairmanships of De Beers, Amgold and Minorco: Julian Ogilvie Thompson. It is an astonishing concentration of power that begs many questions: is it possible for one man to give worthwhile attention to all the varied corporate activities undertaken or controlled by the greater group? What is the opportunity cost of

THE CRISES OF ANGLO AMERICAN

that control in terms of the initiative it denies to others? Minorco has now become JOT's Achilles Heel. Unease about the combination of, so to speak, foreign secretary, head of the party, prime minister and state president will accelerate change.

Equally problematic is Hank Slack's position. The failure to win Gold Fields deprived the son-in-law of a proper job in the United States where he moved his home. Slack now holds a key position in the new management line-up at Minorco as senior man in the Cabinet. But the arrangement looks uncomfortably makeshift. Relly looks set to spend considerably more time on Minorco.

Meanwhile, Nicholas Oppenheimer, settled with his family in Britain, but committed to spend increasing time on Anglo American affairs at 44 Main, remains reticent about his immediate intentions despite a climate of political change that has become more charged by the month. Such reticence at such a time compounds the sense of a fast-developing vacuum at the top of Anglo American with Relly due to retire in two years. With the growing expectation of real political change in South Africa, never before has the need for a defined strategy, plan of implementation and leadership been more paramount. In this gathering crisis of management succession, it is not at all clear what new ideas will inform Anglo American's new leadership. It is not just a vacuum of personality, but a vacuum of idea.

Takeover would certainly be one option were Anglo American a conventional company. But its corporate structure, as complex and as self-interlocking as a printed circuit board, denies the opportunity for external change, close though some have looked. Much now depends on Anglo American's 'revco' – the impressive inner group of Young Turks, comprising of Spicer, Godsell and Sunter – and the movement of the 'idealist monkeys' into the key seats of power. The choice of Clem Sunter to succeed Peter Gush as head of the gold and uranium division is evidence of the Relly commitment to rolling reform.

In South Africa, involvement in the political crisis is inescapable: unlike Britain, where businessmen are disinclined to get involved in politics, no such option is open here. Indeed, one of South Africa's most striking features is the extent to which a constitution designed to exclude some 85 per cent of the population has dramatically politicized everyone.

Anglo American's attempt to escape the fall in earnings of its core operations at home by investment abroad has been increasingly frustrated by South Africa's pariah status and its position as Number One target on the media hate-list. The external criticism has failed to distinguish between those actors who have acquiesced in the system and those who, like Anglo American, have opposed Apartheid and actively worked for change. What is now crucial for the international investment community is distinguishing between the two in order to help sustain the process of reform through to genuine constitutional change. To do this, Anglo American must talk to the world.

Anglo American has sought to hasten this process, though international recognition is not as marked as it might be: indeed, for all its efforts through its pay and personnel policies, the Chairman's Fund, the support for the anti-Apartheid Democratic Party, the Urban Foundation and black entrepreneurship, Anglo American has been given little credit – all stick and no carrot is a frequent and justified complaint. But it now needs to attend, not just to 'getting its message across' on the international stage, but also to thinking more deeply about its post-Apartheid structure and role.

The economic outlook for Anglo American is challenging. The combination of sanctions, disinvestment and Western debt repayment schedules has brought about massive capital outflows totalling R25 billion over four years, bringing a weakened currency, high inflation and a prime overdraft rate of 20 per cent, the principal consequence of which has been a slowing in the rate of economic growth and employment opportunity. Far from helping black empowerment, sanctions and disinvestment now threaten to create an economic wasteland for the post-Apartheid system. The economy, growing at 3.2 per cent in 1988, is reckoned to have slowed to 2.3 per cent in 1989 and growth is forecast to decline further to one per cent in 1990. But it needs to grow by some four per cent a year to keep pace with new entrants to the job market.

Failure to achieve that growth deepens the crisis of black expectations and opportunity denial. Anglo American felt it could make little headway in the United States theatre because in the political address to South Africa was a fundamental ambivalence, if not indifference, to the final outcome. Anglo American and, indeed, most of the South African business community sees a sanctions lobby in the United States driven by domestic political and public relations considerations and swollen by corporate pull-outs that are motivated by fear of post-Apartheid black majority rule. In recent months, there have been encouraging signs of a shift in US attitudes: *Barrons*, the leading investment newsletter, has called on American investors and brokers 'to replace the clenched fist with a helping hand'. Meanwhile, Merrill Lynch, the brokerage giant, met with a barrage of criticism for a move in December 1989 to stop extending buy and sell orders for South African stocks. The step misread a growing change of mood among investors to South Africa in the light of the release of political detainees by the De Klerk administration. It is this process, more than any other, that will unlock doors for both Anglo American and Minorco. But there is still a need for strong leadership at Minorco.

*   *

At 44 Main, the moment of change has arrived. The opening months of F W De Klerk's presidency have not just raised expectations of reform but mark the crossing of a Rubicon for South Africa. At this critical junction of danger and opportunity, Anglo American cannot afford to be an idle spectator.

The danger that it faces is on two levels: the first, and most pressing, is to help secure a peaceful transition to a pluralist constitution acceptable to all parties. The second is to secure a market economy that will deliver on black expectations while the main opposition forces are anti-capitalist in outlook. Both the main black political groups – the ANC and Inkatha – espouse economic agendas that appear to leave, at best, a limited role for the private sector. Significantly, however, the ANC's constitutional guidelines have dropped references to wholesale nationalization and it appears to be following a similar course to SWAPO in Namibia in moving to a mixed-market system. Anglo American, because of its concentration of economic power, would be a prime target for reform. It thus has to create around itself a culture supportive of entrepreneurship: a necessary consent.

But one issue which the Minorco bid had highlighted was the perception of Anglo American as an enterprise-stifling animal at heart, unconcerned for outside shareholders and bottom-line earnings performance.

A vast and complex organizational cobweb testified to Anglo

American's near paranoic concern with control, if necessary at the expense of entrepreneurial success. The demise of the holding company and unbundling of conglomerates that have come to be a prominent theme in corporate development in the industrialized West was passing Anglo American by. The patriarchal culture seemed to be frozen into a bureaucratic one, closed to change and incapable of re-innervation. Anglo American is perceived as a dinosaur that would not survive in the economies of the West, where bids, break-ups and demergers have transformed the landscape.

The challenge presented to Anglo American, both externally and from within, is formidable. It requires of the group a release and encouragement of entrepreneurial talent within the group and a much broader equity constituency than is at present the case.

There are broadly three ways in which Anglo American might achieve this: accelerated support for small business development by further contracting out of activities; greater encouragement of employee share ownership, both in the Anglo American group and also its quoted associates; and a radical overhaul of group structure and functions with a programme of management buy-outs and sales of share stakes. These approaches may be viewed as a series of concentric circles of change, with Anglo American moving from one phase to another, although there is no reason why a mixed package of initiatives cannot be chosen from each area. In each case, the process of black empowerment could be significantly helped.

JCI's economic adviser, Ronnie Bethlehem, places this at the top of the list of priorities for South African business: 'What is really needed from the business community', he wrote recently, 'is a gesture sufficiently generous and demonstrative of goodwill that it would deal a serious blow to black mistrust and transform the structure of its relationship with the black community.' He cited as an example the transfer in the mid-1960s of the control of General Mining from Anglo American to the Sanlam-Federale Group. This had the effect of transforming relationships in the mining industry: prior to the transfer, there was a sharp polarization between the English-speaking employer groups and owners and the Afrikaners trade unions. The change-over defused this situation by giving the Afrikaners an ownership foothold. Something on a similar scale, he urges, is now needed to establish the involvement of blacks in the entrepreneurial sector of the economy.

Critics of the Bethlehem view point out that this was not a free sale, but a transfer for which the Afrikaners paid their ticket; the leadership of the white-dominated corporations cannot be expected to hand over ownership of their operations for nothing, even if it was in their gift to do so.

Nevertheless, Bethlehem has raised an issue that is set to emerge as a central concern of 44 Main. What alternative can it offer to the real possibility of state intervention in its affairs? Here the Sanlam-Federale example is not without conceptual value.

Anglo American has made a start through its employee share ownership scheme. But even after it has run its course over five years, the aggregate amount of equity transferred to employees will be miniscule – around £100 million, or less than two per cent of Anglo American's current market capitalization. It is gesture capitalism at this level, effective more in changing labour attitudes towards industrial action and strikes than in black empowerment *per se*. Yet, wider share ownership has the potential to serve the double function of motivating staff and assisting the process of black empowerment through the transfer of ownership of assets, one area of South African life where progress has been notably slow.

This raises a number of challenges for Anglo American. The current group structure has been shaped by a concern to prevent predatory attack and takeover. Officially, De Beers, JCI and Minorco are each independently administered. but in effect, they are all part of the greater group, interlinked by crossholdings and common directors.

This complex web of crossholdings not only protects the central Anglo American and De Beers pillars from takeover – Anglo American holding 32.25 per cent of De Beers, and De Beers 38 per cent of Anglo American – but the pillars themselves have bound key industrial and commercial enterprises to their base by crossholdings which deny the passage of equity control to non-group companies. It is a complex and byzantine tangle driven by a concern for possession rather than performance. By contrast, other mining houses, such as Gencor under the highly-regarded Derek Keys, have dramatically transformed and streamlined their operations.

Quite what the strategic or synergistic benefits are to Anglo American of maintaining shareholdings in so many disparate companies is not clear, other than psychological reluctance to let go. The result in many cases is power removed from the operational centre, a share price permanently lagging the earnings behaviour and asset strength of the businesses, and a structure impregnable to takeover – the ultimate sanction against indifferent performance. All this inhibits initiative and entrepreneurial flair. The entire Anglo American grouping is in need of a radical restructuring to provide far greater clarity and focus of activity. At present, no corporate theme unifies its activities: it is not clear how Anglo American adds value to the assets that it holds or what its unique business mission is.

At the same time, the shareholder base on which the edifice rests is tiny. For all that the greater group extends into commanding heights of the South African economy, it does so on the most narrow platform. Anglo American itself has a total of 20,680 individual shareholders, of whom 20,240 hold 1,000 shares or less, or 11.7 million in aggregate, equivalent to barely 5 per cent of the equity. The shareholder base of De Beers is even more constricted. The challenge to Anglo American now is how to broaden its equity constituency before an impounding solution is forced upon it.

The lack of constituency is more marked the deeper one looks. Highveld Steel and Vanadium, for example, the 52 per cent owned company associate, has no employee share scheme in place, though it is a publicly quoted company. It has just 2,000 shareholders with private individuals accounting for only 2.35 per cent of the equity. While Highveld's employees are encouraged to join the Anglo American group scheme, there is no means by which they can share more directly in the earnings performance of their own company.

AMIC is also publicly quoted, but individuals hold just 3.8 per cent of the equity; Amcoal, one of the biggest private sector mining groups in the world and with a stock market capitalization of R1.7 billion, has just 2,500 individual shareholders, and they hold less than three per cent of the equity. Its 18,000 employees are also encouraged to join the Anglo American share scheme in lieu of an Amcoal equivalent. Then there are the wholly-owned subsidiaries which would merit a management buy-out and/or stock market quote of their own: forestry, timber and paper group Mondi (profits R353 million) is an obvious example. Anglo Farms is another.

But there are other areas, such as mining equipment, metals handling and electronics, where buy-out/flotation would provide considerable opportunities for extensive staff and management equity participation. The idea is not totally alien: Samcor, for example, is 24 per cent owned by its staff.

A radical model for Anglo American to consider would be the manner of the British Government privatizations of the 1980s: in each case, powerful incentives were provided for employee subscription. Privatization, after an inauspicious period of industrial relations in the 1970s, became a popular and innervating font of the British economy after decades of tired, 'mixed economy' solutions.

The most vivid example was the spectacularly successful National Freight Consortium, where the workforce became 85 per cent owners of the business in a management-led buy-out. Two years prior to the buy-out in 1982, it was lossmaking. When it came to the stock market in 1989 price tagged at £600 million, profits had soared to £62 million. The average initial investment of £700 made by thousands of shop-floor staff had climbed to £37,600 apiece. Such is the co-operative experiment that Anglo American could consider for some of its subsidiaries. Anglo American could also usefully note from the British privatizations that loan schemes were in place to help the least well-off to get started on the equity ownership ladder.

More urgent and arguably more practicable is to step up venture capital support for black entrepreneurs and to accelerate the 'contracting out' of service activities and functions. Progress has been made in transport, the retail trade, personnel sevices and construction. But the process now needs to strike deeper into manufacturing.

Meanwhile, more needs to be done to meet the immediate needs of a black urban workforce where higher standards of education, training and housing are a priority. The amount paid into the Anglo American and De Beers Chairman's Fund for housing, education and community projects, for example, is based on a formula under which the Fund receives the equivalent of one per cent of Anglo American and De Beers dividend payments.

In 1988, the Fund received some R50 million (£11 million). It is a modest sum in relation to the net assets of Anglo American alone which currently stand at R28.5 billion (£6.3 billion). Clearly it has to be related to the greater group's ability to pay dividend income, but since De Beers dividend is covered 2.8 times and Anglo American's 4.3 times by equity accounted earnings, there is scope for a substantial uplift without jeopardizing shareholder interest, however narrowly defined.

And what is the shareholder interest? Anglo American is, in the words of Richard Stuart, analyst at the Johannesburg brokers, Martin & Co, 'one of the last of the great undervalued situations available'. James Capel in London is forecasting a 21 per cent rise in equity accounted profits in 1989 to R3.2 billion. As for De Beers, pre-tax profits are forecast to increase by 41 per cent to R4 billion, with cash reserves totalling $1,440 million; and Minorco, with a cash pile of $2.5 billion, is attracting interest of some $270 million a year on top of the dividend income from its equity investments. The balance sheet and earnings position of these companies is immense. But their future crucially rests on there being a political overhaul in South Africa.

Both for external political reasons and internal managerial ones, Anglo American has urgently to consider whether its present equity distribution and system of centrifugal control is any longer appropriate to what lies ahead – or, indeed, sustainable. Anglo American has much to learn from the wisdom of necessary losses: ones that are needed so that the body can again grow.

It starts with the handicap and advantage of the Oppenheimer legacy: an obsession with control when a letting go is now required. But how? And to whom? In the library of the man who has built the Anglo American–De Beers group to such world pre-eminence in gold, diamonds and platinum, the crisis of empire and its survival has never been more pressing.

For the patriarchy, it looks ominously terminal: a closing in by a new world on the old. But never before has the Corporation had such an opportunity to raise itself into the top ten of the world's most popular global equities. The patriarchy now needs to adapt, but the values it sought to sustain are never more necessary than now. They carried a wisdom, more evident at Anglo American than perhaps any other corporation in the world, that wealth creation is not an end in itself, but brings obligations to pursue and achieve wider goals and ideals. It has brought to Anglo American a tradition of being South Africa's most progressive employer, and a commitment to social policies that deserves recognition in any international reappraisal of South Africa.

It is these ideals that now require Anglo American to devolve, disengage and change. And it is in the execution of them that its gift to the country now lies. In the Oppenheimer library, the apocalyptic painting of The Bridge is not yet a prophecy. But now more than ever it is an opportunity.

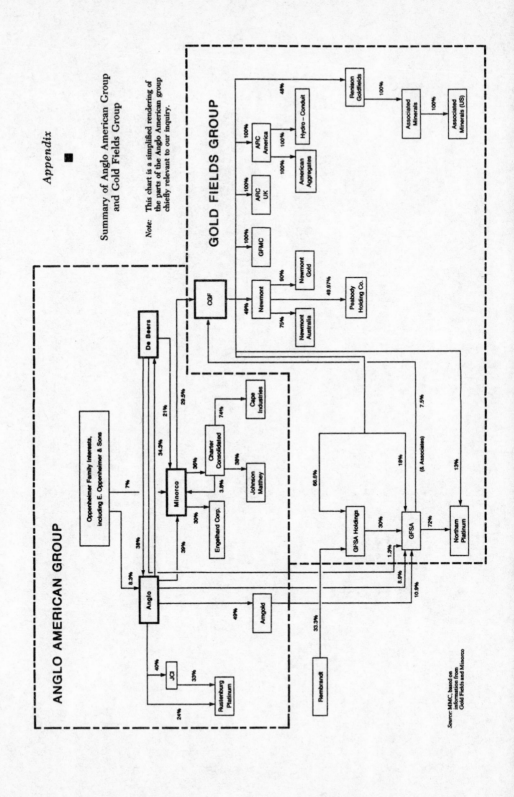

Appendix

Summary of Anglo American Group
and Gold Fields Group

Note: This chart is a simplified rendering of
the parts of the Anglo American group
chiefly relevant to our inquiry.

ANGLO AMERICAN GROUP

GOLD FIELDS GROUP

Source: MMC; based on
information from
Gold Fields and Minorco

Bibliography

■

Annual reports of:
Amcoal
AMIC
Anglo American Corporation
Charter Consolidated
Consolidated Gold Fields
De Beers Consolidated Mines
Highveld Steel and Vanadium
Johannesburg Consolidated Investments
Minorco
Newmont Mining Corporation

Analysts' reports from:
Barclays de Zoete Wedd, London
James Capel, London
Kleinwort Benson Securities, London
Martin & Co, Johannesburg
Phillips & Drew, London
Shearson Lehman Hutton, London
Williams de Broe, London

Monopolies Commission Report: Minorco and Consolidated Gold Fields plc. February 1989.

Annual Gold Review, published by Consolidated Gold Fields.
World Gold Industry Review, published by Shearson Lehman Hutton.

Platinum Review, published by Johnson Matthey.
International Currency Review, London 1989.

Berger & Godsell (eds) *A Future South Africa*: Human & Rousseau Tafelberg, Cape Town, 1988.

Bethlehem, Dr Ronald *Economics in a Revolutionary Society*: A D Donker, 1988.

Chilvers, Hedley *The Story of De Beers*: Cassell & Co, 1939.

Edwardes, Sir Michael *Back from the Brink*: Collins, 1988.

Green, Timothy *The Prospect for Gold*: Rosendale Press, London, 1987.

Gregory, Sir Theodore, *Ernest Oppenheimer and the Economic Development of South Africa*: Oxford University Press, 1962.

Hocking, Anthony *Oppenheimer & Son*: McGraw Hill.

Johnson, Paul *Gold Fields: A Centenary Portrait*: Weidenfield & Nicholson.

Lang, John *Bullion Johannesburg*: Jonathan Ball, Johannesburg, 1986.

Macnab, Roy *Gold Their Touchstone*: Jonathan Ball, Johannesburg, 1987.

Oxley, John *Down Where No Lion Walked: The Story of Western Deep Levels*: Southern Book Publishers, Johannesburg, 1989.

Roberts, Brian *Kimberley, Turbulent City*: David Philip, Cape Town, 1976.

Sampson, Anthony *Black & Gold*: Hodder & Stoughton, 1987.

Sunter, Clem *The World and South Africa in the 1990s*: Human & Rousseau Tafelberg, Cape Town, 1987.

de Villiers, Les *Doing Business with Southern Africa*: Business Books International, Connecticut, 1989.

Speeches and lectures by Gavin Relly, Michael Spicer, J H Steyn and Ann Bernstein.

Index

Buthelezi, Mangosuthu, 44
Byron, 3
BZW, 206

Cadbury, Peter, 122–3, 133, 147, 164,
 184, 191, 196
California, 82
Callaghan, James, 128
Calvinism, 45
Campbell, Colin, 137
Canada, 15, 28, 121, 155, 194, 204
Cape Town, 106
capital accumulation, 6
capital equipment, 30
capital spending programme, 32
car industry, South Africa, 23, 30
car industry, Europe, 29
Caradon, 109
Carrington, Lord, 127
Carbon Leader Reef, 79
Carden, Stephen, 165, 173
Carlin Trend, 105, 107–9, 146, 192
Carlton Club, 165
cartelized markets, 19
Casey, Michael, 165
Castleman, Christopher, 195
Cazenove, 69, 72, 165, 173
Central Holdings Ltd, 6, 10, 69, 173,
 176
Central Intelligence Agency (CIA), 48
Central Selling Organisation, 15–20, 32,
 51, 66, 213
Cerillos, 82
Chairman's Fund, 35, 228, 233
Chajo Properties, 66
Challen, David, 110
Chamber of Mines (Johannesburg), 27,
 62, 64
Chapman, Neil, 165
Charter Consolidated, 30, 51–60, 69, 71,
 76, 114–15, 117–19, 153, 164, 166,
 176, 213, 224
Chemical Bank, 136, 158, 205
Chilvers, Hedley, 11
Chimney Creek, 82, 108
Chloride, 127, 153, 167
Chocolate Mountains, 82
Churchill, Randolf, 20
civil engineering, 60
Clare, Robert, 98, 119
Clarke, John Neil, 38, 57–9, 65–9, 74,

84, 86–7, 98–9, 100, 102, 119, 121,
 153, 224
Clarke, Sonia, 38
coal, 16, 23, 30
Cleveland Potash, 53–4
Close Brothers, 81
Colesberg Kopje, 11
Commonwealth Committee of Foreign
 Ministers on Southern Africa, 158
Committee on Foreign Investment
 (US), 172, 179
Companies Act (UK), 67–8, 71, 73, 75,
 136–7, 149
Competition Board of South Africa, 145,
 169
Comprehensive Anti-Apartheid Act of
 1986 (US), 47
'concert party' operations, 141, 150
Conservative Party (UK), 64
Consolidated Diamond Mines, 17
Consolidated Gold Fields, 5, 7, 12, 19,
 38, 62–227 *passim*; cash drain, 84–7,
 92–3, 120, 131; dawn raid by Anglo,
 1980, 64–77, 81, 136, 182–3;
 headquarters (Charles 11 Street), 98,
 106, 121–2, 138, 144, 157, 165, 167–8,
 172, 206–7, 214–15, 220–1; merger
 plan with Minorco, 1986, 89–103;
 Minorco bid, 1988, 7–8, 120–224
 passim; and Newmont, 105–9;
 operations, 62–3, 79–83, 93, 105–9;
 share price, 74, 83, 92, 107, 120–21,
 123, 131, 136–41, 162, 167–71, 174–7,
 183–4, 190, 201, 204, 214–16;
 takeover by Hanson Trust, 210–21
Consolidated Mines Selection, 13
Coopers and Lybrand, 164
copper, 16, 30, 32, 53–4, 81–3, 113–4
Craven, John, 129
Cromwell, Oliver, 127
Cuba, 149
Cuckney, Lord, 190

Daily Telegraph, 162
Dali, Salvador, 37
Davies, Robert, 109, 225
Davis, Borkum, Hare & Co, 66–8
De Beer brothers, 10
De Beer, Zach, 40
De Beers, 3, 5, 9–20, 23, 30–2, 34, 65,
 66, 68–9, 73, 75–7, 84–5, 87, 93,
 118–20, 125, 128–9, 139–41, 146, 150,